FOAL

Praise for *Fuel to the Fire*

"In light of President Donald Trump's aspirational (and contradictory) tweet-nouncements, this book provides a road map for citizens and scholars to understand the direction of actual U.S. foreign policy. An impressive work of sensemaking in an era of unusual uncertainty."

—Micah Zenko, national security scholar and coauthor of *Clear and Present Safety: The World Has Never Been Better and Why That Matters to Americans*

"Reading this book won't cheer you up, but it will make you smarter. *Fuel to the Fire* is a comprehensive and dispassionate account of Donald Trump's failing foreign policy, and it points the way toward a more effective grand strategy. Trump ran for office pledging to rein in U.S. global commitments, but as president he has repeated most of his predecessors' errors while adding new ones of his own. Americans want a more restrained and successful foreign policy, but this clear-eyed, hard-hitting book explains why Donald Trump is not providing it."

—Stephen M. Walt, Robert and Renée Belfer Professor of International Affairs at Harvard University's John F. Kennedy School of Government

"At a time when American foreign policy is badly in need of a reboot, this provocative, powerfully argued call to move past a failing insistence on militarized primacy is a welcome addition to the debate."

—Ben Rhodes, deputy national security adviser to President Barack Obama, 2009–2017

"In an age where news channels struggle to keep up with Twitter, keeping things in perspective is next to impossible. That's why *Fuel to the Fire* is so critical, looking to the long-term implications of America's ailing approach to foreign policy and offering necessary policy prescriptions to set things back on track. A book for our current times and beyond."

—Ian Bremmer, Eurasia Group and GZERO Media

"*Fuel to the Fire* is an excellent analysis of contemporary U.S. foreign policy. Glaser, Preble, and Thrall explain how Donald Trump has made existing policies worse while introducing harmful changes of his own. They make a persuasive case that Trump's foreign policy is so destructive because it pursues the same strategy of primacy as his predecessors, but with less competence and fewer constraints.

They do a great service in identifying the core of Trump's world-view and understanding how that affects his foreign policy decisions. Their most important contribution is their argument for a strategy of restraint that guards against primacy's excesses and failures. It is essential reading for everyone who wants to understand why our foreign policy has failed Americans so badly and what can be done to fix it."

—Daniel Larison, senior editor, *The American Conservative*

"As scholars, students, and practitioners debate the legacy of American primacy and the virtues of a more restrained U.S. foreign policy, *Fuel to the Fire* should jump to the top of their reading list. Arguing that the younger generation correctly favors strong international engagement through trade and diplomacy while eschewing military intervention, the authors argue for a new grand strategy they believe will prove less costly for American interests and will enable a rules-based international system to flourish. The authors' deep expertise and engaging writing style make this book a must-read as Americans assess their past, present, and future foreign policy."

—James Goldgeier, American University

FUEL TO THE FIRE

FUEL TO THE FIRE

HOW TRUMP MADE AMERICA'S *BROKEN* FOREIGN POLICY EVEN WORSE (AND HOW WE CAN RECOVER)

JOHN GLASER,
CHRISTOPHER A. PREBLE,
AND A. TREVOR THRALL

Print ISBN: 978-1-948647-46-5
eBook ISBN: 978-1-948647-47-2

Library of Congress Cataloging-in-Publication Data available.

Cover design: Derek Thornton, Faceout Studio
Cover illustration: Mike Trukhachev / Shutterstock.com

Printed in Canada.

CATO INSTITUTE
1000 Massachusetts Avenue, NW
Washington, DC 20001
www.cato.org

CONTENTS

ACKNOWLEDGMENTS

We are grateful to the editors at Cato Books, especially Jason Kuznicki and Eleanor O'Connor, and to our many Cato colleagues for their help. We received research help from a number of Cato research assistants and interns, including Jonathan "J.E." Allen, James Knupp, Courtney Nadeau, Madison Parkhill, and Lauren Sander. Thanks to Roshni Ashar for her help with the many charts and graphs and to Karen Coda and Karen Ingebretsen of Publications Professionals LLC for copyediting.

INTRODUCTION

"There is no Trump doctrine." So said Mike Dubke, President Donald Trump's communications director in the early months of Trump's presidency.[1] The comment, offered in private during an internal White House staff meeting about how to brand Trump's foreign policy during his first 100 days in office, was perhaps more perceptive than its utterer appreciated at the time.

To many, Donald Trump's rise in the Republican primaries and eventually to the presidency represented an astonishing break with the Washington, DC, foreign policy consensus that had prevailed from Harry Truman to Barack Obama. The broad pillars of post–World War II U.S. grand strategy, pursued with remarkable continuity from 1945 to 2016, prescribed an international order made dependent on U.S. military predominance. Washington extended security commitments to scores of allies and client states and deployed a permanent globe-straddling forward military presence. It installed itself as leader of the major political and economic international institutions established after World War II and relied on the frequent threat and use of force in pursuit of a wide range of perceived national interests, not merely to protect America's physical security. The foreign policy preferences of candidate Trump, many argued, were a radical departure from these long-standing grand strategic imperatives.

"I think NATO is obsolete," Trump said in an interview with ABC News in March 2016, roughly two months before he would secure the nomination of the Republican Party.[2] The North Atlantic Treaty Organization (NATO), a security alliance established in the early years of the Cold War to contain Soviet influence in Europe, had until this moment been an unassailable element of bipartisan foreign policy doctrine. It obligates member nations to treat an attack on any member as an attack on them all. When the Soviet Union collapsed in 1991, the United States kept the alliance in place and later expanded it to the far eastern reaches of Europe. NATO has come to represent much more than a defensive security alliance. Washington largely sees it as the fulcrum of peace in Europe and an institutional model for promoting democracy, extending economic integration, and allowing the United States to maintain its leadership of the so-called liberal international order.

Trump's dismissal of NATO as "obsolete" in a world without the Soviet Union was consistent with his expressed frustration with allies' free riding on U.S. protection. "We are being ripped off by everybody," Trump said in October 2016. "We have to renegotiate these agreements, because our country cannot afford to defend Saudi Arabia, Japan, Germany, South Korea, and many other places."[3] In addition, candidate Trump spoke somewhat cavalierly of the prospect of nuclear weapons proliferation in South Korea and Japan, countries that had abstained from building their own nuclear deterrents thanks in part to American security guarantees. This position also sharply deviated from the foreign policy consensus in Washington, DC, which understands the U.S.-led international security architecture—centered on U.S. security commitments and extended deterrence—as a vital and incontestable American responsibility.

Trump repeatedly called for an accommodative posture toward Moscow. In verbiage he would use again and again, Trump told Fox News in April 2016, "If we can make a great deal for our country and get along with Russia, that would be a tremendous thing."[4] And he told a crowd in Scranton, Pennsylvania, "Wouldn't it be a great thing if we could get along with Russia?"[5] Such comments sounded dissonant coming from a Republican candidate for president, but they became particularly controversial in light of subsequent assessments by the U.S. intelligence community that Russia had used cyberwarfare tactics to interfere with the 2016 election on Trump's behalf.

Trump also boldly attacked regime-change and nation-building wars, missions that the United States had taken up with increasing frequency in the post–Cold War era, and with conspicuously bitter results. In the aftermath of the Iraq War debacle and the ongoing military quagmire in Afghanistan, public opinion soured on costly ground wars intended to replace far-off regimes with nominally democratic ones. However, the national security establishment continues to value such operations as critical tools of U.S. foreign policy and seems to view Trump's rhetorical attacks as a ploy to exploit public war fatigue in a way that threatens to sap support for even limited military action. Because the post–World War II order requires a generous dose of U.S. military activity, Trump's brickbats led to much establishment handwringing over the possible crumbling of that order.

Richard N. Haass, president of the Council on Foreign Relations, argued that Trump stood for a "new isolationism," a "turning away from global engagement."[6] Hal Brands, a professor at Johns Hopkins University who served for a year in the Obama administration as special assistant to the secretary of defense for strategic planning, warned that a Trump foreign policy could develop into "Fortress America—a hard-line, nearly zero-sum approach that would actively roll back the postwar international order and feature heavy doses of unilateralism and latter-day isolationism."[7] In an essay with Colin Kahl, who served as deputy assistant to President Obama and national security advisor to Vice President Joe Biden, Brands wrote that "Trump's 'America First' grand strategy diverges significantly from—and intentionally subverts—the bipartisan consensus underpinning U.S. foreign policy since World War II."[8] Thomas Wright, a scholar at the Brookings Institution, similarly wrote that Trump "wants to undo the liberal international order the United States built."[9] Mr. Trump, argued Princeton University's G. John Ikenberry, "has made pronouncements that, if acted on, would bring to an end the United States' role as guarantor of the liberal world order," breaking "with 70 years of tradition" in U.S. foreign policy.[10]

Eliot Cohen, a political scientist at Johns Hopkins who also served in
the State Department from 2007 to 2009, wrote a lengthy essay in *The
Atlantic* titled, simply, "How Trump Is Ending the American Era."[11]

These frenzied fears about the demolition of America's enduring
grand strategic duties and prerogatives have proved overwrought. As
president, Trump reaffirmed[12] America's Article 5 security commitment
to NATO countries, expanded the U.S. military presence in Eastern
Europe, welcomed Montenegro as the 29th NATO member country,
and vowed to challenge Russia's "destabilizing activities" in Eastern
Europe.[13] He even exceeded his predecessor's commitment to America's
role as Europe's security guarantor by approving the delivery of lethal
arms to Ukraine—not a NATO ally—to battle Russian-backed separatists. Trump also committed to defend South Korea and Japan and took
a leading role in confronting North Korea's nuclear weapons program.

Trump carried out other policies that fit perfectly within the traditional post–Cold War U.S. foreign policy playbook. In April 2017, and
again a year later, he ordered missile strikes against Syrian military sites
in retaliation for alleged chemical weapons use by the Bashar al-Assad
regime, fulfilling, in a rather uncanny imitation, America's familiar role
of the purportedly indispensable nation and punisher of rogue states.
Elliott Abrams, a veteran of Ronald Reagan's and George H. W. Bush's
administrations, described the first set of strikes as evidence that Trump
had "finally accepted the role of Leader of the Free World."[14] Democratic
leaders Sen. Chuck Schumer and Rep. Nancy Pelosi publicly endorsed
the strikes, while Trump's hawkish Republican antagonists, including Sens. John McCain, Lindsey Graham, and Marco Rubio, praised
Trump for the move. Ian Bremmer, a well-known political scientist and
Washington insider, assessed that "among the U.S. political establishment," Trump's Syria strike was "the most popular action [he] has taken
to date as President."[15]

Similarly, though in the past Trump had decried the war in
Afghanistan as a wasteful quagmire and pledged to "[get] out of the
nation-building business,"[16] as president he decided to send an additional
4,000 U.S. troops to Afghanistan, thus indefinitely continuing the lon-
gest war in U.S. history. Again, this does not fit the model of Trump as

a determined opponent of the Washington foreign policy establishment and the U.S.-led hegemonic order.

In the following pages, we will explore the reasons for these apparent inconsistencies in Trump's foreign policy vision and implementation. One inherent challenge plaguing virtually all analysis of Trump's foreign policy doctrine, however, must be addressed at the outset. This point goes back to the offhand comment of Trump's former communications director, Mike Dubke: "There is no Trump doctrine."

Expert examinations of Trump's foreign policy preferences consistently give the president more credit for having a clear vision of foreign policy than is warranted.[17] While it is certainly true that, as candidate and president, Trump has expounded prolifically on various foreign policy issues, it does not follow that he has firm views on international relations. Indeed, there are compelling reasons to doubt that the president has ever systematically contemplated the foreign policy issues over which he now has ultimate authority. Devising an informed and coherent grand strategy requires a baseline of knowledge about international relations that the president apparently lacks.

President Trump is probably the least informed, least experienced, and least intellectually prepared U.S. president in modern memory—perhaps in American history. "He didn't know a lot of details," Steve Bannon said of candidate Trump. "He knew almost no policy."[18] His rhetoric reveals mostly policy illiteracy, and he seems to lack the rigor and acuity to digest new information in a sophisticated way. In an op-ed in the *Wall Street Journal*, George W. Bush's senior adviser and deputy chief of staff, Karl Rove, lamented that "it appears Trump lacks the focus or the self-discipline to do the basic work required of a president. . . . Mr. Trump may have mastered the modes of communication, but not the substance" of his own policy agenda.[19]

In June 2017, the *Washington Post* reported that "[i]n private conversations on Capitol Hill, Trump is often not taken seriously," and that many "Republican lawmakers . . . are quick to point out how little command he demonstrates of policy."[20] Trump's national security team has had to develop novel ways of briefing the president, relying on one-page, bullet-pointed memos and lots of visual aids to cope with his "notoriously short attention span."[21] As national security advisor, H. R. McMaster reinvented the process. According to the *New Yorker*, the "multi-page explications of policy and strategy" that used to accompany daily briefings were traded for one-page memos after the National Security Council (NSC) received "an edict" from the White House to "thin it out." Even then, the White House reportedly said single-page memos were still too long and suggested briefing Trump "pictorially."[22]

Yet Trump's confidence in his own expertise has never wavered. "I understand what's going on around the world far better than these politicians do," Trump declared during the campaign.[23] On another occasion, he bragged that he "know[s] more than the generals" about national security issues. These prideful boasts faded somewhat once Trump had to confront the issues as president. For example, he had set out a bold position that China was the root of the problem on the Korean Peninsula and that resolving the impasse with Pyongyang simply required U.S. pressure on Beijing. But the president later admitted in an interview with the *Wall Street Journal* that, "after listening for 10 minutes" to Chinese president Xi Jinping explain the history of China and Korea, "I realized it's not so easy."[24]

However, it is far from obvious how much Trump has internalized these brief introductions to the policy basics by advisers and world leaders. "[M]any of America's closest allies have concluded that a hoped-for 'learning curve' they thought would make President Trump a reliable partner is not going to happen," the *Washington Post* reported in October 2017. A top European diplomat said, "The idea that he would inform himself, and things would change, that is no longer operative."[25]

One of the most remarkable on-the-record assessments of President Trump's policy ignorance and unpreparedness came from Republican Sen. Bob Corker. He had been an early backer of Trump in 2016 and was chair of the Senate Foreign Relations Committee when he tweeted that "the White House has become an adult day care center."[26] He later explained to the *New York Times* that the president was treating the presidency like "a reality show." "I know for a fact that every single day at the White House," Corker explained, "it's a situation of trying to contain him," referring to "the tremendous amount of work that it takes by people around him to keep him in the middle of the road."[27] The senator went so far as to say that the "adults in the room"—experienced but now departed practitioners including Secretary of Defense James Mattis, Chief of Staff John Kelly, Secretary of State Rex Tillerson, and National Security Advisor H. R. McMaster—were acting as a buffer between the volatile Trump and the real world. These officials, Corker declared, "separate our country from chaos."[28]

Most, if not all, of Trump's foreign policy pronouncements, from his time as a candidate into his third year as president, have been contradicted by his own separate utterances and outbursts. It is therefore probably a mistake to ascribe much of a coherent foreign policy doctrine, or grand strategy, to the president. Serious inquiry into Donald Trump's foreign policy views is highly susceptible to overinterpretation and errant postulation. Inevitably, though, the president's sentiments set the tone and agenda that his administration, however disjointedly, sets out to actualize. Even if he lacks a coherent and informed set of foreign policy views, Trump does have certain impulses that inform his view of the world.

Specifically, Trump represents a contemporary iteration of the nationalist ideologies found throughout 19th- and early 20th-century Europe and America. However, the president's crude domestic isolationism—his penchant for protectionist economic nationalism and his desire to close off immigration to sociocultural, racial, and religious "others"—does not extend to the realm of foreign policy. Trump's version of "America First" is not about retreating from the outside world. Rather, it is chauvinist in orientation and militarist in method. It extols martial glory and evinces a constant readiness to respond to foreign enemies who have besmirched our honor or defied our will. Like Trump the man, Trumpism harps on righteous victimhood and a fearful frustration with perceived cultural decline and political and economic vulnerability.

Trump is skeptical of allies and antagonistic toward adversaries, while seeming to harbor a soft spot for authoritarian strongmen (e.g., he has praised, variously, Russian president Vladimir Putin, North Korea's Kim Jong Un, Filipino president Rodrigo Duterte, Turkey's Recep Tayyip Erdoğan, and the Saudi monarchs). He believes that projecting toughness and issuing threats yields capitulation from rivals, while a willingness to negotiate or accommodate the interests of other powers is tantamount to weakness and surrender, a naïveté dangerously susceptible to exploitation by competitors.

Yet some of Trump's rhetoric, when taken out of context, does resemble certain ideas in the field of international relations, particularly certain strains of academic realism that advocate for a more restrained U.S. foreign policy. Opponents of these ideas in the policy community have frequently mischaracterized Trump's America First views as variously isolationist, noninterventionist, realist, or restrained. Some have even gone so far as to explicitly associate Trump with these restraint-oriented schools of thought, suggesting that he had even the vaguest understanding of these well-developed ideas. We took particular interest in these claims, as they implicated our own views. We and other scholars at the Cato Institute, the libertarian think tank for which we work, have long criticized primacy and questioned the necessity of America's leadership role in the international system. Unfortunately, attempts to characterize Trump's foreign policy views have resulted in respectable critics of the so-called liberal international order, or anyone with a more restrained view of U.S. foreign policy, being dragged through the mud—guilt by a tenuous association with Trump, or in many cases, an imaginary one.

Undeniably, Trump was elected despite saying things deeply at odds with the view of the U.S. role in the world that prevails in Washington. In practice, however, Trump has come to represent something like the *inverse* of restraint. Most restrainers tend to emphasize the importance of low-tariff free trade, liberal immigration policies, robust diplomatic engagement via multilateral institutions, and a reduced U.S. military role in the world. Trump, on the other hand, has pursued economic protectionism, restricted immigration, neutered the diplomatic corps, and engaged in belligerent militarism based on the frequent threat and use of force on the global stage.

Furthermore, aside from questions of grand strategy, Trump in many ways represents the antithesis of the liberal democratic values strongly preferred by most in the restraint camp. Indeed, one of the major lines of argument in favor of a more restrained foreign policy is that massive military establishments and the permanent security state necessary to sustain an activist foreign policy can have a corrosive effect on liberal democratic values in the domestic sphere. Donald Trump's political and ideological inclinations are unusually authoritarian by the standards of contemporary U.S. political culture. He is prone to conspiracy theories bordering on paranoia, he demands loyalty from officials in federal departments that are supposed to be independent and nonpartisan, and he seems to relish violating long-standing political norms.

For example, Trump pledged during the campaign that he was prepared to accept the results of the election, but only if he won.[29] As president, he has repeatedly threatened to target his political opponents with criminal prosecution.[30] He has condemned the news media as "the enemy of the American people," while calling for revoking the licenses of cable news channels that are critical of him. In true Nixonian fashion, Trump claims to have absolute power to pardon himself for any crime and threatened to terminate the special counsel investigation into his campaign's contacts with Russian operations to influence the 2016 election. He has a general disrespect, albeit based in ignorance, for constitutional constraints on his executive powers, though in practice it seems more of a continuation of a long tradition of postwar U.S. presidents to leave the office more powerful and unchecked than they found it.

This book seeks to properly characterize Trump's foreign policy doctrine, such as it is. It will explain why Trump's policies have hewed closer to conventional U.S. foreign policy than his rhetoric foreshadowed. And finally, it will make the case for a genuinely restraint-oriented departure from America's expansive global military role in the world. This last part is crucial. Restraint is an idea whose time has come; actually, it is long overdue. Despite hysterical news headlines and the ubiquitous elite haranguing about existential national security threats, today's international system is remarkably peaceful and stable. The United States, thanks to its geographic isolation and its outsized economic and military power, is particularly insulated from foreign threats.

Yet our foreign policy does not reflect this benign security environment. America has been at war for two out of every three years since the end of the Cold War. About 46 percent of Americans have lived the majority of their lives with the United States at war.[31] Washington has engaged in more military interventions in the past 30 years than it had in the preceding 190 years.[32] This hyper-activist, heavily militaristic foreign policy has not just been unnecessary, costly, and counterproductive for U.S. interests, but it has also occurred in a period of declining relative U.S. power. Following World War II, after the other great powers had been devastated by conflict, the United States accounted for roughly 50 percent of global economic output, making it hard for our ambition to truly exceed our means. That figure stood at 22 percent as recently as the 1980s, but today the U.S. share has fallen to 15 percent, and the International Monetary Fund projects that it will slip to 13.9 percent by 2023.[33] Such figures mostly reflect the fact that billions of people around the world have lifted themselves out of grinding poverty, a process aided by the embrace of liberalism and market economics. Such human progress should be celebrated. Still, U.S. foreign policy has not adapted; its goals are suited to a time long since passed, when the available resources seemed nearly limitless.

Change has been slow in coming owing to the policy consensus around the grand strategy of *primacy*, which prescribes an expansive conception of the U.S. role in the world that requires overspending on the military and the elevation of peripheral interests to the level of vital ones. A grand strategy of *restraint*, by contrast, counsels prudence, nonintervention in the affairs of other countries, and a more modest set of objectives and interests. It eschews elective wars, unrealistic nation-building schemes, and the pursuit of hegemony. It draws from a rich history of U.S. foreign policy in which, as one of America's preeminent statesmen (and eventual president) John Quincy Adams put it, America "goes not abroad in search of monsters to destroy," and "is the well-wisher to the freedom and independence of all," but "the champion and vindicator only of her own." Adams warned that if America went down the path of global dominion,

> she would involve herself beyond the power of extrication, in all the wars of interest and intrigue, of individual avarice, envy, and ambition, which assume the colors and usurp the standard of freedom.

The fundamental maxims of her policy would insensibly change from liberty to force. . . . She might become the dictatress of the world. She would be no longer the ruler of her own spirit.[34]

Restraint in U.S. foreign policy is ripe for a revival. Primacy has indeed entangled us in gratuitous wars of interest, intrigue, and hubristic ambition, but not, we believe, beyond the power of extrication. Trump's entry into the presidency and onto the world stage has fortuitously prompted a much-needed debate about grand strategy. What America needs is not Trump's America First, nor a return to the status quo ante, but a radical reevaluation of its role in the world.

CHAPTER 1
U.S. Foreign Policy since the Cold War and 9/11

In his farewell message to the American people, George Washington urged his countrymen to "avoid the necessity of those overgrown military establishments" that posed a critical threat to liberty. Rather than relying primarily on military power to advance the nation's security and prosperity, Washington and his successors relied instead on trade and skillful diplomacy. His "great rule of conduct" with respect to foreign nations was to have extensive commercial relations, but "as little political connection as possible."[1]

Washington's contemporaries, and the generation that followed him, echoed these sentiments. As noted in the Introduction, John Quincy Adams explained that America would support the cause of liberty with "her heart, her benedictions and her prayers" but "goes not abroad in search of monsters to destroy." To enlist under foreign banners, he explained, even for just causes, would tear at the fabric of what made the United States truly exceptional.[2]

These guiding principles formed the bedrock of the nation's foreign policy for decades. The greatest threat to the Republic during the 19th century came not from foreign enemies, but rather from those within. The Civil War remains to this day the costliest war in American history. By the end of that century, however, the U.S. government had consolidated its control over the landmass that we know today as the contiguous United States. It acquired territories in Alaska and Hawaii. And it wrested away a decrepit Spanish empire's few remaining possessions in the Caribbean, chiefly Cuba and Puerto Rico, and even the vast Philippine archipelago, some 7,000 miles away.

Such conquests whetted U.S. leaders' appetite for a more active role in world affairs. Woodrow Wilson made the case for U.S. entry into World War I, not on the grounds that it was necessary to preserve U.S. security, but that the world "be made safe for democracy."[3] In effect, Wilson's belated intervention bought the upstart United States, by then the world's wealthiest nation, a seat at the big kids' table. He explained to midshipmen at the U.S. Naval Academy, that the "idea of America . . . is to serve humanity."[4]

Still, the American people retained Washington's and Adams's skepticism of foreign military adventures. They briefly forgot, however, Washington's positive vision for global engagement through commerce. Faced with a sharp economic downturn following the stock market crash in October 1929, Congress erected barriers to foreign trade, deepening a global financial crisis. For years, Americans watched anxiously but from a great distance as Japan rampaged through China and as Nazi Germany rose and overran its neighbors in Europe. When U.S. aid to Great Britain and the Soviet Union failed to reverse the tide, America eventually became directly involved in the fighting in both theaters.

After World War II, U.S. policymakers took away several lessons from the first half of the 20th century: first, that global trade was a force for peace; second, that aggression must be challenged; and third, that the world needed a single dominant power to enforce global norms—and that the United States would be that power. The ensuing decades of great-power peace were taken as proof that these three precepts were correct.

In fact, many factors explain the emergence of peace and prosperity globally after World War II, including economic interdependence and the spread of liberal values, such as respect for the rule of law and human rights. The deterrent of nuclear weapons—not to mention the still-fresh memory of devastating conventional wars—also contributed to the relative decline of organized state-on-state violence. But U.S. leaders focused particular attention on the role that U.S. military power played in tamping down the rest of mankind's warlike impulses.

This elevation of military power as the *sine qua non* of American influence did not sit well with all U.S. leaders. In his own farewell address to the nation, President Dwight Eisenhower conceded that the nation had, for the first time in its history, "been compelled to create a permanent armaments industry of vast proportions." Ike rarely doubted that such a military establishment was needed to compete with the Soviet Union, but he worried that a failure to reconcile the nation's means (resources, public will) and ends (strategic goals) would pose as great a threat as the Soviet menace. Accordingly, he stressed the need for "balance between actions of the moment and the national welfare of the future."[5]

Eventually the United States would prevail over the Soviet Union. But by then the "permanent" aspect that Eisenhower spoke of had become clear: the United States retained a military far larger than necessary to defend U.S. vital interests after the Soviet Union's collapse.

Indeed, as Ike anticipated, the mere existence of a massive "military-industrial complex" created pressures that earlier presidents rarely contended with. Providing for the military became big business, and a sizable constituency within the United States—and a key voting bloc in Congress—was committed to keeping military spending high, irrespective of the actual threats to the nation. These same voters were favorably inclined to foreign military adventures.

To be sure, there were countervailing pressures. The bitter experience in Vietnam, for example, cast a long shadow over U.S. foreign policy in the 1970s and into the 1980s. The U.S. military competed for funding with an expanding welfare state, and the Pentagon's budget ebbed and flowed. And more money didn't always mean more wars. President Ronald Reagan promised to achieve "peace through strength" and pushed through a substantial increase in the military's total budget in the early and mid 1980s; spending on procurement of new equipment more than doubled.[6] But, with a few notable exceptions (e.g., Lebanon in 1982, Grenada in 1983, and Libya in 1986), Reagan generally resisted the urge to use this suddenly expanded force. Like his Cold War predecessors, he worried that even small-scale skirmishes on the periphery could easily spiral into large-scale wars with a formidable, nuclear-armed adversary.

All told, as the Cold War dragged on, the competition between the two superpowers was largely confined to the shadows, or obscured behind proxies and third parties. The United States backed Afghan "freedom fighters" in the Soviets' backyard; Moscow supported Cuban and Nicaraguan allies in ours. Granted, these so-called low-intensity conflicts did entail risk. Support for the Afghan *mujahideen* helped them stymie and eventually expel the Soviet invaders, and it engendered little domestic opposition in the United States. Only later did critics note the problems associated with funding and arming a transnational movement fueled by Islamic extremism.[7] Meanwhile, Reagan's bid to undermine Daniel Ortega's government in Nicaragua by providing aid to the Contra rebels—in direct defiance of congressional prohibitions on such assistance—resulted in the most serious crisis of his presidency.

Such activities were conducted within the context of the Cold War and under the broad rubric of containment. U.S. policymakers debated how to fight the Soviet Union, not whether to do so. That started to change around 1987. Although Reagan had railed against the Soviet Union as "the focus of evil in the modern world" during a 1983 speech and famously called on Soviet leader Mikhail Gorbachev to tear down the Berlin Wall, the two men managed to establish a working relationship by the end of Reagan's second term. When Reagan left office in January 1989, the threat of war between the two countries seemed at its lowest ebb in recent memory.

But Reagan's vice president, George H. W. Bush, wasn't initially won over by Gorbachev's charm offensive. Elected in his own right in November 1988 to succeed the Gipper in the Oval Office, the one-time director of the Central Intelligence Agency, along with key lieutenants National Security Advisor Brent Scowcroft and Secretary of State James A. Baker III, moved cautiously. During the dramatic days of the late summer and early fall of 1989, they mostly watched and waited as the Soviet Union's allies in Eastern Europe distanced themselves from Moscow.

★★★★★

The first act of post–Cold War U.S. foreign policy began on November 9, 1989, if one counts the fall of the Berlin Wall as the critical moment signifying the end of that decades-long conflict. The second act began within hours of the terrorist attacks on September 11, 2001, and led to the ensuing wars in Afghanistan and Iraq and the veritable panoply of military operations, intelligence gathering, and law-enforcement activities associated with waging a global war on terrorism. Understanding each is crucial to understanding where matters stand today.

Act I: The Post–Cold War Era and the New World Order

Faced with an opportunity to make the world anew, President George H. W. Bush was purposeful and deliberate. Opportunities to use the U.S. military in a post–Cold War environment presented themselves before the full extent of the Soviet Union's demise became clear. The brief intervention in Panama in December 1989 to depose the one-time U.S. ally Gen. Manuel Noriega was consistent with a long pattern of U.S. involvement in the Western Hemisphere. The Bush administration's show of force, involving approximately 27,000 U.S. military personnel, might have occurred even if the Berlin Wall hadn't come down the month before.

But the decision to throw the full weight of the U.S. military behind reversing Iraqi leader Saddam Hussein's attempted annexation of Kuwait in August 1990 signaled an important departure from past practices. Bush and his national security team portrayed U.S. intervention as necessary—and, indeed, inevitable. "We don't have the option to be inactive in reversing this," Scowcroft wrote.[8] In fact, a decade earlier, the United States had refused to take action to halt Iraq's invasion of Iran and had even provided Saddam Hussein with weapons—including technology, equipment, and precursors for chemical weapons—to prosecute a brutal war that may have claimed as many as 2 million lives.[9]

In the case of Iraq's invasion of Kuwait, the Bush administration also invoked a variation on the domino theory—if Hussein succeeds, others may try the same thing—and threat exaggeration, including over-the-top comparisons between Iraq circa 1990 and Nazi Germany in the late 1930s. But the critical context was the end of the Cold War and the crafting of a new post–Cold War order. "At stake is the shape of the world to come," Bush explained to his senior aides.[10]

By January 1991, more than 500,000 U.S. military personnel were stationed in the region, on Iraq's border, in Saudi Arabia, and on ships at sea. Congress passed a resolution authorizing the use of force by a comfortable 250–183 margin in the House but by a narrower 52–47 in the Senate. Aircraft pounded Iraq's defenses for more than five weeks before ground operations commenced on February 24. A few days later, Operation Desert Storm was over.[11]

George H. W. Bush could barely conceal his glee. On March 1, following an address to a group of state legislators, the president exulted, "It's a proud day for America. And, by God, we've kicked the Vietnam syndrome once and for all."[12]

Given the incongruity between the *claims* of what was at stake (an Iraq poised to overrun a vital region) and what was *actually* at stake (governance of a tiny petrostate), Bush biographer Jeffrey Engel posited a different explanation for Bush's enthusiasm for waging a massive U.S. military operation in the Persian Gulf. "What . . . ultimately drove Bush to act?" Engel asks. It wasn't so much any intrinsic principle about the inviolability of national sovereignty and recognized borders, or even a compelling U.S. national security interest with respect to access to the region's oil. Rather, Bush and his team saw the Persian Gulf War of 1991 as a critical test case to prove the utility—indeed, some might later claim, indispensability—of American power. "It was [an] opportunity," Engel concludes, "to demonstrate American leadership, on American terms."[13]

After the dust from the Persian Gulf War settled, the Bush administration set about framing U.S. foreign policy for the post–Cold War era in earnest.

An early draft of the Defense Planning Guidance leaked in March 1992. According to the document prepared by aides to Secretary of Defense Dick Cheney, the primary object of U.S. foreign policy was to "prevent the re-emergence of a new rival" capable of challenging U.S. power in any vital area of the world, including Europe, the Middle East, and East Asia. U.S. power would be deployed in a way that deterred not only potential adversaries but also critical democratic allies such as Japan and Germany from "even aspiring to a larger regional or global role."[14]

The logic undergirding this document was consistent with what Harvard political scientist Samuel Huntington called primacy. "A world without U.S. primacy," he wrote in 1993, "will be a world with more violence and disorder and less democracy and economic growth."[15]

"With the close of the century's three great Northern civil wars (World War I, World War II and the Cold War)," explained columnist Charles Krauthammer, "an ideologically pacified North seeks security and order by aligning its foreign policy behind that of the United States."[16]

Huntington and Krauthammer were both worried about renewed security competition leading to arms races, or even nuclear proliferation. The Pentagon's draft guidance echoed these sentiments. If "Germany, Japan and other industrial powers" were tempted "to acquire nuclear weapons to deter attack from regional foes," that "could start them down the road to global competition with the United States and, in a crisis over national interests, military rivalry."[14] U.S. policy would attempt to nip that in the bud. Accordingly, the document pledged to use U.S. military power to construct a security order that protected the major powers in Europe and Asia, and thus effectively eliminated the need for any of them to acquire nuclear weapons of their own.

Bush administration officials acted swiftly to distance themselves from the leaked document, though they seemed more troubled by the impolitic tone than the grandiose substance. A watered-down version dropped references to blocking U.S. allies from attaining greater global influence and instead called for greater burden sharing among like-minded parties. "Where our allies interests [sic] are directly affected," it read, "we must expect them to take an appropriate share of the responsibility, and in some cases play the leading role."[17]

That isn't how it played out. Rather than developing capabilities that might have been useful both for their own defenses and for advancing global peace and prosperity, U.S. allies largely stood on the sidelines as the U.S. military deployed hither and yon—from Somalia to Kosovo—in the ensuing decade.

★★★★★

Americans' attitudes toward these peripatetic interventions on the periphery ranged from casual enthusiasm to anxious indifference.

None of these missions had anything to do with U.S. security narrowly defined. Success or failure threatened neither Americans' safety nor their prosperity. Accordingly, the public supported—or at least tolerated—small wars, as long as the costs were low and the intended objective noble. Such support was always fragile, however; military operations that did not advance U.S. vital interests were rarely deemed worthy of the loss of even a single American soldier.

For example, the first substantial military mission after Desert Storm entailed some 25,000 U.S. troops delivering food aid to starving Somalis in late 1992. By the summer of 1993, the operation had morphed into a hunt for murderous warlords in Mogadishu. It ended with a firefight in October that killed 18 American soldiers. The cover of *Time* magazine spoke for many Americans when it asked, "What in the World Are We Doing?"[18] Within months, all U.S. forces were withdrawn. Historian Andrew Bacevich writes, "Senior U.S. military leaders had never pressed for an answer to the question of how much bringing order to Somalia was actually 'worth.' The firefight [in Mogadishu] revealed the answer: not much."[19] Thereafter, U.S. policymakers went to often absurd lengths to ensure that images of flag-draped coffins never made it on the evening news.

But with the specter of a hot war with the now-departed Soviet Union no longer on the table, U.S. officials contemplated other military adventures—believing that the risks were low and knowing full well that the actual dangers of such operations would be borne by the tiny sliver of the population that had chosen to serve in the nation's military.

Writes Bacevich, "the passing of the Vietnam Syndrome" after Operation Desert Storm

> portended . . . a heedless absence of self-restraint, with shallow mor-
> alistic impulses overriding thoughtful strategic analysis. . . . As a con-
> sequence, in debates over possible U.S. armed intervention, wariness
> now gave way to "why not?". . . . The possession of matchless military
> capabilities not only endowed the United States with the ability to
> right wrongs and succor the afflicted, it also imposed an obligation to
> do just that.[20]

Put differently, the various decisions pertaining to the use of force in the early post–Cold War period seem to confirm the old saying, "when all you have is a hammer, everything looks like a nail."

Such sentiments are apparent in a famous exchange between then ambassador to the United Nations Madeleine Albright and former national security advisor Colin Powell. "What's the point," Albright asked Powell, who chaired the Joint Chiefs of Staff at the time, "of having this superb military that you're always talking about if we can't use it?" Powell later recorded in his memoir that he "nearly had an aneurysm." U.S. soldiers, he complained, were not geopolitical pawns to be moved around some "global game board."[21]

Albright didn't merely have unbounded confidence in the American military's ability to deliver great things. She also possessed an expansive view of America's purpose in the world and the U.S. military's central role within U.S. foreign policy. She expressed less concern about whether a particular military intervention served a "vital national interest." Rather, she wanted to know whether that military power would allow the United States to do good. Most of the time, she believed, it could.

"My mind-set is Munich, most of my generation's is Vietnam," Albright explained. "I saw what happened when a dictator was allowed to take over a piece of a country and the country went down the tubes. And I saw the opposite during the war when America joined the fight. For me," she continued, "America really, truly is the indispensable nation."[22] She was hardly alone.

Overwhelming American military power, explained William Kristol and Robert Kagan in the summer of 1996, "is the only reliable defense against a breakdown of peace and international order." They explicitly rejected "the charming old metaphor of the United States as a 'city on a hill'" and scorned John Quincy Adams's admonition that "America ought not go abroad in search of monsters to destroy." "Because America has the capacity to contain or destroy many of the world's monsters, most of which can be found without much searching," they wrote, "and because the responsibility for the peace and security of the international order rests so heavily on America's shoulders, a policy of sitting atop a hill and leading by example becomes in practice a policy of cowardice and dishonor."[23]

With the passage of time, we can now see that U.S. leaders' decisions to use the military didn't always confirm the efficacy of American hard power; sometimes they revealed its limits. And whereas Kristol and Kagan confidently predicted that "the American people can be summoned to meet the challenges of global leadership if statesmen make the case loudly, cogently, and persistently," that wasn't always the case either.

Instead, Americans' enthusiasm for foreign adventures waxes and wanes in rough proximity to the most recent war. Unpleasant or indecisive wars, such as those in Korea or Vietnam, engender resistance. Seemingly successful wars (for example, Panama or Desert Storm), breed confidence—and then, often, overconfidence.

The 1990s were emblematic of this dichotomy. Consider, for example, how U.S. leaders approached the nations of post–Cold War Europe.

The United States and Europe

George H. W. Bush tread carefully in his first year in office. Signs of the Soviet Union's steady decline were apparent by the spring of 1989, and Soviet leader Mikhail Gorbachev had given numerous signals of wanting to reset bilateral relations. But Bush was cautious. "Faced with uncertainty, and unsure of the best response, he paused, considered, and learned," explains biographer Jeffrey Engel.[24] Ultimately, however, after a period of thoughtful reflection, Bush and his cohort came to believe certain things about the post–Cold War order. In their view, Engel writes, "real long-term peace could be assured only through continued American vigilance, oversight, and strength."[25]

The sentiments reflected in the Defense Planning Guidance, especially the notion that other countries simply could not be trusted to provide security for themselves, shone through in the Bush, and later Clinton, administration's approach to Europe. Bush administration officials believed, Engel explains, that "there was simply something innate to Europeans that made them unable to live peacefully with their neighbors." Accordingly, "The United States . . . needed to remain [Europe's] nurse and nanny."[26]

"The basic lesson of two world wars was that American power is essential to any stable equilibrium on the continent," Brent Scowcroft reminded Bush. James Baker reached a similar conclusion, but he expressed it more succinctly: "we prevented for 40 years war in Europe."[27]

"The pronoun is what mattered," Engel writes. "The 'we' was not NATO. Neither was it a grand democratic alliance. It was the United States." "The central lesson of the twentieth century, to Bush and those he gathered around him," Engel concludes, "was their own indispensability."[28]

By treating U.S. power as the essential tool for ensuring peace in Europe, Bush and his team subverted alternative arrangements that might have encouraged greater self-reliance by U.S. allies and partners. By framing U.S. policy around the "basic lesson" that "American power" had been essential, U.S. officials simultaneously sought to ensure that it always would be.

Candidate Bill Clinton knocked George H. W. Bush for his timidity in adapting to the new realities of the post–Cold War world, but as president he mostly followed along the trail blazed by Bush and his advisers. The Clinton administration envisioned NATO as more than a military alliance to balance against a much-diminished Russian threat. The decision to expand NATO eastward, despite the Bush administration's implicit promise to Russian leaders that former Warsaw Pact states would not be included, reflected this new approach—but critically ignored Russia's security concerns.[29] Instead, Clinton and key advisers, including National Security Advisor Anthony Lake and Deputy Secretary of State Strobe Talbott, believed that an expanded NATO could be used to stabilize the states emerging from the Cold War's shadow and to boost nascent democracies in Eastern Europe.[30] The goal was to reintegrate the various European states—both the old anti-Soviet West and the former Soviet-allied Warsaw Pact—into a single entity. The notion of a Europe "whole and free"—George H. W. Bush's phrase from a speech in West Germany in 1989[31]—was equally important to his successor and became the basis for NATO expansion in the decade after the fall of the Soviet Union. Post–Cold War Europe would be defined, according to U.S. policymakers, by a common commitment to democracy and by the spread of market liberalism and the rule of law.

Eventually, advocates of U.S. intervention in the Balkans in the mid-1990s portrayed NATO's apparent easy victory over Serb forces in Bosnia as a further affirmation of this vision. The alliance created to deter the Soviet Union had seemingly found a new rationale.

But that wasn't initially apparent. Indeed, NATO's failure to halt fighting between ethnic Croats, Serbs, and Muslims in the former Yugoslav republics might have demonstrated the alliance's waning utility. Ultimately, however, the Dayton Agreement that sealed the Serbs' fate in Bosnia also helped solidify support for the alliance.[32]

NATO's advocates claimed that uniting the countries of Europe would foster peace in a historically unstable region. The allure of NATO membership, expansionists argued, would encourage countries—even historic foes—to resolve disputes peacefully. Supporters pointed to the experience of Germany and France in the 1950s and '60s, and Turkey and Greece in the 1980s, as evidence of the pacifying effect of binding former adversaries together as allies.

National Security Advisor Lake explained that Americans must remain committed to NATO—even in the absence of the Soviet threat— because insecurity in any part of Europe would inevitably affect security in the United States. "History has taught us that when Europe is in turmoil, America suffers, and when Europe is peaceful and prosperous,

America can thrive as well," Lake explained.[33] Clinton echoed these sentiments in a speech at the U.S. Military Academy at West Point: "Europe's fate and America's future are joined."[34]

There was broad, bipartisan support for expansion within the U.S. foreign policy establishment. Liberal Democrats rallied to Clinton's side, endorsing his vision for NATO as a stabilizing force for Europe and a vehicle for spreading liberalism and democracy. Most Republicans, from harsh Clinton critics like Sen. Jesse Helms (R–NC) to moderate internationalists like Sen. Richard Lugar (R–IN), saw NATO expansion as a means to seal the United States' victory over the Soviet Union.[35] Locking Eastern Europe within the U.S. orbit might even ensure that Russia would never reemerge as a credible challenger to U.S. power in the region or globally.

Unsurprisingly, most Russians were opposed. U.S. and NATO officials worked to assuage Moscow's concerns that NATO expansion into former Warsaw Pact countries posed a threat to Russia. In May 1995, during a summit in Moscow, Russia joined NATO's Partnership for Peace Program. Separately, Clinton and Russian President Boris Yeltsin traded ideas on creating a NATO–Russia alliance.

Clinton initially did not set a timetable for NATO expansion. He knew the Russians would not be receptive to the idea. The decision to delay may have helped tamp down the issue within Russia, and Yeltsin won reelection in 1996. Thereafter, Clinton administration officials interpreted the result of that election as proof that Russians would ultimately, if begrudgingly, tolerate NATO expansion. The alliance would expand eastward, while the NATO-Russia Permanent Joint Council gave Russia a voice in NATO affairs—but no actual power within the alliance.[36]

In May 1997, U.S. Secretary of State Madeleine Albright laid out guidelines for the expansion—subsequently codified as a Membership Action Plan (MAP). Going forward, she explained, NATO would not exclude any European state that met the MAP requirements.[37] Later that year, at a summit in Madrid on July 8, 1997, NATO members invited Poland, Hungary, and the Czech Republic to join the alliance. On May 1, 1998, the United States became the 5th of the 16 NATO members to approve admission: the U.S. Senate voted 80–19 in favor. The opponents included 10 Democrats and 9 Republicans.[38] Other NATO members followed suit, and on March 12, 1999, the three new members were formally admitted into the alliance. It was the first such expansion in nearly 17 years; Spain had joined in May 1982. The process whereby the three countries gained admission became a model to guide other countries aspiring to join NATO.

Even so, NATO expansion did engender opposition and criticism. The fights between Clinton and Yeltsin over the issue were among the most contentious during their overlapping presidencies. Russian officials disputed that the alliance was truly needed to safeguard Europe's security and were equally skeptical of U.S. and NATO claims that the alliance posed no threat.[39]

Many critics within the United States agreed. Military leaders worried that continuing or expanding the American commitment to Europe's defense would strain a shrinking force. An array of foreign policy experts—including elected officials, retired diplomats, military officers, and prominent academics—viewed expansion as unnecessary and warned that it threatened to raise the temperature on U.S.–Russia relations during what could have been a long post–Cold War thaw. The veteran diplomat and scholar George Kennan called NATO expansion "the most fateful error of American foreign policy in the entire post–Cold War era."[40]

Other factors contributed to the controversy over NATO's eastward expansion. Threats within and to Central and Eastern Europe had never been a core U.S. national security concern. The region's geography made it difficult for outsiders to defend, and cross-border ethnic tensions portended trouble in the future. For example, Hungary had always taken an interest in the plight of the Hungarian diaspora (numbering some 5 million people) in Romania and elsewhere. Unrest in Belarus threatened to spill over into neighboring Poland.[41]

The second round of NATO expansion raised similar issues. Seven nations—Bulgaria, Estonia, Latvia, Lithuania, Romania, Slovakia, and Slovenia—were invited to join in November 2002, and all gained full membership on March 29, 2004, the largest single expansion of the alliance since its founding. All had followed MAP guidelines, as would three additional members who joined later—Albania and Croatia in 2009, and Montenegro in 2017.

Looking back on a process that ultimately doubled the number of states within NATO, even some supporters of the decision to move forward with NATO expansion allow that it might have had unfortunate side effects.

"Historians will debate the wisdom of NATO enlargement," according to Council on Foreign Relations president Richard N. Haass, and "there is no way of knowing whether the trajectory of relations with Russia would have been better" had there been no expansion. "All that can be known for sure," Haass continues, "is that NATO enlargement contributed to the alienation of Russia."[42]

The Brookings Institution's Michael O'Hanlon agrees, calling NATO expansion "the fundamental cause of the problem" that is U.S.–Russia relations today—at least in Vladimir Putin's mind. The prospect of further expansion, O'Hanlon writes, amounts to a "doomsday machine that raises the likelihood of conflict in Europe."[43]

The United States and China

Just as Bush, Clinton, and others took as an article of faith that U.S. power would remain central to keeping peace in Europe, so too did both the Bush and Clinton administrations believe in the ultimate triumph of liberal democracy over illiberalism and autarchy, with the United States leading the way to that promised land. These beliefs saw their clearest expression in U.S. policy toward the People's Republic of China.

According to historian Engel, after the Chinese government's brutal crackdown on pro-democracy protesters in Tiananmen Square in May 1989, "Bush worked . . . hard to keep the 'butchers of Beijing' a part of the world."[44] The decision elicited considerable scorn. Clinton blasted Bush for coddling the regime and promised to get tough with the communist government. Indeed, write Derek Chollet and James Goldgeier, "Clinton saw China as a key test of the commitment to defend liberal ideals." In a major speech after Clinton took office, his foreign policy adviser Anthony Lake explained that the United States needed an approach toward China that "reflects both our values and our interests."[45]

Sino–U.S. relations grew tense in the ensuing years even though Clinton generally avoided criticizing China's human rights record and stressed instead the benefits of increased trade with China. In June 1995, China withdrew its ambassador in protest over the U.S. government's decision to allow Taiwan president Lee Teng-hui to speak at Cornell University. The following spring, the United States sent two aircraft carriers plus associated escorts into the Taiwan Strait to block Beijing's military exercises there, the first such show of military force against China in more than four decades. But Clinton moved swiftly to reset relations. "Rather than seeking to isolate or contain or punish China," Chollet and Goldgeier explain, "the Clinton team decided to try to integrate the rising economic and military power into the global community."[46]

The move offended critics on both ends of the political spectrum in the United States. James Woolsey, an outspoken hawk who had briefly served as CIA director under Clinton, accused the president of "outright appeasement" and claimed that "the United States [had] actually helped create a new superpower threat."[47] Liberals were equally dismayed by Clinton's decision to ignore China's poor human rights record. They also complained that China's low wages and lax-to-nonexistent environmental standards put U.S. workers and producers at a competitive disadvantage.

But Clinton persisted. Determined to draw China into an international order that the United States had helped create, he pushed Congress to grant China Permanent Normal Trade Relations, a step that eventually paved the way for China's admission into the World Trade Organization. Clinton downplayed the economic benefits that might accrue from increased trade with what would soon be the largest economy in Asia, stressing instead the geostrategic rationale: it was better that China have a seat at the table than to be left, angry and resentful, on the fringes.

But while Clinton's attention was fixed on dealing with a future great power in Asia and on containing possible unrest in Europe, a worrisome nonstate threat was arising in the still-roiling Middle East.

Act II: Al Qaeda, 9/11, and the Hijacking of U.S. Foreign Policy

During the 1980s, the U.S. government supported insurgents inside Afghanistan who fought against the pro-Soviet government in Kabul and the tens of thousands of Soviet troops sent there to prop it up. The U.S. effort culminated in billions of dollars of aid, including weapons, flowing into the country through neighboring Pakistan. The Kingdom of Saudi Arabia also provided funding and rallied the world's Muslims to help drive out the infidel invaders. Over the decade, thousands of "freedom fighters" flowed into Afghanistan, and they had reason to celebrate after the Soviet troops withdrew in 1989.

One of those foreign fighters, Osama bin Laden, later offered his services to Saudi Arabia, when Iraqi troops invaded Kuwait in August 1990 and seemed poised to overrun the kingdom. He was appalled when Riyadh instead welcomed U.S. troops onto Saudi lands. Bin Laden thereafter dedicated himself to toppling the apostate rulers of, as he called it, the Land of the Two Holy Places (i.e., Mecca and Medina). He later allied himself with a medical doctor from Egypt, Ayman al-Zawahiri, who was equally disgusted by the Egyptian government's alliance with the United States.

Their organization, al Qaeda ("the base"), carried out a series of terrorist attacks in the 1990s. These included an attack in late December 1992 on a hotel in Yemen that had housed U.S. soldiers and a 1993 truck bomb in the basement of the World Trade Center that killed five and injured hundreds, but failed to bring down the building. In 1995, a bombing at a Saudi National Guard training center killed seven Americans. Investigators at the scene found a terrorism how-to CD which celebrated bin Laden as a hero. The following year, a truck bomb attack on the Khobar Towers, an apartment building in Dhahran that housed U.S. Air Force personnel, killed 19 Americans; another 372 were injured. Saudi officials convinced American investigators that Hezbollah, with

Iranian support, was responsible, though all of those involved in the attacks were Saudis.[48]

That same month, bin Laden issued a public call for Muslims to join a *jihad* that would drive the United States out of Saudi Arabia. Less than two years later, a second public message called on Muslims to kill Americans anywhere they could.[49] The 9/11 Commission's review of bin Laden's writings and statements during the 1990s noted that he had "stressed grievances against the United States widely shared in the Muslim world." In addition to his familiar complaint about the presence of U.S. forces in Saudi Arabia, he also blamed Americans for the suffering of the Iraqi people caused by sanctions imposed after the first Gulf War, and he protested America's long-standing support for the state of Israel.[50]

Bin Laden's various statements, and even al Qaeda's occasional attacks, failed to mobilize the American people to embark on a campaign to eradicate him and his organization. Officials within the U.S. government tracked al Qaeda's activities but were unable to kill or capture its leaders.

Then, on August 7, 1998, the eighth anniversary of the arrival of U.S. troops in Saudi Arabia, nearly simultaneous attacks on the U.S. embassies in Nairobi, Kenya, and Dar es Salaam, Tanzania, killed more than 220 people. Thousands were wounded. Bin Laden finally had the world's attention.

He had fled Saudi Arabia for Sudan in 1991, but by 1998 he had set up operations in Afghanistan. The ruling Taliban were happy to afford him safe haven, and some Taliban fighters even trained in al Qaeda camps. Unsurprisingly, after the embassy bombings, the U.S. government pressured the Taliban to hand over bin Laden and separately planned operations to destroy al Qaeda camps and incapacitate its leaders. Again these operations failed. By 2000, bin Laden and al Qaeda—and the threat of terrorism, generally—had been the subject of some media attention. A commission chaired by former senators Gary Hart and Warren Rudman warned in September 1999 that "America will become increasingly vulnerable to hostile attack on our homeland, and our military superiority will not entirely protect us." The report further predicted that "Americans will likely die on American soil, possibly in large numbers."[51]

An attack on a U.S. Navy destroyer in the port of Aden, Yemen, in October 2000—killing 17 sailors, and wounding another 39—generated outrage but little tangible action. Some in the outgoing Clinton administration advised George W. Bush and his senior aides to pay more attention to the anti-terror fight, but that did not happen until after the devastating attacks on September 11, 2001.

On that day, al Qaeda terrorists hijacked three American airplanes and dove them into both World Trade Center towers in New York City and into the Pentagon. A fourth plane, believed to have been bound for the U.S. Capitol or some other target in Washington, DC, was commandeered by passengers and crashed in a field in rural Pennsylvania. All told, 2,973 were killed. It was by far the single worst act of terrorism ever recorded worldwide and also the largest loss of life on American soil as a result of a hostile attack in U.S. history.[52]

In an address before a joint session of Congress nine days later, Bush explained that the United States would "starve terrorists of funding" and "drive them from place to place until there is no refuge or no rest." Equally important, he pledged to "pursue nations that provide aid or safe haven to terrorism. . . . Every nation in every region," he continued, "now has a decision to make: Either you are with us or you are with the terrorists. . . . From this day forward, any nation that continues to harbor or support terrorism will be regarded by the United States as a hostile regime." Bush said that the U.S. War on Terror would not look like the wars fought during the previous decade, for example in the desert against Iraq and over the skies of Kosovo. "Americans should not expect one battle, but a lengthy campaign unlike any other we have ever seen."[53]

Yet fear of terrorism served as a rationale for two major land wars launched after 9/11. The war against the Taliban government that had harbored al Qaeda in Afghanistan was a logical response to the attacks. It was important to disrupt the training camps there and put the group under unrelenting pressure. The need to send a message to other regimes that might have tolerated the presence of anti-American terror groups in their midst was also a key rationale.

Within hours of the attacks, however, a small but important group of Americans saw an opportunity to go after another target that they had kept in sight for years: Saddam Hussein's Iraq.

The Road to Iraq

The Project for the New American Century (PNAC) played a unique role in building the case for war against Iraq, beginning well before 9/11. The organization was founded in 1997 by William Kristol, editor of the *Weekly Standard*, and Robert Kagan, a scholar at the Carnegie Endowment for International Peace and later a senior fellow at the Brookings Institution. PNAC organized a series of open letters making the case for regime change in Baghdad. The first of these, released in January 1998, called on President Clinton "to enunciate a new strategy that . . . should aim, above all, at the removal of Saddam Hussein's regime from power," by military means if necessary. Signatories included a slew of Ford, Reagan, and Bush administration officials, such as former vice president Dan Quayle, Elliott Abrams, William Bennett, Donald Rumsfeld, and Paul Wolfowitz. Other prominent writers and pundits signed on, including Steve Forbes and Norman Podhoretz. Bush's son and future Florida governor Jeb Bush also signed the PNAC letter.[54]

That same month, Kristol and Kagan coauthored an op-ed in the *New York Times* urging Clinton to block "Iraqi biological and chemical weapons" by deploying more U.S. troops to the region. An op-ed in the *Washington Post* the following month reiterated that Hussein was in possession of chemical and biological weapons and called for his removal by force. Several months later, a second PNAC letter again called for Hussein's overthrow.[55]

This concerted pressure campaign bore fruit in October 1998 when Congress passed the Iraq Liberation Act. The act committed the U.S. government to regime change in Iraq as official policy. The law also stipulated that opposition groups dedicated to Hussein's overthrow would be eligible for U.S. direct financial assistance. The Iraqi National Congress (INC) emerged as the leading beneficiary of U.S. taxpayers' largesse. The INC's leader, Ahmed Chalabi, had been carefully cultivating allies in the United States for years. His family had fled Iraq in the 1950s, when Chalabi was still a teenager, and the INC had been receiving support from the CIA since its founding in 1992. But Hussein remained in power through the mid and late 1990s, even as the INC's coffers filled with American cash.

The 9/11 attacks proved the crucial catalyst in finally driving Hussein from power in Baghdad—and ultimately to the gallows. This was odd, given that Hussein and Iraq had not been involved in the 9/11 attacks, a key fact that advocates for war with Iraq worked diligently to obscure. At times, the misdirection bordered on outright deception.

For example, on December 9, 2001, Vice President Dick Cheney appeared on the NBC News program *Meet the Press*. Asked by host Tim Russert whether there was any information showing that "Iraq was involved in the September 11" attacks, Cheney mentioned "a report that's been pretty well confirmed," that 9/11 lead hijacker Mohamed Atta had met with the Iraqi intelligence service in Prague several months before the attacks.[56] In fact, the CIA concluded that no such meeting occurred and had just informed the White House as much.[57] Cheney chose to ignore the agency's finding and continued to peddle the Atta-in-Prague story. Two years later, Cheney again appeared on *Meet the Press*. Russert asked if he was surprised that 69 percent of Americans believed Saddam Hussein was involved in 9/11. Cheney didn't find it surprising at all, pointing to "a relationship between Iraq and al-Qaeda that stretched back through most of the decade of the '90s." He linked Iraq to the first attack on the World Trade Center in 1993. And he repeated "the story that's been public out there" of lead hijacker Atta's supposed meeting "with a senior Iraqi intelligence official" in Prague "five months before the attack."[58] He neglected to mention that he'd been a key figure behind making the story public.

Chalabi and the INC were a major source of false or misleading material on Iraq and 9/11, often funneled through *New York Times* reporter Judith Miller. Sometimes the stories appeared under her byline. On other occasions, she shared the information with her colleagues: Patrick Tyler and John Tagliabue, for example, broke the story claiming that Atta had been in Prague. Another account purported to show

terrorists training to hijack airplanes at a camp near the Iraqi city of Salman Pak. Chalabi later confirmed to Miller that he had been the source
of both tales.

Another incident involving INC-supplied information was Secretary of State Colin Powell's infamous speech before the United Nations
(UN) on February 4, 2003. Relying in part on material provided by a
source nicknamed "Curveball," Powell alleged that Iraq had an active
chemical weapons program that it was concealing from international
inspectors. He showed satellite images of bunkers and buildings purportedly containing Iraqi chemical munitions. Powell reported that "the
existence of mobile production facilities used to make biological agents"
had been made known to U.S. government officials by "an eyewitness,
an Iraqi chemical engineer who supervised one of these facilities."[59] As
with the claims of Saddam's supposed links to 9/11, however, these allegations ultimately proved false.

Although Chalabi and the INC are responsible for the lies that they
told to build the case for war with Iraq, U.S. officials are responsible for
believing them—and for ignoring the many warnings that the information being provided was selective and self-interested. Indeed, many
in the Bush administration—and a number of key outsiders—chose to
ignore evidence that might have undermined the case for war.

Experienced intelligence professionals describe a concerted campaign on the part of key figures within the Bush administration to find
information potentially helpful to the war effort—even if not necessarily
accurate. "We were being asked to do things and make sure that that
justification was out there," explains John Brennan, then deputy director
of the CIA.[60] Veteran CIA analyst Paul Pillar agrees: "A policy decision
clearly had been made," and the intelligence community was expected
"to support that decision."[61]

All told, according to a 2004 report by minority staff of the House
Committee on Government Reform, Bush administration officials had
made "237 misleading statements about the threat posed by Iraq." Those
implicated included Bush, Cheney, and Powell, as well as Secretary of
Defense Donald Rumsfeld and National Security Advisor Condoleezza
Rice. The report cites at least 61 separate statements "misrepresenting

Iraq's ties to al-Qaeda."[62] A Senate investigation in 2006 reached similar conclusions.[63]

Key outsiders had also made the case for war with Iraq. In 2002, Kenneth M. Pollack's book, *The Threatening Storm: The Case for Invading Iraq*, called for "a full-scale invasion of Iraq to smash the Iraqi armed forces, depose Saddam's regime, and rid the country of weapons of mass destruction." Such an undertaking, the Brookings Institution scholar insisted, would not be very costly to the United States. "It is unimaginable," he wrote, "that the United States would have to contribute hundreds of billions of dollars and highly unlikely that we would have to contribute even tens of billions of dollars." He even seemed to doubt that many U.S. troops would be killed or injured, pointing to the recent conflicts in Bosnia and Kosovo in which U.S. forces "have not suffered a single casualty from hostile action."[64]

To be sure, there was opposition to the war in Iraq, including marches that drew hundreds of thousands in New York and Washington, DC. Even larger protests erupted in cities around the world. A handful of think tank scholars, including some at the Cato Institute, made the case against war with Iraq.[65] A letter signed by 33 prominent political scientists and published on September 26, 2002, as a paid advertisement in the *New York Times* explained that "war with Iraq is not in America's national interest." The editors had refused to run it as an op-ed.[66]

When the first bombs fell on Baghdad on March 19, 2003, 72 percent of Americans supported the decision to go to war, and that number rose to 78 percent by early April.[67] When President George W. Bush spoke before sailors on May 1, 2003, onboard the USS *Abraham Lincoln* under a banner that proclaimed "Mission Accomplished," the naysayers and skeptics might have seemed overly pessimistic. Saddam Hussein had been driven from power, American casualties had been light, and resistance had been disorganized.

But the passage of time would prove the war skeptics correct. The Pentagon's official statistics in May 2019 counted 4,423 U.S. military and Department of Defense civilians killed and another 31,957 wounded.[68] As of this writing, the direct costs of the Iraq war to American taxpayers almost surely total more than $2 trillion. According to some reasonable estimates, the war's final tally, including disability payments to veterans and their families over the next several decades, could eventually rise to $6 trillion.[69] Proponents' estimates of what the war would cost American taxpayers had been wildly off the mark.

Meanwhile, estimates of the number of Iraqis killed during the war range well into the hundreds of thousands.[70] A study published by The Watson Institute for International Studies at Brown University in March 2013 concluded that the war had killed at least 134,000 Iraqi civilians, but, because such deaths often go unreported, the true toll could be twice as high. "In addition," the report's author Neta Crawford notes, "many times the number killed by direct violence have likely died due to the effects of the destruction of Iraq's infrastructure."[71]

The RAND Corporation's Michael J. Mazarr calls the "ill-conceived invasion of Iraq" "a historical misjudgment of the first order."[72] Conservative columnist George Will noted in 2018 that "it is frequently said that the decision to invade Iraq was the worst foreign policy decision since Vietnam." Will, who had supported the invasion in 2002 and 2003, disagreed. "Actually," he continued, "it was worse than Vietnam, and the worst in American history."[73]

Steven Bucci, a former military assistant to Secretary of Defense Donald Rumsfeld, and now a scholar at the Heritage Foundation, admitted, "If we had had the foresight to see how long it would last and even if it would have cost half the lives, we would not have gone in."[74]

★★★★★

A few politicians had the foresight and were willing to buck the bipartisan march to war in Iraq, long before the true scale of the debacle had become obvious to nearly everyone. In October 2002, a University of Chicago law professor and Illinois state senator explained:

> After Sept. 11 . . . I supported this administration's pledge to hunt down and root out those who would slaughter innocents in the name of intolerance, and I would willingly take up arms myself to prevent such tragedy from happening again. I don't oppose all wars. And I know that in this crowd today, there is no shortage of patriots, or of patriotism.

What I am opposed to is a dumb war. What I am opposed to is a rash war. What I am opposed to is the cynical attempt by . . . armchair, weekend warriors in this administration to shove their own ideological agendas down our throats, irrespective of the costs in lives lost and in hardships borne.[75]

Less than two years later, Barack Obama would deliver the keynote address at the Democratic National Convention in Boston, Massachusetts. And four years hence, U.S. Sen. Barack Obama accepted his party's nomination for the presidency.[76] His opposition to the war was a critical factor in helping him defeat other, more experienced and better-known Democrats, including Hillary Clinton, John Kerry, and Joe Biden, who had all voted for the war in 2002. And Obama's Iraq war stance similarly helped him to best Republican John McCain, one of the war's most outspoken supporters, in the general election. Young people seemed particularly responsive to Obama's message on Iraq.

Ben Rhodes was one such person. The aspiring novelist was living in New York City when the planes struck the Twin Towers, and he thereafter turned his attention to national security affairs. He was eventually attracted to a political figure willing to buck the foreign policy establishment. Looking back on the Iraq decision in particular, Rhodes observes that "the people who were supposed to know better had gotten us into a moral and strategic disaster." "You can't change things unless you change the people making the decisions," Rhodes concludes.[77] He went to work for Obama's long-shot campaign in 2007 and remained with Obama through the end of his second term.

And at least one other aspiring politician agreed with Rhodes about Iraq, even though they disagreed on nearly everything else. Donald Trump declared in one of his first major foreign policy speeches as a presidential candidate that "foolishness and arrogance" had "led to one foreign policy disaster after another" since the end of the Cold War. He promised to "look for talented experts with new approaches, and practical ideas."[78]

Barely six months later, he was president-elect. The next chapter explores how the dominant strategy undergirding U.S. foreign policy for the past half century—primacy—tends to lead the country into disasters like Iraq and therefore why some aspects of Trump's critique had merit.

CHAPTER 2
Why Primacy Doesn't Pay

For the past several decades, and especially since the end of the Cold War, U.S. leaders have pursued a foreign policy built on American military dominance. The strategy hinges on the belief that overwhelming American power and especially military power is the linchpin of global order. This approach draws on hegemonic stability theory, which holds that a world order with a single dominant power will be more stable than one with many such actors. In its role as the global superpower, the United States facilitates international cooperation by convincing states to forgo arms races and war. This, in turn, generates trust among potential adversaries, allowing them to engage in mutually beneficial trade.[1] Last, because the United States is a liberal country with good intentions, the order it oversees is ostensibly liberal and benign. Indeed, some defenders of U.S. foreign policy describe their approach as liberal hegemony, or "benevolent global hegemony."[2] The order under American tutelage is seen as relatively respectful of human rights and self-determination, and it privileges norms of nonviolence over the mere rule of the strong, where power alone dictates who wins and who loses. Or, say its defenders, at least liberal hegemony is more attentive to these principles than the alternatives on offer.

By definition, then, a world with less American military power would be less stable, less prosperous, and more prone to violence. "A world without America," explains Michael Mandelbaum, "would be the equivalent of a freeway full of cars without brakes."[3] Former secretary of state George Shultz puts it even more succinctly. "If the United States steps back from the historic role [it has] played since World War II," he explains in the documentary *American Umpire*, "the world will come apart at the seams."[4]

As such, the United States is "the indispensable nation," a phrase popularized during the 1990s. Primacists contend that active U.S. leadership is required to solve the world's problems; a failure to lead will inevitably result in the problems growing worse. Such a view presumes much about the wisdom and foresight of U.S. leaders, and the efficacy of U.S. power. "We [Americans] stand tall and we see further than other countries into the future," explained Secretary of State Madeleine Albright in 1998, "and we see the danger here to all of us."[5]

Both sets of claims—one, that world order depends upon a single dominant power to enforce it, and two, that the United States benefits from, and is uniquely suited to, playing that role—deserve scrutiny. Assessing these claims is the purpose of this chapter. It aims to show that primacy fails a basic cost–benefit analysis: indeed, the benefits are ephemeral, whereas the costs are enormous.

U.S. military power is not necessary for maintaining peace and prosperity. The international system is safer, and the international economy more durable, than the advocates of primacy allow. Accordingly, by initiating numerous conflicts during the past quarter century, and by threatening to launch even more, U.S. government officials have undermined global order. They have incentivized states that fear they might wind up in Washington's regime-change crosshairs to desire nuclear weapons as a deterrent. International trade operates independently of U.S. efforts to manage it and might have been impeded by U.S. threats of punishment or retaliation, including unilateral sanctions. Americans' ability to access global markets is not contingent upon, and therefore does not justify, the enormous expenses that purport to keep the global commons open. The costs, meanwhile, go well beyond what U.S. taxpayers spend on the nation's military. Americans enjoy fewer freedoms at home and are exposed to greater risks on account of the militarism on which primacy depends. Washington's many wars, meanwhile, which are also an essential element of primacy, have disrupted countless lives both at home and abroad.

On the whole, primacy is synonymous with military hyperactivity. America's frequent interventions have caused many observers, both at home and abroad, to question U.S. global leadership, writ large. This crisis in confidence, however, is not primarily a problem of implementation. We shouldn't aspire to better primacy; we should seek a genuine alternative to it. Rather than relying on a single dominant United States to "stand taller" and "see further," Americans—and the rest of the world—should favor an arrangement whereby the many beneficiaries of a peaceful global order contribute meaningfully to maintaining it.

Our (Not So) Dangerous World

For the first 100 or so years of American history, U.S. leaders relied on what the University of Chicago's John Mearsheimer calls "the stopping power of water" as the country's principle means of defense.[6] Despite its relative military weakness, the young nation had the luxury of choice. "Separated as we are by a world of water from other Nations," George Washington explained in a letter to a friend, "if we are wise we shall surely avoid being drawn into the labyrinth of their politics, and involved in their destructive wars."[7] In his farewell address, Washington urged his countrymen to take advantage of "our detached and distant station" and maintain a neutral stance with respect to other nations.[8]

It didn't always work. The British set Washington, DC, ablaze during the War of 1812, when the U.S. Navy was weak and the British Navy was strong. But that was the exception that proved the rule. At the time, the United States was in no position to defend itself against determined adversaries. But other countries mostly left the United States alone. Today, by contrast, the United States possesses overwhelming military superiority, including a prodigious nuclear deterrent. Indeed, the United States continues to enjoy near strategic immunity by virtue of geography. We *still* have wide oceans to the east and west, and friendly and weak neighbors to the north and south.[9]

What other types of threats are there, besides land invasion and occupation by foreign armies? We cannot rely on oceans to halt nuclear missiles or cyberattacks. Terrorists can still infiltrate by land, sea, or air—or grow right here at home. So while our nuclear weapons are a powerful deterrent against state actors with return addresses, military dominance is all but irrelevant when dealing with terrorists and hackers. Law enforcement agencies, aided by timely intelligence, are often more effective in rolling up criminal gangs, which are a better parallel to terrorist organizations. The use of deadly force may be appropriate—to thwart an imminent attack, for example—but such operations should be combined with nonkinetic measures that advance a broader agenda and drain away support from terrorists or nonstate actors. Well-intentioned and carefully planned military strikes that nonetheless result in civilian casualties and collateral damage often have the opposite effect.

In short, there have always been dangers in the world, and there always will be. We can identify myriad threats that our ancestors couldn't fathom, but primacy finds even more. By calling on the United States to deal with all threats to all people in all places, primacy ensures that even distant problems become our own.

Not So Pacifying

Primacy holds that American military power explains the absence of major war since the end of World War II. The first half of the 20th century witnessed grueling conflicts in Europe and Asia that claimed tens of millions of lives. Nothing of the sort has occurred since. This long peace coincides with the network of far-flung alliances that the United States established after World War II. It also coincides with the formidable forward military presence that the United States maintained throughout the Cold War, and has kept up ever since. But correlation does not prove causation. At a minimum, the claim that U.S. power is *the* determining factor behind relative peace and prosperity ignores or at least underplays the numerous other explanations, including the deterrent effect of nuclear weapons, the spread of democracy, increasing globalization and economic interdependence, and evolving norms against violence in general.

Nor is it clear that the American pacifier is as pacifying as claimed. The continued presence of U.S. military forces in post–Cold War Europe, and especially NATO expansion to Russia's borders after the Cold War ended, has provoked fear and consternation in Moscow. In East Asia, China views the continued American naval presence with equal alarm, fearing the prospect that these ships and submarines could be used to close off vital waterways and deny access to global markets, effectively strangling the Chinese economy.

Meanwhile, advocates of primacy claim that U.S. military power reassures nervous allies, effectively discouraging them from taking steps to defend themselves. Whereas Donald Trump often points to free riding by allies as a problem to be solved, primacists view such behavior as both reasonable and desirable. Hal Brands approvingly notes in his book *American Grand Strategy in the Age of Trump* that the United States provides "protection that allows other countries to underbuild their militaries."[10] *New York Times* columnist Bret Stephens agrees. "America is better served," he wrote in 2015, "by a world of supposed freeloaders than by a world of foreign policy freelancers."[11]

Primacists are particularly concerned that freelancing and self-help could lead to nuclear proliferation. Countries evicted from under the American nuclear umbrella might be tempted to develop a deterrent of their own. But so far only a handful of countries, including several U.S. allies and partners who were capable of building such weapons, have chosen to do so (the United Kingdom, France, Israel, India, and Pakistan).[12] On the other hand, some countries that might have considered building an indigenous nuclear force have stopped well short of doing so, and might reconsider their decision in the absence of American security guarantees. More important, other countries seem to believe that such weapons are the only effective way to deter America's vast military power. That is the lesson North Korea appears to have learned from U.S.-led operations against Serbia, Iraq, and Libya.

On balance, "all-out efforts to prevent [nuclear proliferation] would also be costly and may not succeed," explains Harvard's Stephen Walt.

"Nuclear proliferation will remain a concern no matter what the United States does."[13] Cato Institute senior fellow John Mueller takes a slightly different tack but arrives at a similar conclusion: the costs of counterproliferation may well be higher than the benefits. This is especially so when counterproliferation requires preventive wars aimed at denuding nascent nuclear-weapon states of their costly devices or deterring aspiring ones from ever obtaining them. While nuclear nonproliferation might reasonably be a high priority, Mueller writes, it should be subsumed below "a somewhat higher one: avoiding policies that can lead to the deaths of tens or hundreds of thousands of people."[14]

There are still other drawbacks under primacy. To be sure, U.S. security guarantees to wealthy allies *may* have discouraged harmful arms races that *might* eventually have led to offensive wars, though advocates of primacy would be hard pressed to name even one obvious recent example. This much is certain: reassurance has caused other countries to underprovide for their own defense. That was as intended. The promise of security that Americans extend to others, explains the Brookings Institution's Robert Kagan, encourages U.S. allies to "spend less on defense and more on strengthening their economies and social welfare systems."[15] This also means, however, that other countries have little hard power capacity for dealing with common security challenges, from ethnic violence in the Balkans in the 1990s, to combatting terrorism and piracy in South Asia or the Horn of Africa in the 2000s, to averting state collapse in North Africa and the Middle East and the rise of the so-called Islamic State (ISIS) in the 2010s.

This tendency of the weaker members of a security alliance to free ride on the strong cannot be easily reversed by a concerted campaign to shame the free riders into paying their fair share. Individuals are generally disinclined to pay for things that others are willing to buy for them, and countries are no different. Moreover, the United States derives little leverage over allies' behavior; threats to cut off alliance partners for failing to do as we ask are generally not believed, because they are not true. The United States has never cut off an ally for failure to contribute its "fair share" to the common defense. The result of U.S. foreign policy under primacy, therefore, is that the United States has many allies with liabilities and few with capabilities. Even fewer possess an inclination to use the limited power they have.

Primacy has had at least one other unfortunate side effect. Whereas U.S. security guarantees may have encouraged some U.S. allies to resist pressure from the likes of Russia or China, other allies have become emboldened in less constructive ways. Indeed, some have been known to act recklessly, or to stand firm against regional rivals when reasonable accommodation might be the best course. Saudi Arabia's ruinous war in Yemen, which began in 2015, certainly falls in the first category. The Saudis employed a punishing air campaign to root out Houthi rebels and a naval blockade to cut off their supplies, but the effects were felt mostly by millions of innocent civilians in one of the world's poorest countries. U.S. military and intelligence assistance proved critical. Saudi rulers mostly ignored pleas from the international community to stop the war and relieve the suffering, apparently confident that the United States would give them diplomatic cover. Meanwhile, several nations with claims to disputed rocks and shoals in the East and South China Seas might come to believe that the United States will back them to the hilt against China, effectively forestalling a more durable settlement.[16]

In short, the American pacifier is neither a sufficient explanation for the long global peace nor always a force for regional stability and peace. The United States certainly has played an important role in the world, but it would be a mistake to presume that peace and security have necessarily and inevitably flowed from U.S. primacy.

PRESERVING THE GLOBAL ORDER: FRAGILE OR RESILIENT?

Accordingly, U.S. military dominance is not essential to sustain the global order going forward. Indeed, less American military power being deployed in fewer places might be more conducive to peace.

To be sure, the U.S. military presence in Europe and Asia after World War II helped the countries there recover more quickly than they would have if left to fend for themselves. This presence might even have played a constructive role well into the 1950s and '60s. G. John Ikenberry, one of the most articulate defenders of the postwar order under U.S.

global hegemony, points to "the hallmarks of liberal internationalism—openness and rule-based relations enshrined in institutions such as the United Nations and norms such as multilateralism." He worries that these norms "could give way to a more contested and fragmented system of blocs, spheres of influence, mercantilist networks, and regional rivalries."[17] On other occasions, however, Ikenberry retains his confidence that such a reckoning can be avoided, provided that U.S. leaders take adequate account of the legitimate interests of other states.[18]

Others are not so sanguine. Robert Kagan is convinced that the end of the liberal order is fast approaching—or has already arrived. "The democratic alliance that has been the bedrock of the American-led liberal world order is unraveling," he wrote in July 2018, days after Donald Trump berated NATO allies for failing to spend more on their militaries. "At some point," a gloomy Kagan continued, "and probably sooner than we expect, the global peace that that alliance and that order undergirded will unravel, too. Despite our human desire to hope for the best, things will not be okay. The world crisis is upon us."[19]

According to Hal Brands, "the international order ultimately rests on the credibility of U.S. commitments," and any "weakening of America's reputation for diplomatic steadiness and reliability," as has occurred under Donald Trump's presidency, could do irreparable damage to the entire system.[20] Frank Ninkovich expresses similar concerns. Although some worry that Trump's policies "might trigger a catastrophic collapse," Ninkovich doubts that "a frontal assault on the existing order is . . . the immediate cause for concern." "Even benign neglect has its dangers," however, "because all systems . . . even if not abused, inevitably break down without regular maintenance and the occasional overhaul. There is no sign that Mr. Trump aims to be Mr. Fixit."[21]

But these same scholars put too little faith in the durability of the order that they celebrate. It persists, and is likely to in the future, precisely because so many actors are now invested in it. That was not always the case. There was one very important challenger to the U.S.-led order in the immediate aftermath of World War II—the Soviet Union under Joseph Stalin—and too few actors willing or able to resist it. Today, the many beneficiaries of a global order that has delivered decades of human progress are determined and strong, whereas the challengers are mostly divided and weak. Nihilistic disruptors like al Qaeda and ISIS simply do not compare to a nuclear-armed superpower.

Even a rising China, which arguably already rivals in power and influence the Soviet Union at the height of the Cold War, is more invested in sustaining critical elements of the global order than in destroying them. This reflects the extent to which critical norms and values—including respect for national sovereignty, protection of trade and free movement of goods through the global commons, and strong prohibitions against the use of force except in self-defense—have effectively become locked in. To be sure, Chinese leaders are not above working within these rules to gain advantages for themselves. In fact, considerable benefits accrue to countries that conform to global order.[22] They don't wish to the see the United States use its privileged position atop this order to thwart them, as it has done in the past. Indeed, under primacy, the United States essentially reserves for itself the right to violate these rules. By and large, however, global norms might be more widely accepted and obeyed in the future if they were broadly beneficial, and not primarily because they were backed by U.S. threats or coercion.[23]

Put differently, the international order has achieved a degree of institutionalization that no longer relies on the power of a single state. A number of empowered nation-states and multilateral bodies, plus the plethora of rules-enforcing nongovernmental organizations— from the Internet Corporation for Assigned Names and Numbers to the International Olympic Committee—possess a degree of authority and legitimacy far greater than what U.S. policymakers can muster by themselves.[24] The United States is still important, but no longer indispensable. Much good occurs in the world without Uncle Sam's guiding hand or threatening fist.

PRIMACY AND INTERNATIONAL TRADE: LESS THAN MEETS THE EYE

Last, a related point, primacists argue that the United States must maintain a global military presence to protect global commerce. Some go so far as to argue that U.S. military power is *essential* to the proper functioning of the world economy. The United States sets the rules of the game and punishes those who defy them. And by discouraging security competition among states, primacy creates the conditions for trade to flourish.[25] If the United States were less inclined to intervene in other people's disputes, the primacists say, the risk of war would grow, roiling skittish markets.

But the international economy is far more resilient than the advocates of U.S. military primacy allow. And the case for hegemonic stability theory, dating from the 1950s and '60s, has been further weakened by the experience of the recent past. While primacy's defenders claim that America's role as global hegemon confers unique benefits on Americans, it is not clear that the benefits outweigh the costs.

For one thing, the forward U.S. military presence undergirding primacy has not always been stabilizing. The presence of foreign troops often undermines the legitimacy of elected governments and engenders local resistance. Terrorist organizations often seize upon these feelings of resentment and humiliation to draw support to their cause and increase their ranks. Meanwhile, the United States' forward military presence does allow U.S. leaders to intervene quickly in distant disputes. But, given that these purportedly small-scale interventions often evolve into large and protracted conflicts, it is hard to see how the resulting disorder is conducive to global prosperity. The U.S. military interventions in Iraq and Afghanistan, for example, have devastated those countries and spread chaos throughout their respective regions.

Political scientist Daniel Drezner finds that America's massive military power "plays a supporting role" in stabilizing the international economy, but by itself does not confer great benefits for the American economy. What's more, those benefits are diminishing over time. "The principal benefits that come with military primacy," he writes, "appear to flow only when coupled with economic primacy." "An excessive reliance on military power, to the exclusion of other dimensions of power," Drezner concludes, "will yield negative returns."[26]

Stephen Walt agrees. "On the whole, the purely economic benefits of liberal hegemony and global military dominance are less than their proponents claim." The risk that the United States will be cut off from vital resources and lucrative markets is overblown. Few other countries are interested in raising "new protectionist barriers" or demolishing the institutions that facilitate global trade. Such actions, after all, "would only make them poorer." He allows that "U.S. security commitments and U.S. prosperity" are connected and acknowledges that major conflicts in Europe, the Middle East, or Asia would disrupt global trade and harm the U.S. economy. But he considers such extreme scenarios far-fetched.[27]

Short of preventing wars, defenders of primacy typically argue that the hegemon—in this case the United States—is able to derive other substantial benefits by virtue of its central place in the international system. This process can work in various ways. For example, the dominant power may be able to negotiate favorable terms for the extraction of natural resources, either through coercion, reminiscent of the imperial powers of old, or in a more cooperative fashion ("informal empire"), as the elites of protected states craft policies that also serve the hegemon's interests. Also, by providing security throughout the global commons, and by bringing order to poorly governed spaces, the hegemon creates an international system that is more conducive to trade and commerce.

Primacists also claim that the U.S. military's global policing mission gives Americans leverage in economic negotiations with others, allowing us to shape the rules in a way that confers special advantages for U.S. producers and consumers. A 2005 study by the Peterson Institute for International Economics estimated that the post-1945 global trading order adds $1 trillion to the U.S. economy every year.[28]

To be sure, everyone has gained—but the United States as the hegemon, *the* dominant power, the rulemaker, and the de facto enforcer of global norms supposedly gains the most. In support of this claim, primacists note that the United States after World War II was often able to coerce weaker players into following its lead. On several occasions, Washington threatened and cajoled alliance partners to accede to its demands, particularly when it came to sustaining the United States' capacity for spending well beyond its means. U.S. allies acted to shore up the dollar on a number of occasions when inflation worries mounted.

But, on the other hand, U.S. policymakers often sacrificed the United States' own economic well-being for geopolitical interests, including those of our allies. For example, Francis Gavin's study of economic statecraft between the United States and Europe in the 1960s finds in U.S. policy "a repeated pattern of sacrificing economic for geopolitical interests." And when European officials did bow to Washington's wishes, their concessions served mostly to fix problems created, or at least exacerbated, by the U.S. military presence in their countries.[29]

The net economic benefits of U.S. primacy have declined since the end of the Cold War. Following the fall of the Soviet Union, fewer security clients were willing to defer to Washington on matters of trade and economic policy. The nature of the threat had changed, and the ever-evolving international economic order offered them practical alternatives to the dollar-dominated system of the 1950s, '60s, and '70s. The 2008 financial crisis delivered a second major blow to U.S. influence. Looking ahead, as U.S. military and economic dominance wanes relative to other international actors, America's ability to extract benefits for itself will further diminish.[30]

Another dubious suggestion is that U.S. companies' ability to sell in foreign markets, and American consumers' taste for goods produced outside of the United States, would be seriously affected by the relative decline of U.S. military power. However, if U.S. leaders were less prone to intervening in foreign conflicts, trade would continue and likely increase. "It is not American troops deployed overseas that make American products and services attractive to foreign consumers," note Eugene Gholz, Daryl G. Press, and Harvey M. Sapolsky in a seminal critique of primacy, "it is the quality of American goods, the image of America's prosperity, and the productivity of American workers."[31]

Last, primacists assert that countries are more inclined to cut trade deals with the United States if the U.S. military protects them. It isn't obvious, however, that such negotiations are much influenced by the nature of the *security* relationships between trading partners. Many people would want to sell to some of the wealthiest consumers on the planet, even if U.S. policymakers didn't promise to defend them from threats. Meanwhile, it is hard to extract concessions from security clients because

U.S. threats to leave alliances are not credible. On balance, primacy looks like Americans paying others "for the privilege of defending them."[32]

There is ample historical evidence to suggest that commerce is conducive to peace, and, conversely, that barriers to trade can lead to war. Trade flows, however, do not depend upon U.S. ground troops in overseas bases or even U.S. naval ships at sea or American aircraft in the skies. The international economy doesn't need a Leviathan and has almost surely suffered whenever Uncle Sam actually attempts to exert influence militarily.

In general, primacists overstate the role that the U.S. military plays in facilitating global trade and ignore the extent to which U.S. military activism has disrupted markets and upset vital regions. At best, American military dominance is a double-edged sword when it comes to defending the liberal trading order, and a costly one at that.

Spending a Lot, But Needing More

Primacy requires the world's most capable and most expensive military. U.S. military spending remains near historic highs, and well above the Cold War average. Defense spending in the eight years under Barack Obama exceeded that under George W. Bush, and by a wide margin. Average annual spending in 2009–2016 was nearly 17 percent higher than in 2001–2008, after adjusting for inflation.[33]

Within his first two years in office, Donald Trump presided over a further expansion in U.S. military spending. As a result of these increases, the Office of Management and Budget estimates that projected outlays for national defense will be $53.4 billion higher in 2019 than in the preceding year, and it anticipates that spending in 2024 will reach $784.9 billion—a 14.6 percent rise over the previous five-year period.[34]

Yet despite such increases in U.S. military spending over the past two decades, policymakers and many national security experts worry that the U.S. military is unprepared to fulfill its missions. So say the members of a bipartisan group tasked by Congress with providing an independent assessment of the nation's defense strategy. Describing the "crisis of American military power," the National Defense Strategy

Commission concludes, "America's military capabilities are insufficient to address the growing dangers the country faces," and it questions "whether the desired outcomes of the [Trump administration's National Defense Strategy (NDS)] can be realized within anticipated resource constraints." Elsewhere in the report, released in November 2018, the commissioners warn, "Without additional resources . . . the Department will be unable to fulfill the ambition of the NDS. . . . There must be greater urgency and seriousness in funding national defense."[35]

Two members of the commission, former senator Jon Kyl and Roger Zakheim, director of the Ronald Reagan Institute, followed up with an op-ed calling for "3 to 5 percent real growth annually" in military spending, but they warned that "even with this level of investment, it will take a decade or more" to meet "America's global strategic objectives."[36] One study calculated that increases of that magnitude could boost the Pentagon's budget to nearly $972 billion by 2024, or 51 percent higher than 2018 outlays.[37] Even if one disputes that U.S. defense requirements are as onerous and inflexible as these voices claim, the costs merely to maintain the status quo are obviously growing.

The bigger issue is why we seem to be falling behind even as our spending remains historically high. Part of the explanation lies in the fact that the active-duty force, although smaller than during the Cold War, is also better trained and better compensated. The costs of developing new military equipment, and maintaining such equipment in fighting condition, are rising as well. In 2017, the Congressional Budget Office reported that operation and maintenance costs were eating up approximately 50 percent of the total defense budget. This was consistent with long-term trends. "Over the past few decades," the report noted, "funding for [operations and maintenance] has increased substantially, accounting for a growing share of DoD's [Department of Defense] budget. That growth has occurred even as the number of active-duty military personnel has remained flat or declined."[38]

Defenders of primacy point out that military spending both as a share of gross domestic product (GDP) and as a share of total government spending is not particularly high, suggesting that we *could* generate much more military power. But that too is misleading because military spending is competing with popular domestic programs, and tax revenues are not making up the difference. Together, rising spending and rising deficits pose a greater threat to America's long-term prospects than our most insidious foreign enemies. The National Defense Strategy Commission agrees. "Policymakers must address rising government spending and decreasing tax revenues as unsustainable trends that compel hard fiscal choices," the commissioners write:

> No serious effort to address growing debt can be made without either increasing tax revenues or decreasing mandatory spending—or both. Without such an effort, it will be impossible to stabilize the nation's finances, and to fund and sustain an adequate defense. Rather than viewing defense cuts as the solution to the nation's fiscal problems, Congress should look to the entire federal budget, especially entitlements and taxes, to set the nation on a more stable financial footing. In the near-term, such adjustments will undoubtedly be quite painful. Yet over time—and probably much sooner than we expect—failing to make those adjustments and fully fund America's defense strategy will undoubtedly be worse.[39]

This might seem a reasonable proposal—if there was evidence that the public would tolerate cuts in Social Security and Medicare, for example, to maintain U.S. foreign policy along its present course. The defenders of primacy might claim that the resources needed to carry out the strategy could easily be found, but only one in four Americans believes that the country spends too little on the military, while a clear majority believes the military is already strong enough.[40] Meanwhile, although the commissioners portray the costs of the U.S. military as paying for "an adequate defense," U.S. foreign policy under primacy doesn't merely seek adequacy and doesn't focus on the defense of U.S. vital interests. U.S. grand strategy also purports to provide security for others—but defending our allies consistently ranks among Americans' lowest spending priorities. It seems particularly unlikely that Americans will gladly endure higher taxes, lower domestic spending, higher debt, or all three of those things, so that U.S. allies can continue to underspend on their defenses. Primacists appear to believe that a well-crafted marketing strategy can change people's minds, but Americans are already well aware of the costs of U.S. foreign policy and seem indisposed to new arguments to sustain it.

This political reality is a dagger pointed at the heart of primacy. The benefits of American military dominance and activism are ostensibly enjoyed by many. But the monetary costs of primacy fall mostly on the backs of current U.S. taxpayers and those yet unborn, and the risks to life and limb are borne almost exclusively by U.S. soldiers, sailors, airmen, and marines. And, as already noted, U.S. military personnel are having to work harder and deploy longer, and U.S. taxpayers are having to spend more, just to keep up. The proliferation of various technologies, from crude explosives to advanced robotics, has made it easier for even relatively small and weak actors to challenge the big and powerful United States. And truly determined nation-states, even very poor ones like North Korea, can develop nuclear weapons to deter attacks.

Senior U.S. national security officials understand well the nature of the challenge. The Trump administration's National Defense Strategy speaks of "an ever more lethal and disruptive battlefield," and worrisome "trends" that "will challenge our ability to deter aggression." The document predicts that U.S. allies will lose faith and U.S. global influence will wane unless U.S. taxpayers commit to "devoting additional resources in a sustained effort to solidify our competitive advantage."[41]

In sum, according to figures compiled by the International Institute for Strategic Studies, the United States *already* spends more on its military than the next nine nations combined and nearly three times more than China and Russia put together.[42] Nonetheless, leaders at the Pentagon, in Congress, and elsewhere throughout the government, as well as outside experts, including the members of the National Defense Strategy Commission, all believe that Americans must spend even more. Anyone committed to maintaining primacy not only believes that the costs of doing so are reasonable and manageable; they also believe that additional spending is required.

The high cost of primacy is not its greatest shortcoming. The United States probably *could* spend more on its military, if it were truly essential. However, as described above, Americans demonstrate little interest in increasing military spending at the expense of domestic priorities. They want to nation-build at home.[43]

The central problem with primacy is that it isn't necessary to maintain U.S. security or to maintain the American or global economy. The earliest advocates of American military dominance after the end of the Cold War couldn't imagine that it would eventually run out of gas. The United States retained an enormous military apparatus and deployed it more often and in more places than ever before. U.S. leaders and policy-makers expanded America's global role and rarely considered plausible alternatives. The core assumption underlying primacy is that a single dominant power is needed to forestall dangerous arms races and insecurity spirals and to make global commerce possible; that assumption merited wider debate than it received at the time.

So far, this chapter has challenged the primacists' claims. But a U.S. grand strategy built upon primacy is also flawed because it hinges on a particular misconception about the utility of military power in the 21st century and a misplaced faith in the United States' ability to wield this power. We explore those problems next.

The Limits of Military Power—A Quarter Century of Failure

Madeleine Albright isn't alone in believing that the United States is "the indispensable nation" and that Americans stand taller and see farther. Indeed, those beliefs have informed U.S. foreign policy, under both Democratic and Republican presidents, for decades.

The track record alone should have prompted some self-reflection. After all, while the United States of America is obviously a powerful country, it is not omnipotent. It cannot actually see into the future. It does not correctly anticipate dangers to itself, let alone to others. When it does act, it often fails. It hasn't discovered a magic formula for deploying force with such surgical precision that it can easily shape the international system in a way that works for everyone's benefit and harms no one. With respect to U.S. efforts at regime change, for example, Admiral Mike Mullen, former chair of the Joint Chiefs of Staff, noted in 2016, "We're 0 for a lot."[44] Military historian Andrew Bacevich similarly concludes that "having been 'at war' for virtually the entire twenty-first century, the United States military is still looking for its first win."[45]

Unsurprisingly, others around the world don't trust the United States to perform the role of disinterested global policeman. Many don't even believe U.S. leaders' professions of good intent. In fact, when the Pew Research Center asked people around the world to name the greatest threats facing their respective countries, substantial numbers cited "U.S. Power and Influence." Fifty percent or more of respondents in nine different countries identified *the United States* as their top threat, including treaty allies Turkey (72 percent), South Korea (70 percent), Japan (62 percent), Mexico (61 percent), and Spain (59 percent).[46]

For the most part, U.S. leaders mean well. They are often motivated by a genuine desire to shape the international system in ways that are conducive to peace and prosperity. But they err in believing that they have the capability to do great things, and they end up causing harm. By privileging the military over other instruments of U.S. power and influence, primacy undermines Americans' safety. It increases the likelihood that the United States will become drawn into other people's fights. Once involved, the United States becomes responsible for bringing those fights to an acceptable conclusion—or it will be blamed for failing to do so. These individual interventions often become quagmires where victory is impossible, but decisionmakers are reluctant to quit. The process typically proceeds in several stages.

First, with the help of the news media's morbid attraction to human suffering, the White House espies some outrage. For George H. W. Bush, it was Saddam Hussein's invasion of Kuwait. In the waning days of his presidency, Bush also opted to send U.S. Marines into Somalia to avert a deepening famine. Bill Clinton inherited that mission and expanded it, choosing to go after the warlords who were controlling access to food. In subsequent years, he sent U.S. troops into Bosnia and later Kosovo to protect Muslims from Serbs. George W. Bush, shaken by the events of 9/11 and convinced that democracy was the cure for terrorism, pledged to end tyranny in our world. For Barack Obama, Muammar el-Qaddafi's threat to the eastern Libyan city of Benghazi prompted U.S. military intervention from the skies and aid to favored

Libyan rebels on the ground. Even Donald Trump, who routinely castigated his predecessors' meddlesome instincts, has succumbed to the interventionist lure as president and has twice ordered missile strikes on targets in Syria to punish the Assad regime for using chemical weapons in the civil war there (see Chapter 3). He also toyed with the idea of overthrowing Nicolás Maduro's government in Venezuela.

Each case follows a similar pattern. Convinced that U.S. action is necessary to reverse an act of aggression or avert a great suffering—or halt it before it begins—the president prepares to deploy U.S. military forces. The debate over whether U.S. action will succeed is often stunted and incomplete. The White House dominates the discussion owing to the president's institutional advantage, including privileged access to the media; opponents of intervention generally lack sufficient information to mount a campaign against it.[47]

Indeed, those making the case for war often deploy stories that heighten public outrage or anxiety, while at the same time suppressing information suggesting the military mission might be more difficult than the advocates claim. Vice President Dick Cheney in 2001 and 2003 spoke of furtive meetings between Iraqi agents and the 9/11 hijackers, even though U.S. intelligence agencies found no evidence that they had ever actually occurred. Others in the Bush administration knocked down suggestions that war in Iraq might require hundreds of thousands of troops and cost hundreds of billions of dollars. Larry Lindsey, a top economic adviser, and Army Chief of Staff Eric Shinseki were effectively fired for even suggesting that the war wouldn't be quick, cheap, and easy.

After winning the stunted and lopsided debate, the White House plunges the country into a foreign conflict, determined to defeat the bad guys even if there aren't any good guys to support. The impulse to get in quickly often precludes adequate vetting of potential allies. The entire debate over involvement in Libya in 2011, for example, took less than three weeks.

On other occasions, self-interested expatriates manage to dominate the discourse. The Iraqi National Congress (INC) did this in the years leading up to Saddam Hussein's overthrow, and the cultish Mujahideen-e-Khalq (MEK) does the same with respect to regime

change in Iran. No serious experts on Iranian politics believe that the
MEK can establish a durable political order in a post-ayatollah Tehran,
just as Iraqi experts saw through the INC's charade. But these types of
organizations are adept at building support in Washington.[48]

Once engaged militarily, U.S. leaders often define success too
expansively, setting forth grandiose objectives but lacking the resources
or the support of the American people to achieve them. On other occasions, they declare victory too quickly, often on the basis of emotion
rather than strategic calculations. In either case, the result is predictable:
failure. For example, George W. Bush proclaimed "Mission Accomplished" in Iraq within a matter of months, long before a durable political settlement had been established. Likewise, U.S. officials called Libya
"a model intervention," and after Qaddafi's murder Secretary of State
Hillary Clinton crowed, "We came, we saw, he died!"[49] The chaos that
ensued in both countries belied U.S. officials' confidence that anything
had actually been won and raised many questions about the price paid in
treasure and lives.

With respect to Libya, for example, Alan Kuperman, in a policy brief
for Harvard's prestigious Belfer Center, concluded that "NATO's action
magnified the conflict's duration about sixfold and its death toll at least
sevenfold . . . while also exacerbating human rights abuses, humanitarian
suffering, Islamic radicalism, and weapons proliferation in Libya and its
neighbors."[50] Perhaps mindful of these realities, Obama eventually came
to regard the failure to plan for the aftermath of Qaddafi's overthrow
as the worst mistake of his presidency, though he also stated his belief
that intervening was "the right thing to do."[51] On another occasion, he
allowed that Libya was "a mess" and "a shit show."[52]

But such introspection is rare and, as with Obama, usually too late.
In most instances, when failure looms, policymakers recognize the need
to try something different, but the most common impulse is to double
down. The introduction of additional military power, either as U.S. aid
to local combatants or through the direct involvement of U.S. forces,
amplifies the conflict and fuels higher levels of violence. Research shows
that foreign-imposed regime change rarely succeeds, and foreign intervention in civil wars often simply prolongs the suffering of the innocents

caught in the middle. Meanwhile, the American public, having been told that the war was already won, or that victory is around the corner, either grows impatient or loses interest. The war fades from memory, and television news stops running stories.

If forced to confront an unambiguous, worsening problem during an ongoing intervention, U.S. officials aim merely to forestall an unambiguous defeat. They contend that America can't walk away. But, given meager public support, they opt instead for a light footprint. This strategy avoids the need to spend political capital at home but is insufficient to achieve actual victory abroad. It is, in short, a recipe for quagmire.

Tragically, U.S. efforts to produce change through the use of force have often caused instability, deepened conflicts, and engendered anger and resentment, precisely the opposite of what the proponents of such interventions have promised. One need look no further than the Middle East, where public attitudes toward the United States have cratered.[53] Support for democracy, economic freedom, and protection of human rights have also faltered.[54] The fundamental reason for this failure is that American officials have too much faith in their power to shape events around the world and often fail to take account of the negative unintended consequences of their actions.

America's impulse to confront the world's evils is noble, but the refusal to accept the world as it is prevents a clear-eyed assessment of costs and benefits. Of course the desire to prevent oppression everywhere is understandable, and wanting to end "tyranny in our world," which George W. Bush pledged to do, is admirable. But endless military intervention has caused more problems than it has solved. Indeed, without a clear national security rationale, military intervention stops being a useful tool for foreign policy and becomes instead an instrument of folly. Failure to align strategic ends with diplomatic and political (as well as military) means, or to define a clear plan for victory, puts lives at risk while at the same time robbing the American people of the opportunity to participate in an open debate.

It wasn't always this way. The doctrines coined by Ronald Reagan's secretary of defense, Caspar Weinberger, and Weinbergers's principal military aide, Colin Powell, encouraged presidents to identify limited missions, with a clear military objective; to use overwhelming force in a decisive manner; and to deploy such force only when vital interests are at stake.[55]

That last point is critical because such doctrines help ensure proper backing from the American people. In recent years, the United States' inability to deliver on its grandiose promises has been partly a function of limited resources. This might seem odd, given that U.S. military spending exceeds $700 billion annually. The sum total of national security expenditures, including for veterans' care and homeland security, approaches $1 trillion. That so much spending could ever seem inadequate is mostly a reflection of the scale of U.S. leaders' ambitions, not the paucity of resources dedicated to achieving them.

An Ambivalent Public

These ambitions, however, do not align with the wishes of the American people, who are willing to spend vast sums to support a military that defends this country but not to pay for large-scale nation-building projects abroad. In fairness, we shouldn't expect others to trust the United States to behave in a disinterested way, and we shouldn't expect Americans to wish to do so. A better approach would be to call on all countries to attend to their most urgent security challenges and mobilize the resources necessary to manage them—in collaboration with others as much as possible, but unilaterally when absolutely necessary.

Primacy has discouraged precisely this sort of self-help behavior. Instead, it has gambled the safety and security of the entire planet on Americans' willingness to bear the burdens of leadership. It has also gambled on the belief that no American would ever be elected president promising to put "America First."

And then 2016 happened.

Donald Trump won by espousing views that the foreign policy establishment, both Republicans and Democrats, had previously said would prove disqualifying. He criticized America's alliances, questioned the benefits of global trade, and doubted the value of human rights. He even dared to criticize a Republican president's wars—during a *Republican* primary debate.[56]

It is not accurate to suggest that Trump won high office *because of* his foreign policy views, but it is obvious that they didn't prevent him from becoming president. And it is equally clear that another person could come along in the future and actually implement an America First–style foreign policy, even if Donald Trump ultimately fails to do so. For several years, polls have revealed Americans' skepticism of the benefits of U.S. global leadership, at least as it has been practiced for the last quarter century. The Pew Research Center found in 2013, for example, that 52 percent of Americans agree with the statement that the United States "should mind its own business internationally and let other countries get along the best they can on their own." Fewer than 4 in 10 (38 percent) disagreed.[57] A follow-on study in 2016 reached a similar conclusion, with 57 percent of respondents calling on the United States to deal with its own problems, while letting other countries get along as best they can. The 2016 survey also found that just 27 percent of Americans believed that the United States was doing too little to solve the world's problems, while 41 percent said that the United States was doing too much.[58]

MANY HANDS, RATHER THAN JUST ONE

The United States' power relative to that of other states is slowly declining. This trend will not be reversed by a concerted campaign to Make America Great Again, because other countries are rising too. Indeed, in many respects, what journalist Fareed Zakaria calls "the rise of the rest" is a testament to the effectiveness of the post–World War II order.[59] One could say, however, that the United States succeeded too well. In the past, U.S. leaders could behave hypocritically, holding others to standards that they did not always apply to themselves. Before other countries approached the United States in terms of relative economic power or political influence, U.S. leaders were confident that others wouldn't challenge American dominance.

"As the ordering superpower," explains international relations professor Patrick Porter, "the United States did not bind itself with the rules of the system. It upended, stretched, or broke liberal rules to shape a putatively liberal order." The United States, he continues, underwrote "a liberal world order not by adhering to its principles but by stepping outside them, practicing punishment, threats, and bribes that it would not accept if directed at itself."[60]

Duke University's Bruce Jentleson partly agrees, stating that

> for many decades, the United States had the power and wealth to sponsor and buttress the [international] system. What it gave the world (e.g., Marshall Plan aid and NATO protection for Europe, bilateral security and economic dispensations for Japan while it rebuilt its economy in the 1950s–60s) and what it took (e.g., control over alliance policy, selective protection for its own politically sensitive sectors like agriculture and textiles) were generally seen as in balance. To the extent they weren't, as with military and covert interventions installing friendly governments and deposing unfriendly ones in Third World countries, others had limited power to do much about it.[61]

Now, however, others are less inclined than before to defer to Washington's wishes. This defiance was likely to grow more acute over time, but the Trump presidency has served as an accelerant. The lack of commitment to liberal values by the putative leader of the liberal order is inherently problematic. And the general ineptitude of Trump's diplomacy has only compounded the problem. In the past, leaders of other countries might have been more inclined to trust the United States to do right, because the U.S. government was at least run by people who seemed to know what they were doing (though the many failures of U.S. statecraft of the last quarter century, noted above, surely undermined these beliefs).

Fortunately, there is an alternative to simply spending more and trying harder. This alternative hinges on the expectation that there are many responsible and credible actors in the world. Indeed, some countries, including a number of longtime U.S. allies, are trying to move away from their dependence upon the United States. Unsettled by President Trump's threats to renege on American security commitments or offended by his attempts to extract tribute in exchange for U.S. protection, these countries' leaders are thinking seriously about different security arrangements. In November 2018, for example, French president Emmanuel Macron and German chancellor Angela Merkel both called for an integrated European Union military, one that could operate independently of the United States—though both pledged that such a force would not undermine the U.S.-led NATO alliance. "The times when we could rely on others are over. This means we Europeans have to take our fate fully into our own hands," Merkel told the European Parliament. "We should work on a vision of one day establishing a real European army."[62]

Such moves are not driven merely by Donald Trump's erratic behavior and belligerent tweets. Skepticism about Washington's competence and its capacity for performing its self-appointed role as global hegemon is propelling the consideration of new approaches to global security. Many are upset about Americans' habit of initiating new conflicts, or adding fuel to existing ones, and then expecting others to help with the cleanup. In short, other nations around the world might welcome the chance to show that they know best how to maintain their security.

Americans should welcome this change. Instead of treating U.S. allies like reckless teenagers that can't be trusted without Uncle Sam's constant supervision, or like feckless weaklings that will jump at the chance to capitulate to rapacious neighbors, U.S. foreign policy should expect—and, in some cases, demand—that mature, like-minded states will deal with nearby challenges before they become regional or global crises. U.S. military power was a key factor in shaping the postwar global order, but other factors—including deepening economic interdependence, widespread cultural exchange, and evolving norms that privilege diplomacy over violence—were important as well. Human beings are generally reluctant to go to war, and more so now than 70 years ago, or 500 years ago. Harvard University's Steven Pinker has documented the dramatic decline in all forms of violence committed by humans against other humans.[63] These welcome factors will persist even as America's relative power recedes.

Some worry that U.S. allies will show less deference and be less willing to comply with Washington's dictates if they become less dependent on U.S. power. But, as noted earlier, U.S. allies have been known to act recklessly when they believe that we have their back. Greater independence could induce greater caution. And the benefits flow both ways. If Washington was slightly less confident that it could count on others to support its decisions, that might help us avoid some costly mistakes.

The United States is the most important country in the world, and it will remain so for many years by virtue of its strong economy and its prodigious military capabilities. But advocates of restraint also take account of our favorable geography, weak neighbors, and devastating nuclear arsenal. A strategy of restraint indicates relative optimism about regional balances of power and confidence that the international economy is robust and resilient. Restraint as a strategy hinges on the belief that peace results from the widespread realization among most states that war does not pay. Although the United States undoubtedly played a critical role in establishing institutions after World War II, the need to continue to do so is not obvious. Just as most people have concluded on their own that peace is preferable to war, so too have most come to appreciate the benefits of a relatively open economic system. U.S. leaders need not lecture others—or threaten them.

Restraint appreciates the inherent limits of military power. The use of force beyond self-defense is unjust and unnecessary. It almost always causes more problems than it solves. The military is a blunt instrument, ill suited to rooting out extremist ideologies, spreading democracy, or implanting liberal values. Military intervention often turns small conflicts into medium or large ones, and can create new enemies along the way. Renewing the United States' commitment to primacy, and discouraging greater self-reliance among current allies and partners, will be a massive undertaking, far more onerous than any the United States has attempted since World War II. It is also unlikely to work. In short, U.S. foreign policy was ripe for a fundamental revision long before Donald J. Trump emerged on the political scene. Any number of alternatives to primacy were available to him or any other aspiring politician. What he brought to the table is the subject of the next chapter.

Spoiler alert: it wasn't restraint.

CHAPTER 3
Defining Trump's "America First" Worldview

As we have seen, the strategy of restraint has long been anathema within the Washington, DC, foreign policy elite. Despite a good deal of support among international relations scholars, restraint is generally unwelcome in the halls of power. The vast network of elected representatives and their staffs, career national security analysts, military and intelligence professionals, Foreign Service officers, and civil servants deep within the bowels of the bureaucracy—from the National Security Agency to the National Security Council—almost universally supports primacy.

This should come as no surprise. After all, restraint prescribes a humble, modest foreign policy that eschews the vigorous exercise of U.S. power. Few decisionmakers in the national security bureaucracy stray from the dominant ideology of American exceptionalism and indispensability that has prevailed since World War II; even fewer are eager to forfeit their broad policy mandates or embrace massive budget cuts that may lose them their jobs. Restraint is unpopular not just in government, but also in the Washington think tank community. Most policy experts in such organizations share the ideological commitment to U.S. foreign policy activism and also face powerful incentives to conform to official preferences.[1]

Therefore, as Donald J. Trump rose to power, his foreign policy vision, such as it is, was considerably out of step with the establishment foreign policy community. He even occasionally stumbled upon some of the same arguments frequently made by advocates of restraint. Trump, for example, excoriated the decades-old policy of extending security guarantees to rich, powerful, and safe allies abroad while America foots the bill and assumes the risk. He questioned the need to have hundreds of thousands of U.S. troops permanently stationed all over the world and decried America's global policeman role. He even waved aside the notion that American foreign policy is guided by benevolent higher values and liberal principles, dispensing with the crusading spirit that drives much U.S. interventionism.[2]

Regrettably, in their frustration at the rise of Trump, many staunch defenders of the status quo erroneously lumped him and his foreign policy pronouncements in with the advocates of restraint. Notwithstanding sporadic and shallow likenesses, however, the substantive similarities between Trump's vision of U.S. foreign policy and that prescribed under a grand strategy of restraint are scarce. Indeed, in a certain sense, Trump's foreign policy is closer to the *inverse* of restraint. Advocates of restraint tend to favor low-tariff free trade, liberal immigration policies, robust diplomacy, and a reduced military role for the United States. By contrast, Trump favors economic protectionism, restricted immigration, weakened diplomacy, and energetic militarism. Advocates of restraint emphasize the relatively peaceful state of world politics, disparage Washington's habit of inflating trivial threats, and complain that America devotes too much blood and treasure to fighting minor problems like terrorism. Trump, on the other hand, warns that the world is as dangerous as ever and demands that we must do more to fight terrorism.

Some of Trump's detractors mistake his foreign policy views in another way, by labeling him an isolationist.[3] Thomas Wright of the Brookings Institution argues that Trump's views are reminiscent of a certain "pre–World War II" tradition in U.S. foreign policy that is skeptical of alliances, sympathetic to authoritarian strongmen, and contemptuous of free trade.[4] Wright compares Trump to the "staunch isolationist and mercantilist" Robert Taft, the prominent mid-century Republican senator and presidential candidate, and to Charles Lindbergh, "who led the isolationist America First movement" and opposed aiding Britain in the war against Nazi Germany. Trump's "America First" campaign slogan does explicitly revive the one used by isolationists during the interwar period, and Trump's views on trade and immigration certainly suggest strong isolationist impulses.

However, isolationism was always a poor label for someone who advocated seizing Iraq's oil, unleashing an open-ended air war on ISIS, and picking fights with weak adversaries like Iran, North Korea, and Venezuela.[5] Far from turning inward, Trump has evinced a kind of neo-imperialist tendency, going so far as to encourage his cabinet in late September 2017 to prioritize extracting Afghanistan's mineral deposits for our own economic gain.[6] Although Trump has frequently criticized the U.S. military presence in Afghanistan, he reportedly concluded that if we have to be there, we might as well profit by snatching up their natural resources. Isolationist this is not.

Still others claimed that Trump's foreign policy preferences derive from a stark realist vision of the world.[7] As Hal Brands and Peter Feaver put it, Trump's "version of realism has quite a lot in common with the contemporary academic version."[8] Daniel Drezner put it even more bluntly: "This is realism's moment in the foreign policy sun."[9]

Understanding what to make of these claims takes a bit more precision than we have been using so far. Realism as a school of thought in international relations is a wide-ranging category that does not always produce unanimous policy prescriptions. Broadly speaking, realism splits into two schools: classical and structural. Both schools tend to see the international system as a harsh Hobbesian environment of dog-eat-dog competition in which states ruthlessly pursue their own selfish interests in often violent ways. Both place the distribution of power among states at the heart of their analysis. But *classical realists* emphasize the quest for domination inherent in human nature, whereas *structural realists* emphasize how the anarchic nature of the international system imposes constraints on states and conditions their behavior.

In a 1980 interview, Trump, the maverick businessman, said he sees "life to a certain extent as combat." To historians Charlie Laderman and Brendan Simms, that statement reflects Trump's "Hobbesian perspective on international affairs, in which the world is anarchic and strength is paramount."[10] Randall L. Schweller, associate professor of international affairs at Ohio State University and a prominent realist, argues that "Trump's views conform to both the political economy and geopolitics of realism," particularly in his emphasis on economic self-sufficiency, his disdain for free-riding allies, his ambivalence about great power spheres of influence, and his rejection of a liberal, rules-based world order in favor of an unsentimental, almost value-free approach to foreign policy.[11]

Again, Trump's views bear a superficial resemblance to realism but we see negligible substantive overlap. Realism, for one thing, puts a premium on shrewd rationality, utility maximization, objective situational judgments, and long-term strategic thinking.[12] A foreign policy informed by realist sensibilities is empathetic; it assesses the interests and gauges the strategic perspectives of other states, including adversaries. Policy is informed by a calculating and nuanced appraisal of tangible threats to the national interest, rather than ideologically motivated crusades. Clearly, this cautious, deliberative, rational realpolitik approach does not describe Trump's foreign policy temperament, which is frequently erratic, confused, irrational, and unable to see the world through others' eyes.

Indeed, in one way, Trump's disposition more often resembles the school of thought that early 20th-century realists identified as the antithesis of realism. In one of the foundational realist texts, E. H. Carr defended realism against the emerging idealist tendency in international politics, in which "wishing prevails over thinking, generalization over observation, and in which little attempt is made at a critical analysis of existing facts or available means."[13] Hans Morgenthau, one of the most renowned classical realist scholars, also argued that realism requires "distinguishing . . . between what is true objectively and rationally, supported by evidence and illuminated by reason, and what is only a subjective judgement . . . informed by prejudice and wishful thinking."[14] Brian Rathbun, professor of international relations at the University of Southern California, contrasts Otto von Bismarck—the 19th-century Prussian statesman and first chancellor of the German Empire, and widely considered history's consummate realist—with King Wilhelm I, thus: "a contrast between a deliberate, careful, and sober (in other words, rational) statesman and an impulsive, shortsighted, and emotional sovereign."[15] There is no doubt which of these contrasting dispositions best describes President Trump.

The Elusive Trump Doctrine

So, if Trump is not a restrainer, an isolationist, or a realist, what is he? What are the core features of his worldview? Where do they come from? And how do they inform his approach to foreign affairs? Answering these questions with precision is difficult with any president, but several factors make it exceedingly difficult with Trump.

First, Trump is unique in that he has no prior foreign policy experience. Despite their differences, all of Trump's post–Cold War predecessors had served in political or national security positions prior to their presidency and were profoundly molded by the expectations of the DC consensus around primacy. Also unlike his predecessors, he has not adapted his views while in office, despite considerable internal and external pressure to do so. This makes it harder to classify a Trump doctrine than a Bush doctrine or an Obama doctrine.

Second, the record strongly suggests that Trump is a mercurial liar of the highest order.[16] A number of the president's closest advisers and confidants—including his first secretary of state, Rex Tillerson; former director of the National Economic Council Gary Cohn; and former legal adviser John Dowd—have reportedly called him a liar.[17] "One of the distinguishing characteristics of Donald Trump's presidency," wrote the *Washington Post*'s Glenn Kessler, "has been his loose relationship with facts."[18] By April 2019, the *Post* had documented more than 10,000 false or misleading claims from the president, averaging 15 erroneous claims per day.[19] He lies so frequently and so casually that it appears to be almost involuntary.[20] He promulgates false or misleading information even when it is entirely unimportant whether the falsehood is accepted by anybody else (e.g., the size of the crowds at his inauguration or the number of new U.S. Steel plants under construction). Determining the worldview of a habitually dishonest man is not easy.

Third, this "loose relationship with facts" means not only that Trump frequently tells lies or believes things despite clear disconfirming evidence, but also that he habitually changes his position on a great many issues. Rex Tillerson reportedly complained to White House colleagues that Trump "makes a decision and then changes his mind a couple days later."[21] Trump has changed his party identification—from Democratic to Republican, to Reform Party, to Independent—more than any other modern political figure. He expressed support for the Iraq War before condemning it as foolish. In 2011, he criticized the Obama administration for being too slow to intervene in Libya to protect civilians from the Qaddafi regime, insisting that "we should go in . . . do it on a humanitarian basis" and "knock this guy out" and "save these lives."[22] And yet, in the 2016 campaign, he railed against Hillary Clinton for her involvement in the Libya intervention, saying it was a stupid idea and that "We would be so much better off if Gadhafi would be in charge right now."[23]

In 2013, amid intense debate about whether President Obama should bomb the Syrian regime of Bashar al-Assad as punishment for crossing his red-line ultimatum against the use of chemical weapons, Trump tweeted: "President Obama, do not attack Syria. There is no upside and tremendous downside," adding, "Syria is NOT our problem."[24] "The only reason President Obama wants to attack Syria," Trump explained in another tweet, "is to save face over his very dumb RED LINE statement. Do NOT attack Syria, fix U.S.A."[25] He insisted Obama get congressional approval before any strike against Syria and criticized Obama for broadcasting his (soon aborted) plans to attack Syria: "I would not go into Syria, but if I did it would be by surprise and not blurted all over the media like fools."[26]

Trump would subsequently contravene every one of these positions. In April 2017 and April 2018, Trump bombed Syria for precisely the same reason for which he condemned Obama in 2013—to save face over the red line. He did so without congressional approval, and before acting, he broadcast his plan to do so all over the media.[27] During the campaign, even Trump's own running mate, Mike Pence, apparently had trouble deciphering Trump's position on Syria, suggesting in a debate that, if elected, a Trump administration would move to establish safe-zones in Syria, which Trump later contradicted.[28]

Candidate Trump dismissed NATO as obsolete. Less than four months into his presidency, he declared it "no longer obsolete," while paving the way for NATO expansion.[29] By the summer of 2018, Trump declared NATO, and the U.S. commitment to it, stronger than it has ever been.[30] After securing the Republican nomination, the Trump campaign excised the section of the Republican platform calling for sending lethal U.S. arms to Ukraine.[31] But as president, Trump approved the delivery of lethal arms to Ukraine. He frequently disparaged American nation-building missions abroad and insisted we should withdraw from Afghanistan, only to authorize a surge of U.S. troops there to help continue a war he had previously denounced.

Even on the issues on which Trump has been most consistent, trade and immigration, he has prevaricated and flip-flopped. Trump has long advocated protectionist economic policies, criticizing companies that engage in free trade, employ cheap foreign labor, and hire illegal immigrants. As president, Trump has pushed for a "Buy American, Hire American" policy.[32] And yet, as a private businessman, he hired undocumented immigrants and sold an array of Trump products—including ties, suits, dress shirts, eyeglasses, sofas, chandeliers, and bedding—all variously made and manufactured in China, the Netherlands, Mexico, India, Turkey, Slovenia, Honduras, Germany, Bangladesh, Indonesia, Vietnam, and South Korea.[33]

Every politician lies, and most have been on multiple sides of one issue or another. But Trump is especially guilty of this, and in a way that seems almost independent of policy substance. A good example is the Trump administration's policy toward Iran and North Korea. Trump came into office harshly antagonistic toward both countries. In particular, he spent a lot of time denigrating the Iran nuclear deal, or the Joint Comprehensive Plan of Action (JCPOA), secured by the Obama administration after years of negotiations with Iran and the "P5+1" (the permanent members of the UN Security Council—the United States, Britain, France, China, and Russia—plus Germany). In exchange for lifting economic sanctions, the deal rolled back Iran's nuclear enrichment program and imposed strict limits on its expansion over long periods of time. The JCPOA also subjected Iran to the most intrusive international inspections regime in the world. The agreement had broad support in the expert community, and successive reports from the International Atomic Energy Agency confirmed Iran's full compliance with its stringent terms, a finding that was corroborated by assessments from the U.S. military and intelligence community. President Trump claimed that the JCPOA was a weak deal because it failed to eradicate even civilian enrichment in Iran and because it addressed only the nuclear program, while leaving aside other issues like Iran's regional behavior and domestic human rights abuses.

In contrast, after a single face-to-face meeting with the North Korean dictator, during which Supreme Leader Kim Jong Un agreed to vague, jointly expressed aspirations for the eventual denuclearization of the Korean Peninsula, Trump declared the problem solved and said North Korea was "no longer a threat."[34] The parties did not negotiate any specific details, Trump secured no explicit commitments from Kim to roll back his nuclear weapons program or to open it up to international inspections, and he offered no timeline for reciprocal concessions to incentivize North Korean compliance in some future agreement. The joint statement from the summit meeting did not address North Korea's regional behavior or its domestic human rights abuses. Even after intelligence assessments concluded that the Kim regime was continuing to expand its nuclear program, Trump praised the progress in the effort to dismantle Pyongyang's nuclear capabilities.[35]

So, in sum, Trump vehemently opposed, and withdrew from, one of the most robust nonproliferation agreements ever negotiated on the grounds that it continued to allow uranium enrichment for civilian purposes and failed to rein in Iran's regional behavior and human rights abuses. Yet he simultaneously boasted about a flimsy joint communique (not an actual agreement) with North Korea (unlike Iran, already a nuclear weapons state) devoid of any verification procedures or any suggestion that Pyongyang must reform its foreign and domestic policies.

All this suggests that policy is not being made on the basis of substantive considerations or coherent strategy. As an anonymous senior administration official put it in a *New York Times* op-ed, "Anyone who works with him knows he is not moored to any discernible first principles that guide his decision making," a charge Trump has received from multiple people who have worked with him. Thus we come to the fourth major obstacle to accurately divining Trump's worldview: his lack of a worldview. Pinning down the moving object that is Trump's foreign policy is hard enough, but trying to concretize what is essentially a vacuum can seem downright futile.

The most systematic and intelligible presentations of Trump's foreign policy views are found in his major speeches, including those he gave as a candidate at an event organized by the Center for the National Interest, as president to the UN General Assembly, and to some extent his inaugural address. But all of those were written by other people—advisers and close aides like Steve Bannon and Stephen Miller—making it difficult to know where their views end and Trump's begin. In his book *Devil's Bargain*, the journalist Joshua Green, who had extensive access to Bannon in 2015 and 2016, uncovers the extent to which Bannon fleshed out old populist and nationalist ideas to "build an intellectual basis for Trumpism." Trump, Green surmised, "proved to be an able messenger" for a variety of ideas that he hadn't necessarily developed from his own deep study.[36] Alas, scripted speeches are less useful as signposts to Trump's worldview than they might be for the typical president and his speechwriters. This isn't to say Trump has no fixed views on anything, or that he is literally an ideological empty vessel. But he does not seem to have a holistic philosophy about how the world works or ought to work, or any coherent strategic framework within which his foreign policy positions can be situated.

Unsurprisingly, many analysts have concluded that there simply is no Trump doctrine, per se. "Trump has no coherent foreign policy stance," according to the *New Yorker*'s John Cassidy, "he has only instincts."[37] Thomas Otte describes Trump's early foreign policy as "chaotic ad hoc improvisation, impelled by personal impulses and short-term domestic calculations, rather than the fruits of careful strategic cerebration."[38] Rebecca Friedman Lissner and Micah Zenko argue that Trump lacks "the careful patience required to develop and execute a purposive course of action." Scholarly attempts to "impose intellectual coherence on Trump's constellation of instincts and predilections," they say, won't alter the fact that he is "explicitly anti-strategic" and destined to produce unpredictable policy outcomes.[39]

A fifth and final obstacle to accurately divining Trump's true foreign policy views is that analysts must rely more than usual on how his personality traits and apparent cognitive characteristics factor in. The unusually dominant position of the United States in the international system, combined with the incredible expansion of executive war powers over the years, elevates the importance of a president's temperament and personality in foreign policy decisionmaking, while diminishing the importance of external threats and constraints. Moreover, President Trump's lack of prior political or foreign policy experience, his habitual lying and flip-flopping, and his inability to unite even his own cabinet around a clear strategy, leave us with little to draw on in sketching out his worldview. The clues, therefore, are to be found not in official documents like the National Security Strategy, but in Trump's own mind.

This effort raises problems of its own, of course. The psychiatric community is ethically bound by what is commonly called the "Goldwater rule," in reference to 1964 presidential candidate Barry Goldwater, whom some psychiatrists controversially deemed unfit for office despite never having personally examined him. The guideline appears in the American Psychiatric Association's code of ethics Section 7.3; it states, "it is unethical for a psychiatrist to offer a professional opinion [on a public figure] unless he or she has conducted an examination and has been granted proper authorization for such a statement."[40] Yet many psychiatrists and psychologists have felt compelled to publicly voice their concerns about President Trump, despite the ethical guidelines.[41]

We don't want to diagnose anything, but some of Trump's public behavior raises questions about his fitness for office. He has repeatedly, and apparently without shame, referred to himself as a genius,[42] bragged about being "really rich,"[43] and publicly insulted his detractors, including former friends and allies he previously praised. Trump famously called Rosie O'Donnell "a fat Pig,"[44] called his former White House adviser Omarosa Manigault Newman a "crazed, crying lowlife" and a "dog,"[45] ridiculed a disabled reporter, and blamed a female journalist's tough questions on her menstrual cycle, along with many other such instances of verbal abuse. When accused of tax evasion during a presidential debate in September 2016, Trump boasted, "That makes me smart," indicating he expects special treatment not granted to others. In one of the more unusual features of the administration, President Trump occasionally uses cabinet meetings as an opportunity to receive praise from top officials in the presence of the news media.[46]

Trump constantly exaggerates his own abilities and achievements, something psychologists refer to as the Dunning-Kruger effect, a cognitive bias in which people with little expertise possess an illusory superiority over others. In his acceptance speech for the Republican nomination, Trump declared "Only I can fix it!" During the campaign, he said he knew more about ISIS than the generals. This tendency goes back a long way in Trump's history. In 1984, at a time when he was trying to insinuate himself into politics, he advertised his business acumen as the remedy for negotiations with the Soviet Union over nuclear and ballistic missile policy; Trump insisted, "It would take an hour-and-a-half to learn everything there is to learn about missiles. . . . I think I know most of it anyway."[47] This claim rings false, though, given the revelation during the 2016 campaign that he did not know the meaning of "nuclear triad."[48]

He regularly overstates the direct impact he has on the economy and falsely describes his economic guardianship as record-breaking. In September 2018, for example, he tweeted that the GDP growth rate was higher than the unemployment rate for the first time in 100 years; actually, it is a rather common occurrence, having happened 185 times since 1948.[49] He seems to have little awareness of how absurd his boasting appears to others. In a speech to the UN General Assembly in September 2018, he claimed, "my administration has accomplished more than almost any administration in the history of our country." The august audience of emissaries and diplomats broke out in uproarious laughter.[50]

Another worrying tendency is the president's penchant for wild conspiracy theories. His promotion of the "birther" conspiracy, the idea that Barack Obama was not a citizen of the United States, is a case in point. He also claimed, "The concept of global warming was created by and for the Chinese in order to make U.S. manufacturing non-competitive."[51] As a candidate, he alleged that Texas Sen. Ted Cruz's father was an accomplice in the assassination of President John F. Kennedy.[52] Once in office, conspiracy-mongering fused with Trump's own paranoia when he claimed that the Obama administration wiretapped Trump Tower.[53] He repeatedly dismissed the validity of the special counsel investigation into Russian influence operations in the 2016 election, decrying it instead as a politically motivated witch hunt perpetrated by the Democratic Party, the so-called deep state, or some combination of the two (Special Counsel Robert Mueller is a lifelong Republican). Less publicly, a small circle of Trump national security advisers circulated what the *New Yorker* described as a "conspiracy memo" that "read like a U.S. military-intelligence officer's analysis of a foreign-insurgent network," identifying former Obama administration officials as being involved in a coordinated effort "to undermine President Trump's foreign policy." The memo described Ben Rhodes, Obama's deputy national security adviser, as "likely the brain behind this operation" and Colin Kahl, Vice President Joe Biden's national security adviser, as its "likely ops chief."[54]

In addition, numerous public officials have voiced related concerns. Senator Cruz (R-TX), while a rival of Trump during the Republican primary, accused Trump of being "a pathological liar," "utterly amoral," and "a narcissist at a level I don't think this country's ever seen."[55] Sen. Lindsey Graham (R-SC) said of Trump, "I think he's a kook. I think he's crazy. I think he's unfit for office."[56] Mitt Romney warned that Trump is "not of the temperament of the kind of stable, thoughtful person we need as a leader."[57] These are not ordinary rhetorical jabs at a political opponent. Reince Priebus, Trump's first White House chief of staff, told journalist Bob Woodward that "the president has zero psychological ability to recognize empathy or pity in any way."[58] Priebus's successor John Kelly reportedly called the president "unhinged,"[59] and "an idiot" who has "gone off the rails."[60] John Dowd, President Trump's legal adviser from June 2017 to March 2018, inadvertently described Trump as "clearly disabled."[61] Whatever may or may not be diagnosable in a clinical setting, Trump seems to present just the scenario that advocates of restrained presidential power have always warned about—above all in foreign policy, where presidential power has always been comparatively strong and unchecked.

Members of Congress have raised the issue of whether the cabinet should invoke the 25th Amendment to the Constitution, which provides for the removal of a president who is mentally or physically "unable to discharge the powers and duties of his office."[62] According to widespread reports, confirmed by a senior administration official, top cabinet members have actually discussed this option.[63] Indeed, in the early days of the administration, a new phrase entered the political discourse: the so-called adults in the room, a term meant to refer to responsible officials in the president's inner circle who would balance his volatility and counteract his worst instincts. In a public spat with Trump in October 2017, Sen. Bob Corker (R-TN), who was then the chair of the Foreign Relations Committee and had been an early supporter of Trump's campaign, told reporters, "I know for a fact that every single day at the White House, it's a situation of [senior administration officials] trying to contain him."[64] The White House had become "an adult day care center," he said, before warning that, left to his own devices, President Trump would put the nation "on the path to World War III."[65]

In summary, President Trump is a hard case for foreign policy analysts. His policy preferences often defy neat categorization, and many of his positions change with the political winds, sometimes even within a single news cycle. Searching for a Trump doctrine in the president's personality and psychological makeup adds to the challenge of defining his worldview with precision. His lack of a fixed ideology and his turbulent temperament further complicate the task. Nevertheless, despite these obstacles, it is possible to work out certain consistent features of Trump's overall worldview—components of his ideological makeup that drive his approach to foreign policy.

FOUR FRAMES FOR TRUMP'S WORLDVIEW

Several astute analysts have tried to sketch a broad overview of Trump's foreign policy inclinations, sometimes fruitfully. Some attempts to boil it all down have yielded valuable insights, though they risk dramatically oversimplifying things. Harvard University's Danielle Allen, for example, has argued that

> Trump's foreign policy is perfectly coherent—so coherent, in fact, that we could give it a name: pure bilateralism. . . . Less than seeking to disrupt the old order because he has a considered view about it, apparently Trump seeks a global order that turns around him personally, where global politics is conducted as a series of deals with Donald Trump.[66]

Allen provides a perceptive frame for Trump's foreign policy, perhaps, but omits important features of his rhetoric and ideas.

We have identified four frames through which to ascertain and interpret President Trump's worldview. Relying largely on the president's record so far in the White House, his rhetoric and speeches both during the campaign and in office, and an extensive review of his interviews and public statements going as far back as 1980, we argue that the Trump doctrine, such as it is, comprises a shifting blend of four animating features: zero-sum transactionalism; Jacksonian nationalism and militarism; honor, status, and respect; and the authoritarian mind.

Zero-Sum Transactionalism

One of Trump's most prominent early political statements was a full-page advertisement he took out in the *New York Times*, *Washington Post*, and *Boston Globe* in 1987. The central impulses he displayed in the five-paragraph open letter animate his politics to this day. Trump railed against allies, singling out Japan and Saudi Arabia in particular, for benefitting from U.S. security guarantees while America gets nothing in return. "Why are these nations," he asked, "not paying us for the human lives and billions of dollars we are losing to protect *their* interests?" He highlighted Japan's booming economy and Saudi Arabia's vast oil wealth as especially disturbing because of the bitter irony of aiding countries he sees as our economic competitors.

There are a lot of reasons one might be skeptical of the United States' postwar system of alliances, in which America subsidizes the defense of scores of countries abroad, often in formal treaties that obligate the United States to fight on its allies' behalf in case of war. The expense of such policies is certainly a valid concern; other concerns include the strategic risks of becoming entangled or entrapped in unnecessary wars and, say, differing assessments of the threats that allies face now versus during the Cold War. Trump's singular focus on the transactional nature of these alliances is a consistent theme in his foreign policy thinking. Perhaps because of his experience in the business world as a real estate developer, Trump does not believe such arrangements can be mutually beneficial. To his way of thinking, bilateral and multilateral relationships—whether in the security or economic realm—cannot be positive-sum. Every deal has a winner and a loser. Trump is therefore unconvinced by arguments that economic interdependence promotes economic growth beyond what could be achieved in an autarkic system of walled-off national economies. In fact, interdependence can contribute to a convergence of interests among two or more states, but Trump sees this convergence almost exclusively as an economic and national security vulnerability.

This belief largely explains why Trump seems to spend more time criticizing long-standing U.S. allies than adversaries. With the notable exception of China, the U.S. economy is far more intertwined with our friends than our rivals. Since Trump sees the world as a zero-sum arena of competing winners and losers, adversaries with isolated economies that don't trade much with the United States—for example, Russia—are less of a threat than allies with whom we have significant trade relationships. Part of the explanation for this view comes from Trump's tendency to think of global wealth as a fixed pie, rather than an expanding sphere.

In an interview on CNN in 2013, Trump said, "You have to take jobs away from other countries, China, India, all of these countries, they're taking our jobs. . . . You've got to take the jobs, you [*sic*] got to make the economy strong."[67] He sees trade imbalances as inherently exploitative, complaining after a G7 meeting about trade deficits with Canada and Europe that "[w]e are being taken advantage of by virtually every one of those countries. . . . They don't take our agricultural products, barely. They don't take a lot of what we have and yet they send

Mercedes into us. They send BMWs into us by the millions. It's very unfair."[68] These views are roundly rejected by economists and simply do not correspond with the data on trade relations and economic growth.[69] When Trump's former economic adviser Gary Cohn asked him, "Why do you have these views?" Trump answered, "I don't know . . . I just do. I've had these views for 30 years."[70]

In office, Trump has pushed ahead with these protectionist instincts, imposing tariffs on imports worth hundreds of billions of dollars from Canada, Mexico, the European Union, Russia, and China, among other countries.[71] To a substantial degree, economic warfare is the most conspicuous feature of Trump's foreign policy. In some cases, the White House dubiously justified these tariffs as necessary to protect national security. Targeted countries have retaliated in kind, with China imposing countertariffs on U.S. goods worth more than $100 billion. This trade war has harmed the U.S. economy.[72] For example, retaliatory countertariffs hit tens of billions of dollars' worth of U.S. farm and seafood exports, prompting the White House to authorize nearly $20 billion in subsidies to the farming industry, assistance meant to ease the pain caused by Trump's elective trade war in the first place.[73] According to an estimate from J.P. Morgan Chase, Trump's tariff policies might have cost the S&P 500 10 percent of its value in 2018.[74] A study by Goldman Sachs found that the costs of Trump's tariffs against Chinese imports fall "entirely on U.S. businesses and households."[75] The tariffs will cost American households about $106 billion a year, or $831 for the average family in the United States.[76]

Despite the self-harming nature of economic protectionism and despite the failure of Trump's tariffs to bend America's trade partners to his will, the president seems to prefer economic warfare to peaceful trade relations. "Trade wars are good, and easy to win," he tweeted in March 2018.[77] He has tried several times to formally withdraw from long-standing trade agreements—including the North American Free Trade Agreement (NAFTA), the United States–Korea Free Trade Agreement, and even the World Trade Organization (WTO)—only to be blocked or slowed by his own advisers. His antipathy for free trade stems from his zero-sum transactional worldview. Trump seems allergic to the idea of a mutually beneficial, "all boats rise" kind of system. And he doesn't mince words about it. While working up a speech with then White House staff secretary Rob Porter, Trump scribbled a note in the margin in large capital letters: "TRADE IS BAD."[78]

Trump's transactionalism spills over from the economic realm into the security realm. Frustrated with European efforts to uphold the JCPOA following the U.S. withdrawal, Trump accused them of wanting to keep the deal in place because "they're all making money" doing business in Iran following the lifting of economic sanctions.[79] Trump also pressed his advisers to agree to withdraw the 28,500 U.S. troops based in South Korea and to cancel the deployment of an expensive U.S. missile defense system there—not because of the strategic or national security issues at play, but because these were pricey commitments for which South Korea didn't reimburse U.S. taxpayers. "I think we could be so rich," Trump said while arguing with his military advisers about the U.S. troop presence in South Korea, "if we weren't so stupid." In June 2018, Trump suspended U.S.–South Korean military exercises. Again, he didn't frame the decision as a matter of security or as a carrot in negotiations with North Korea. Rather, he criticized the drills as "tremendously expensive," adding, "We save a fortune by not doing war games."[80] Notably, Trump is not opposed to forward deployment as a rule; America just needs to see tangible economic gains from it. In September 2018, for example, he tentatively welcomed Poland's proposal to establish, and fully pay for, a permanent U.S. military base there.[81]

An especially egregious example of Trump's unscrupulous transactionalism arose in October 2018. Amid intense public scrutiny of Washington's relationship with Saudi Arabia as the latter was committing war crimes in Yemen and murdering prominent dissidents, Trump dismissed proposals to halt U.S. military support for Riyadh by pointing to the increased profit margins of defense corporations and the added manufacturing jobs produced domestically by major arms sales to the kingdom.[82] Yet, U.S. jobs tied to arms sales represent less than two-tenths of one percent of the U.S. labor force.[83] He exaggerated the economic benefits by a large margin, but he also warned that canceling U.S. arms sales would make the Saudis look to Russia or China instead, thus giving our geopolitical competitors a win.[84] With this cold-hearted calculation, Trump rather casually prioritized profits for a handful of private corporations over both the moral and strategic costs of U.S. support for Riyadh.

Over and over again, one can find President Trump articulating grievances or justifying policies in zero-sum, transactional terms. His record so far strongly suggests that ethical and strategic imperatives weigh less in his decisionmaking process than how much our side can gain at the expense of others. This mentality pervades his thinking across personal and political domains and explains his views on economics as well as his treatment of allies. It has contributed to his skepticism of the Iran nuclear deal, the Paris Agreement on reducing global carbon emissions, his abandonment of pro-democracy rhetoric, and his hostility to trade deals like NAFTA and the Trans-Pacific Partnership (TPP).

Jacksonian Nationalism and Militarism

In his 2001 book, the political scientist Walter Russell Mead argued that the interplay of four schools of thought have shaped U.S. foreign policy throughout its history. Almost 15 years before Trump descended the escalator at Trump Tower to announce his candidacy for president, Mead described a foreign policy disposition uncannily fitting for the future President Trump: the Jacksonian tradition. *Hamiltonians*, in Mead's paradigm, tend to emphasize the importance of strong national institutions focused on promoting commerce and economic diplomacy. *Wilsonians* believe in the crusading spirit behind U.S. interventionism, the idea that America has a moral obligation as well as an important national interest in spreading democratic values abroad, thereby promoting global peace. *Jeffersonians* are skeptical about exporting democracy, preferring instead to be an example for others to follow, and they are wary of entangling alliances that risk perverting a properly narrow conception of the national interest. Finally, *Jacksonians* stress populist values, economic nationalism, and military might.[85]

Close observers will note that Trump has consciously embraced comparisons with President Andrew Jackson. He even had a presidential portrait of Jackson hung behind his desk in the Oval Office. Trump probably isn't directly familiar with Mead's book, but his campaign manager and later chief White House strategist Steve Bannon made the connection early on. In an interview with *Politico Magazine*, Mead revealed that Bannon phoned him in the summer of 2017 to discuss Trump's classification as a Jacksonian.[86] In the domain of foreign policy, nationalism (of a certain kind) and militarism are at the root of Trump's Jacksonian bent.

"The Jacksonian school," according to Mead, "gets very little political respect and is more frequently deplored than comprehended" by "intellectuals and foreign policy scholars."[87] Jacksonians have "cultural dispositions toward conspiracy thinking"[88] and believe that "while problems are complicated, solutions are simple."[89] Jacksonians are "skeptical about the prospects for domestic and foreign policy do-gooding" and "opposed to federal taxes but obstinately fond of federal programs seen as primarily helping the middle class," and they were "the most consistently hawkish" sect throughout the Cold War.[90] Though occasionally critical of federal power, Jacksonians readily make exceptions in the interest of regulating business or fighting crime, "even at the cost of constitutional niceties."[91] They see immigration "as endangering the cohesion of the folk community and introducing new, low-wage competition for jobs."[92] Other Jacksonian qualities Mead identifies seem particularly apt as well: "bragging about one's physical and sexual prowess, the willingness to avenge disrespect with deadly force, [and] a touchy insistence that one is as good as anybody else."[93]

"Jacksonian political philosophy," Mead explains, "is often an instinct rather than an ideology . . . a set of beliefs and emotions rather than a set of ideas."[94] Adherents are "the least likely to support Wilsonian initiatives for a better world, the least able to understand Jeffersonian calls for patient diplomacy in difficult situations, [and] the least willing to accept Hamiltonian trade strategies."[95] Jacksonians

> believe that international life is and will remain both violent and anarchic. The United States must be vigilant, strongly armed. Our diplomacy must be cunning, forceful, and no more scrupulous than any other country's. At times we must fight preemptive wars.

> There is absolutely nothing wrong with subverting foreign govern-
> ments or assassinating foreign leaders whose bad intentions are clear.
> Indeed, Jacksonians are much more likely to tax political leaders with
> a failure to employ vigorous measures than to worry about the niceties
> of international law.[96]

Indeed, Trump has rarely hesitated to advocate forceful, unscrupulous policies that flout the niceties of international law. During the
campaign Trump argued in favor of torturing detained terrorist suspects
and murdering the families of terrorists.[97] As president, he reportedly directed then secretary of defense James Mattis to assassinate Syrian
president Bashar al-Assad,[98] although that would clearly have been a violation of both U.S. and international law. None of these policies were
actually put into practice as far as we know, but Trump did ramp up
the fight against ISIS by loosening the rules of engagement and giving
the military wider latitude to use force in Iraq, Syria, Yemen, Afghanistan, Somalia, and beyond. No public evidence has emerged to suggest
that the consequent rise in civilian casualties has given Trump second
thoughts about employing ruthless means against enemies.

Widespread reports noted in 2016, particularly in the context of
Trump's verbal assaults against his Republican rivals vying for the nomination, that Trump may leave neutral parties alone, but if targeted, he
would punch back with disproportionate force. "When a person screws
you, screw them back fifteen times harder," he once said.[99] Mead situates
this sentiment firmly in the Jacksonian tradition. For Jacksonians, Mead
explains, "You must hit [enemies] as hard as you can as fast as you can
with as much as you can. Nothing else makes sense. . . . Either the stakes
are important enough to fight for, in which case you should fight with
everything you have, or they aren't important enough to fight for, in
which case you should mind your own business and stay home."[100]

Mead's Jacksonian typology grafts nicely onto many of Trump's
foreign policy inclinations. Trump's antipathy toward international
organizations and free trade institutions fits squarely in the Jacksonian
opposition to Wilsonian and Hamiltonian globalist designs. Trump
sees international law as an affront to national sovereignty that unfairly
constrains U.S. unilateralism. His tough-guy approach parallels Old

Hickory's stubborn resolve and manly dominance. It is important for him to appear aggressive and willing to use overwhelming force, but he also exhibits a willingness to rapidly withdraw from what he sees as peripheral fights that lack a clear enemy. His disinterest in promoting liberal democratic values in other countries, even rhetorically, is a break from his predecessors and consistent with Jacksonian tendencies. Strong disapproval of immigration on both cultural and populist economic grounds is another point of overlap, as evidenced by Trump's unabashed xenophobia. His views on immigration were prominently displayed during the campaign and have been a major element of his administration's policies, particularly the so-called "Muslim ban," the forced family separation and detention of incoming asylum seekers, and the push to abolish the 14th Amendment's birthright citizenship clause.

One final element of the Jacksonian tradition is "a deep sense of national honor" that "must be acknowledged by the outside world" and must be defended, including by going to war over "great things and small."[101] This emphasis on honor is related to concerns about both national and personal status, prestige, and respect. It is such a prominent driver of Trumpian foreign policy impulses that it deserves its own frame.

Honor, Status, Respect

In a review of five hours of recorded interviews with Trump conducted by his biographer in the mid 2000s, the *New York Times*'s Michael Barbaro identifies Trump's "deep-seated fear of public embarrassment" as his most powerful driving force. "The recordings reveal a man who is fixated on his own celebrity" and "anxious about losing his status."[102] In 2013, Trump directed his attorney and personal fixer to have someone pose as a fake bidder at an art auction selling a portrait of himself. Trump used $60,000 in funds from his charity organization, the Trump Foundation, to pull off the ruse intended to create the impression that a painting with his likeness was in high demand.[103]

Trump's grandiose sense of himself and his standing relative to others is so inflated that it rarely matches up with the reality of his experience, which means he constantly feels undervalued and slighted. Relatedly, one of the most consistent themes in all of Trump's public commentary over the course of 40 years has been his belief that America is disrespected around the world, laughed at, and taken advantage of by others, strongly suggesting that his foreign policy outlook is motivated by concerns over status and prestige. Indeed, many of the contradictions in Trump's foreign policy outlook appear consistent when viewed through this frame, and it operates both at a personal level and at the national level as an ordering principle for U.S. foreign policy.

In an October 1980 interview with NBC's Rona Barrett, Trump argued that most of the challenges America faced in the world were due to a lack of respect.[104] If Iran, for example, respected the United States, and feared us, it never would have taken Americans hostage following the 1979 revolution; and Washington's failure to intervene to rectify the slight represented a further blemish on our honor. Trump's aforementioned 1987 newspaper advertisement complained of other nations "taking advantage of the United States."[105] "The world is laughing at America's politicians," he worried. That same year, he told CNN's Larry King that NATO countries "laugh at us."[106] Months later, on the Phil Donahue show, Trump again harped on how Japan, Saudi Arabia, and others "have taken such advantage of this great country."[107] In a 1988 interview, when asked what his political platform would be should he run for office, Trump boiled it down to a single word: "Respect." He added that our adversaries are "beating us psychologically, making us look like a bunch of fools."[108] Again, in a 1989 interview, "They think the United States is made up of a bunch of fools. They're laughing at us."[109] Even more explicitly, in a 1990 interview with *Playboy* magazine, Trump explained that America was "suffering from a loss of respect." "People need ego," he said, "whole nations need ego. I think our country needs more ego" because our leaders have let other countries "literally out-egotise this country."[110]

Trump has been astonishingly consistent on this subject for decades. In a 2004 CNN interview, as the Bush administration's War on Terror was alienating the United States from the rest of the world, Trump again demonstrated the importance he places on international respect and reputation. He lamented that we're "not a very popular country right now."[111] In April 2009, in a discussion with Larry King, Trump offered limited praise to Barack Obama for "trying to restore our reputation."[112] Trump's speech at the 2011 Conservative Political Action Committee (CPAC) conference recycled these themes: "The United States has become a whipping post for the rest of the world," which "is treating us without respect. . . . The United States is becoming the laughing stock of the world."[113] Later that year, in an interview with CNN's Candy Crowley, Trump insisted, "We are not a respected country anymore. The world is laughing at us."[114] A 2013 MSNBC interview featured Trump claiming, "China and lots of other countries . . . are really taking advantage of our country and our people."[115] The world, he said at the 2014 CPAC conference, "has no respect for our leader and . . . no respect any longer for our great country."[116] In a 2016 interview with the *Washington Post*, when asked about his prospective foreign policy, Trump complained about "a tremendous lack of respect for our country" that he planned to remedy "through the aura of personality."[117] In his speech at the Republican National Convention in 2016, Trump warned that "as long as we are led by politicians who will not put America First, then we can be assured that other nations will not treat America with respect." Americans will continue to live "through one international humiliation after another," he warned, citing as recent humiliations Iran's capture (and prompt release) of American sailors in the Persian Gulf, Obama's Syria red-line controversy, and the attack on the U.S. consulate in Libya—"the symbol of American prestige around the globe."[118]

This fixation on international respect and reputation is common in international relations. Preoccupation with honor, status, respect, and reputation has had a major influence on states' foreign policies throughout recorded history, from warring Greek city-states in antiquity to the emerging Sino-American rivalry in the 21st century. In the scholarly literature, "status" refers to collective beliefs about a state's standing or rank in the international system. High-status states are seen to be near the top of the hierarchy and exercise special prerogatives to which weaker, lower-status states defer. The desire for prestige, sometimes used interchangeably with "honor," drives leaders to place special value on international recognition of their country's eminence. Nations that receive what they feel is insufficient status recognition experience it simply as disrespect. "[T]he key to understanding Trump's foreign-policy outlook," according to the political scientist Reinhard Wolf, "lies in his extreme attention to symbolism," where

> questions of substance are eclipsed by an obsession with status and respect. . . . [F]or Trump, America First is not so much about advancing the national interest measured in terms of material wealth or physical survival. It is, first and foremost, about the United States becoming the undisputed 'number one' again, and being treated with due respect.[119]

Symbolism has certainly proved important to President Trump. He called for, and signed into law, a large increase in military spending—less for tangible security reasons than as a symbol of American power. His aborted push to have a military parade in Washington, DC, was similarly indicative of the flair and showmanship important to someone who values prestige for its own sake. And in his relations with foreign leaders, Trump places enormous value on their show of respect for America's high status, even to the point of being easily manipulated by flattery.

On a number of occasions, he has used press briefings to hold up copies of letters sent to him by North Korean leader Kim Jong Un, which shower Trump with respect and praise. The president describes this correspondence as "historic" and "groundbreaking." According to a *Washington Post* report, "Trump is so smitten that he privately shows off the notes to guests in the Oval Office"; former U.S. diplomats privately suggest that "Kim has sized up his mark and showered the president with flattery to soften him up at the negotiating table."[120] In another example, during a White House press conference, Polish president Andrzej Duda proposed establishing a permanent U.S. military base in Poland. To overcome Trump's well-known aversion to providing for Europe's security, Duda suggested naming the base Fort Trump. Visibly delighted, President Trump left Duda's proposal open as a possibility.[121]

Trump's first visit to a foreign country as president was to Saudi Arabia, a country he had previously singled out for disapprobation for taking advantage of the United States. The Saudi monarchy, however, hosted an elaborate red carpet welcome complete with ornate gifts, traditional sword dances, glowing orbs, and obsequious displays of fealty and appreciation. Ever since, Trump has apparently taken Saudi Arabia off the naughty list, arranging for major arms deals and eagerly lending U.S. backing to Riyadh's regional agenda. Japan was the other country that, for decades, Trump had listed alongside Saudi Arabia as an ally that was "ripping us off," even suggesting during the campaign that Tokyo might need to consider obtaining nuclear weapons to make up for the loss of a U.S. security guarantee. Presumably aware of these statements, and intent on maintaining U.S. military support for Japan under Trump, Japanese prime minister Shinzo Abe was the first foreign leader to meet face to face with the president-elect and was determined to get on his good side. Abe presented Trump with a $3,755 gold-plated golf club, sounded all the right notes about sharing the defense burden, and pronounced his firm conviction that "Mr. Trump is a leader in whom I can have great confidence." Abe later followed up on his ostentatious gift with a set of white baseball caps emblazoned with a play on Trump's campaign slogan, "DONALD & SHINZO, MAKE ALLIANCE EVEN GREATER."[122] Coincidentally, Japan, unlike many other prominent U.S. allies, has yet to be on the receiving end of Trump's vitriol.

Symbolic gestures with little or no tangible impact on the national interest are the hallmark of a status-driven foreign policy. The Trump administration's strikes against the Syrian regime of Bashar al-Assad are a good illustration. The attacks did nothing to protect the Syrian people from the Assad regime's brutality and had no discernable tactical or strategic impact on the civil war. According to the White House, the objective was to deter Assad from using chemical weapons in the future and thereby enforce the international norm prohibiting the use of chemical weapons. But the bombings were not authorized by Congress or the UN Security Council and therefore lacked any legal sanction. The only norm the administration really enforced is the one that says the United States is exempt from the laws and norms it commands others to abide by. What the strikes did accomplish was to signal the Trump administration's willingness to use force, thereby reinforcing America's status as the indispensable nation and the policeman of the world. "I think

Donald Trump became President of the United States," CNN's Fareed Zakaria explained in the immediate aftermath of the bombings.[123] "The strikes vindicated America's prestige," Walter Russell Mead wrote at the time, "and dealt a clear setback to those who seek to humiliate or marginalize the U.S."[124]

Status motivations can sometimes inspire peaceful diplomatic efforts, as may have been the case with Trump's unprecedented, and very public, summit with Kim Jong Un. For Trump, whispers of Nobel Peace Prize glory and wall-to-wall television coverage of the first face-to-face meeting between a North Korean supreme leader and a sitting American president redounded with florid praise of skillful statecraft and history being made. However, a status-driven foreign policy more often produces a hawkish approach to the world. In *Why Nations Fight*, Richard Ned Lebow found that, of 94 interstate wars between 1648 and 2008, 58 percent were fought for status and prestige.[125] Foreign policies that seek to reaffirm one's status or redress perceived disrespect can push leaders to pursue more aggressive policies, including military action, for the sake of peripheral interests.

Status and prestige concerns are a major animating feature of Donald Trump's worldview. At a personal level, they explain why he attacks the standing of his detractors, whether "the failing *New York Times*," "low-ratings *Morning Joe*," or "lightweight Marco Rubio." They explain why he so easily takes offense at perceived slights and so readily insults other international actors. These concerns played a significant role in motivating military action against Syria and even surging troops in Afghanistan. And they explain his tactic of harshly criticizing and even withdrawing from "bad deals" negotiated by his predecessors, only to claim credit for fixing them without actually making substantive changes.

The Authoritarian Mind

Trump exhibits distinct authoritarian tendencies. He equates personal loyalty with patriotism and regards disloyalty as treasonous. He has repeatedly attacked federal courts as politically motivated and illegitimate, even going so far as to target individual judges with ad hominem slander for having the gall to overrule his executive orders. He continually denigrates the news media as "fake news" and vilifies the press as "the enemy of the people." He maligned his own attorney general, Jeff Sessions, and ultimately fired him in November 2018 for following protocol and recusing himself from the federal investigation into the Trump campaign's activities in 2016 and Trump's possible obstruction of justice in firing FBI director James Comey. Trump repeatedly expressed frustration that Sessions hadn't used his authority at the Department of Justice to snuff out the special counsel investigation led by Robert Mueller. Trump, as he publicly articulated numerous times, never would have nominated Sessions for the job if he had known Sessions would be disloyal. Trump even criticized Sessions for permitting criminal investigations of Republican members of Congress in a midterm election year, unambiguously implying that the Department of Justice should be an overtly partisan agency in service to the president. According to one report, Trump called Sessions a "traitor."[126]

Indeed, Trump has made something of a habit out of labeling his detractors treasonous. When his top economic adviser, Gary Cohn, submitted a resignation letter, Trump reportedly responded, "This is treason."[127] He said White House officials leaking information to the press "are traitors and cowards."[128] He accused Democrats who refused to stand and applaud during his State of the Union speech of being "un-American" and "treasonous."[129] Following the *New York Times*'s publication of an anonymous op-ed by a senior administration official that was deeply critical of the president, Trump demanded that the newspaper of record "must, for National Security purposes, turn him/her over to government at once!"[130] On one occasion, Trump's intolerance for dissent led him to insinuate that protesting should be illegal.[131] Trump also has a well-known affinity for foreign dictators, as demonstrated by his rhetorical praise for and diplomatic embrace of despots, from Egypt's Abdel Fattah el-Sisi, to Saudi Arabia's Mohammad bin Salman, to Russia's Vladimir Putin, to North Korea's Kim Jong Un.

In a dramatic illustration of his authoritarian tendencies, Trump in May 2019 responded to Congressional inquiries by ordering the executive branch to defy lawful subpoenas from Congress regarding any issue at all. Not only would any request for documents be ignored, but Trump told his advisers and associates called to testify to refrain from doing so, even under subpoena and threats to be held in contempt of Congress. This blanket refusal to comply with any Congressional investigation was unprecedented, according to House Judiciary Committee Chairman Rep. Jerry Nadler, and put the country in a "constitutional crisis."[132]

Steven Levitsky and Daniel Ziblatt, political scientists at Harvard University, spent more than 20 years studying cases of democratic countries in Europe and Latin America being subverted into dictatorships by the election of an autocrat or by the erosion of democratic norms over time. They identify four key indicators of authoritarian behavior in elected leaders: (1) rejection of (or weak commitment to) democratic rules of the game; (2) denial of legitimacy of political opponents; (3) toleration or encouragement of violence; and (4) readiness to curtail civil liberties of opponents, including the press. According to Levitsky and Ziblatt, Trump meets all four key indicators.[133] Trump's verbal encouragement of Russian hacking operations to undermine the Clinton campaign, his refusal in the final presidential debate to promise to respect the results of the election if he was defeated, and his baseless claims both before and after the election of rampant voter fraud all fit under the first indicator. His unprecedented threats (and, as president, active efforts)[134] to have his political rival Hillary Clinton thrown in prison fits under the second. At campaign rallies, Trump frequently encouraged violence against anti-Trump protestors, consistent with the third indicator. And finally, Trump's repeated denigration of critical news media and his successive threats to "open up our libel laws" to prosecute journalists who publish unflattering facts about him, qualifies him for the fourth indicator.[135]

These authoritarian proclivities can shed light on Trump's worldview and his handling of the foreign policy apparatus in the executive branch. Political scientists have been formally researching authoritarian personality traits in political leaders for more than 70 years.[136] Those with authoritarian traits tend to share important psychological habits and decisionmaking styles. They have greater difficulty engaging in critical thinking, are more likely to blame scapegoats for societal problems, are given to superstition and stereotyping, place a high value on power and toughness, and tend to be very assertive and dominant in managing subordinates, thus suppressing an open and deliberative internal decisionmaking process. Authoritarian personalities are also given special attention in the field of international relations, where "regime type" is an important variable in various categories of state interaction, from warfare to multilateral diplomacy.[137]

While Trump may have an authoritarian mind, the political system in which he operates is by no means authoritarian. He is subject to the democratic process via the electorate and constitutionally limited to serving only two four-year terms. His power is also at times curbed by the norms and procedures associated with the professional civil bureaucracy serving under him. His authority faces checks and balances from the two other branches of government, the legislature and the judiciary. And America's free press exposes internal administration debates, sheds light on White House policies, and puts constant pressure on the president's agenda.

That said, there is arguably more raw power concentrated in the single office of the president of the United States than in the thrones of the world's worst dictators. Executive power has been expanded well beyond what is granted in the Constitution and in violation of long-standing norms. Today, U.S. presidents exercise the de facto power to unilaterally launch wars, both big and small, on their own and without the consent of Congress. They can initiate covert actions or conduct air campaigns in any region simply by remote-controlled armed drones. They have at their disposal the most sprawling, sophisticated surveillance system in the world. Presidents even have the power to destroy much of human civilization, with few reliable procedural constraints on the authority to launch nuclear war.[138] Given these awesome powers, Trump's authoritarian tendencies are especially relevant and help determine how he manages his administration's foreign policy priorities, how he perceives foreign threats, and how his impulses translate into actual policy.

CONCLUSION

President Trump's foreign policy doctrine is much more ambiguous than that of his predecessors. However, the truth is that although presidents are typically more explicit in laying out their foreign policy doctrines within some cohesive strategic vision, all administrations engage in some measure of improvisation that may or may not diverge from their stated doctrine.[139] And although Trump's worldview is in many ways unlike his predecessors', he is subject to the same psychological biases and misperceptions that influence every president when dealing with the inherently opaque nature of international politics, where the actions and intentions of other states are often open to interpretation.

Like previous administrations, Trump's is biased toward action rather than passivity. Threat inflation exacerbates this predisposition. Overconfidence in the effectiveness of interventions of all kinds is also common, as is downplaying the potential negative unintended consequences of military action. Concerns about credibility have driven many past presidents to take military action for peripheral interests out of the largely misguided fear that inaction would embolden adversaries elsewhere. Foreign policies are also influenced by what psychologists call the fundamental attribution error, or the tendency to attribute the behavior of other states to the character of the regime instead of the conditions within which the state acts. This bias makes it easier for decisionmakers to interpret defensive measures as offensive and hostile, leading to counterproductive policy responses. Relatedly, Trump joins his predecessors in bringing to the office preconceived "enemy images" of particular states, notably Iran, that bias policy in a more antagonistic direction than is objectively warranted. These kinds of biases influence every president and must be included, along with the four frames we have outlined, as important variables influencing Trump's foreign policy.[140]

Trump's foreign policy preferences do not fit neatly into existing paradigms or labels. They are not consistent or concrete enough to summarize in a "doctrine," as with the Truman doctrine or the Bush doctrine. He is not a realist or a liberal internationalist. Contrary to the assessments of many commentators beholden to the bipartisan consensus around a grand strategy of primacy, Trump is also not an isolationist or an advocate for restraint. Instead, zero-sum transactionalism, Jacksonian nationalism and militarism, status and respect, and authoritarian proclivities represent personal characteristics and political impulses that inform his worldview and motivate the policies he has pursued in office.

We turn to those policies in the next chapter.

CHAPTER 4
Explaining Continuity and Change in Trump's Foreign Policy

Without a doubt, the Trumpian worldview outlined in Chapter 3 represents a dramatic departure from anything espoused by the vast majority of political leaders from either party since World War II. But despite candidate Trump's fiery harangues against the status quo, and in spite of his unorthodox and erratic approach to foreign policy since taking office, Trump's America First vision has had much less impact on the nation's strategic course than most imagined it would. With a few important exceptions, American foreign policy under Trump looks much more like business as usual than a departure from it. Sadly, where Trump has moved foreign policy in an America First direction, the result has been worse than what came before.

Why does Trump hew so close to the path of primacy? Assessing why the Trump administration's foreign policy looks the way it does in practice is important not only for a full accounting of the actions of the administration but also for our ability to understand—and to improve—American foreign policy in the years to come. To the extent that Trump's actions flow from his own worldview, or from the people he has handpicked to guide foreign policy, the obvious solution is to replace him with a better president and a better foreign policy team. But to the extent that Trump's actions reflect bureaucratic constraints, domestic politics, the views and lobbying efforts of the professional foreign policy community, or the pressures of the international arena, we are foolish to imagine the next president will do much better.

Understanding the perpetuation of primacy is even more urgent given how bad Trump's America First version of primacy is—and how much worse things might get if it becomes more fully entrenched over time.

ASSESSING TRUMP'S FOREIGN POLICY

In a few critical policy areas, Trump has undeniably resisted pressure to conform. The four frames of Trump's worldview outlined in Chapter 3—zero-sum transactionalism, Jacksonian nationalism and militarism, status-seeking and respect, and authoritarianism—help explain those instances where he has most conspicuously departed from the basic primacy playbook.

On immigration, for example, Trump exhibits the behavioral and ideological tendencies of three of the four frames. His zero-sum view of the economy makes restricting immigration important to protect American jobs. His xenophobia toward Latin Americans and Muslims springs from his Jacksonian nationalism. And his uncompromising, top-down approach to immigration policy—including his "Muslim ban" executive order, his sending of the U.S. military to the southern border, and his decision to shut down the government until Democrats provided funding for a wall—reflect his authoritarian instincts.

On trade, Trump's essentially mercantilist view of international commerce fits firmly within the zero-sum transactional frame. Although the United States generally maintains low-tariff free trade, some protectionist policies, as in agriculture, have long been tolerated as a political reality under most U.S. presidents. But Trump, in preference and in policy, stands out from the crowd for his unabashed promotion of economic nationalism, particularly on trade with China and Europe. That said, the U.S.-Mexico-Canada Agreement (USMCA), negotiated by the Trump administration to replace NAFTA, while partially protectionist, actually includes only cosmetic changes to NAFTA and even borrows some provisions from the TPP, a trade deal that candidate Trump had vociferously derided. Trump's evident pride in the USMCA as a significant achievement of his presidency, despite its lack of adherence to his protectionist ideology, may simply speak to the difficulty of making abrupt radical changes to U.S. trade policy or his well-documented inattention to detail, but it may also denote status-seeking behavior.

Another clear distinction is Trump's penchant for eschewing multilateral agreements and abruptly withdrawing from international organizations. The United States has a long history of exempting itself from international pacts and associations when it feels they get in the way. In 2001, the George W. Bush administration withdrew from the Kyoto Protocol, an international environmental agreement. Another example is the Rome Statute, which established the International Criminal Court to prosecute officials who commit war crimes or participate in genocide. Although 122 other countries have signed that agreement, successive U.S. administrations have refused to do so. And the United States has acknowledged that the UN Convention on the Law of the Sea, which defines maritime rights and responsibilities, is customary international law, but Washington refuses to ratify it.

That said, the sheer number of agreements and organizations Trump has renounced, and the rapidity with which he has done so, suggests a difference in degree if not in kind.[1] Trump withdrew from the Paris climate agreement; the TPP; the Iran nuclear deal; the Intermediate-Range Nuclear Forces Treaty (INF Treaty); the UN Educational, Scientific and Cultural Organization; and the UN Human Rights Council. Trump and his national security officials have also offered harsh criticisms of NATO, NAFTA, the International Monetary Fund, the WTO, and the World Bank, among others. Past administrations tried to carve out exemptions to ensure maximum freedom of movement, but they generally worked to uphold the broad set of international institutions and agreements. Trump, on the other hand, seems to have an intrinsic distaste for international arrangements, reflecting his Jacksonian emphasis on national sovereignty, rejection of globalist designs, and preference for transactional bilateral relations that capitalize on America's zero-sum power differential.

Trump's marked lack of rhetoric about the importance of promoting democracy and liberal values in U.S. foreign policy represents another departure from the norm. In the past, presidents employed such rhetoric for many reasons. Some genuinely believed that the United States should, as a matter of policy, seek to transform the politics of distant countries along broadly liberal democratic lines. Others used such rhetoric more as cover, to legitimate policies with much less benign motivations. To be fair, the Trump administration still uses some of this rhetoric, most prominently as a bludgeon with which to attack illiberal adversaries like Iran (even while we hypocritically support worse tyrannies such as Iran's rival, Saudi Arabia). But as a matter of policy, the promotion of democracy has taken a back seat under Trump, which could be explained by his authoritarian proclivities and the Jacksonian aversion to nation-building abroad.

A bird's-eye view of President Trump's foreign policy, however, reveals much more continuity with the policies of his predecessors than change. In some cases, the policy prescriptions of primacy overlap with those of Trump's worldview—continued militarism in the Middle East, for example. In other cases, alternative explanations account for policy continuity. We will explore these alternative explanations later in this chapter.

A tour of Trump's foreign policy makes clear that he has not retreated from the world. In his 2019 State of the Union address, the president pronounced that "great nations do not fight endless wars."[2] To date, however, the president has only talked about withdrawing ground troops from some of the active conflicts America is currently engaged in, while continuing the fight with air power and other lighter-footprint tactics. Indeed, the two wars Trump has been most outspoken about withdrawing from, in Syria and Afghanistan, are wars that he expanded significantly during his first two years in office. Trump has maintained all of America's security commitments and has not withdrawn from any overseas garrisons. U.S. military posture still seeks to dominate not only the Western Hemisphere but also Europe, Asia, the Middle East, and even Africa. Primacy remains America's grand strategy, with all its attendant flaws—albeit with Trumpian flavor.

Latin America

In Latin America, Trump's foreign policy mostly looks like his predecessors'. His administration has emphasized building and maintaining military-to-military ties with allies in the region, continuing a decades-long policy of aiding, training, and equipping national forces while ensuring access for U.S. military bases and troops.[3] As in the past, the justifications for this approach are diverse, from fighting drug trafficking to quelling local insurgencies and rolling back alleged regional penetration by Russia, China, Iran, and international terrorist groups. In stark contrast to allegations of stingy isolationism, the administration pledged in December 2018 to supply $10.6 billion in security assistance and economic development aid for Mexico and Central America.[4]

Trump did reverse one Obama administration initiative in the region, but that decision simply affirmed the status quo ante. At the tail end of his presidency, President Obama orchestrated a fundamental shift in U.S. policy toward Cuba. In 1962, the United States imposed an economic blockade on Cuba, and policy had hardly budged since then. Yet the embargo accomplished nothing beyond helping to impoverish Cubans. The Castro regime not only survived decades of the embargo, it also survived the death of its founder and underwent an orderly transfer of power. President Obama acknowledged this policy failure and, though he lacked legal authority to lift the embargo, he established diplomatic relations with Havana and eased restrictions on travel and business. Trump mostly overturned those policy changes, reverting to the outmoded status quo that had been embraced by virtually every president since John F. Kennedy.

During his campaign, Trump laid out a combative posture toward Mexico as perhaps the trademark of his policy agenda. In a speech launching his presidential run, he made sweeping xenophobic generalizations about Mexican immigrants and vowed to build a wall along the southern border, promising to somehow coerce the Mexican government to pay for it. In the 2017 National Security Strategy, the administration described "strengthening control over our borders and immigration system" as "central to national security."[5] The document went on to claim that "terrorists, drug traffickers, and criminal cartels exploit porous borders and threaten U.S. security and public safety."[6]

The facts paint a very different picture. The overall terrorist threat is minor; the annual chance of an American being killed in a terrorist attack on U.S. soil is about 1 in 29.6 million—less than the chance of being struck by lightning. The chance of being killed by a terrorist who illegally crossed the Mexican border is effectively zero. Since 1975, only nine people who entered the United States illegally committed or attempted to commit a terrorist attack, and only three of those entered via the Mexican border. Not a single American in this period has been killed by a foreign-born terrorist who entered the country illegally.[7]

As for drug trafficking, the vast majority of drugs smuggled into the United States come through legal points of entry. Trump also exaggerates the crime rates of illegal immigrants: immigrants, whether legal or undocumented, are about half as likely as native-born Americans to commit violent or property crime.[8]

Nevertheless, President Trump has continuously stoked fear about immigration from the south. In the lead-up to the 2018 congressional elections, he essentially manufactured a "crisis" over a caravan filled with Latin American migrants and asylum-seekers driving toward the U.S.-Mexico border. Trump called it "an invasion" while focusing public attention on the threat it posed, apparently in an attempt to swing the midterm election in favor of the Republican Party. He even ordered Secretary Mattis to send thousands of U.S. soldiers to the border to stem the tide, a rare and extraordinary step that was dubiously justified on national security grounds.[9]

Trump has also escalated tensions with Venezuela. Amid rising political and economic insecurity, as well as the reelection of President Nicolás Maduro in what international observers considered a sham election, the Trump White House has targeted the regime in Caracas with persistent threats and hostility. In 2017, Trump publicly floated the idea of using the "military option" in Venezuela, though no set of objectives accompanied the pronouncement, never mind any mention of a national security rationale.[10] A year later, the president made explicit reference to the prospect of an internal military coup,[11] and administration officials even met with rebel Venezuelan officers to discuss their plans to overthrow the Maduro regime.[12] Meanwhile, the White House heaped punishing economic sanctions on the country and paved the way for Venezuela to be added to the State Department's official list of state sponsors of terrorism, even though experts generally dismiss the allegation.[13]

These moves may seem unusually belligerent, but they are quite typical. As Mark Feierstein, Obama's senior director of Western Hemisphere Affairs at the National Security Council, said, the Trump policy on Venezuela "is on the right track," adding, "I think in many cases they're building on what we did in the Obama administration."[14] Going back further, in 2002, the George W. Bush administration was implicated in helping orchestrate and encourage a coup in Venezuela, which failed when loyalists in the military moved to protect then president Hugo Chavez.[15] As if to emphasize the essentially conventional nature of Trump's approach, National Security Advisor John Bolton coined the phrase "Troika of Tyranny," an implicit allusion to the Bush administration's "Axis of Evil," as a call to confront the regimes in Cuba, Nicaragua, and Venezuela.[16]

In January 2019, Juan Guaidó, the president of Venezuela's National Assembly, declared himself interim president. He did so in accordance with provisions in the Venezuelan constitution that authorize the president of the National Assembly to assume power and call for new elections if the current leadership is deemed illegitimate. To most observers, this development was unexpected and impromptu, but the Trump administration had prior knowledge of it and appears to have had a hand in its orchestration for the purpose of changing the regime in Caracas. Sen. Marco Rubio (R–FL) had reportedly been working closely with the White House on Venezuela policy since the early days of the administration. In February 2017, according to the *New York Times*, "Mr. Rubio arranged for a White House meeting with Lilian Tintori, the wife of Leopoldo López, an opposition leader currently under house arrest and the architect of Mr. Guaidó's rise."[17] The day before Guaidó's declaration, Vice President Mike Pence phoned him, encouraged him to challenge Maduro's rule, and pledged U.S. support and recognition. Pence then recorded a video message addressing the Venezuelan people and encouraging protesters.[18] Rubio met with Trump and Pence to plan the United States' immediate recognition of Guaidó as Venezuela's new leader, while Secretary Pompeo urged regional allies and partners to do the same.

Predictably enough, Maduro did not back down, and the Venezuelan military stuck with him. In response, the Trump administration dug in its heels. The White House began drawing up policy plans to increase sanctions on the Maduro regime and possibly send aid to the opposition. National Security Advisor Bolton warned in a press conference that unless Maduro and the Venezuelan military handed over power to Guaidó, the United States might take forceful action. When asked by a reporter to specify what action, Bolton issued the common refrain that "all options are on the table," a well-known euphemism for military action.[19]

Fulton T. Armstrong, a former CIA analyst with years of experience in Latin America, speculated to the *Military Times* that the Trump administration is "not trying to provoke a war. . . . They're trying to provoke the Venezuelan military to rise up and overthrow Maduro."[20] But by issuing those threats and inserting itself so boldly into Venezuela's internal affairs, the Trump administration is putting U.S. credibility on the line, which could create pressure to act later regardless of intentions at the outset. The costs and risks associated with such an inadvertent escalation are not trivial: according to expert testimony during a House Foreign Affairs Committee hearing in March 2019, an invasion "would be prolonged, it would be ugly, there would be massive casualties." As many as 150,000 U.S. troops would be required to stabilize the country, which is twice the size of Iraq, and more than 350,000 soldiers in the Venezuelan military would be prepared to fight to defend their nation.[21]

Intervention in the domestic politics of Latin American countries comes right out of the traditional foreign policy playbook and has long enjoyed bipartisan support. The United States has an extensive history of foolhardy intervention in Latin America, including attempts at territorial conquest, supporting violent rebel militias, training and arming illiberal regimes that commit human rights abuses, deploying troops, and covertly overthrowing democratically elected governments in favor of dictatorships. The oldest strategic rationale—to block intervention and influence by states outside the Western Hemisphere—persists to this day. But fears of foreign intrigue are substantially inflated, as are the supposed threats from various weak and impoverished states to America's south. With the 2016 peace agreement between the Colombian government and the Revolutionary Armed Forces of Colombia (FARC) rebel group, the last active political armed conflict in the Western Hemisphere came to an end. Overall economic relations have been healthy, with Latin America exporting more than $406 billion worth of goods to the United States in 2017.[22]

Not surprisingly, deep suspicion of the behemoth to the north permeates the region.[23] No doubt, President Trump's xenophobia and open disdain have exacerbated the problem, but anti-American sentiment is mostly explained by opposition to U.S. policies that interfere in these countries' internal affairs, lend support to corrupt security forces, and inadvertently inflame drug gang violence. None of this is essential to U.S. national defense, and much of it produces results inimical to U.S. interests and values.

The Middle East and South Asia

In the Middle East, Trump's policies have also adhered very closely to past practice. He has maintained an extensive infrastructure of forward-deployed U.S. military assets throughout the region. In his first year as president, he increased the number of U.S. troops in the theater by more than 30 percent; almost 60,000 were deployed there as of December 2018. Overall, the use of force in the region increased massively as Trump loosened the rules of engagement and intensified ongoing bombing campaigns across multiple countries.[24] In 2017, the number of coalition airstrikes against the Islamic State in Iraq and Syria rose by nearly 50 percent compared with the previous year, while civilian deaths rose by an estimated 215 percent.[25] The use of drone strikes has also increased markedly.[26]

When Trump took office, his administration doubled down on America's traditional alliances in the Middle East, while reasserting U.S. hostility toward long-standing adversaries. The new White House devoted considerable effort to establishing close working relationships with Israel, Saudi Arabia, and the smaller Arab Gulf states in Saudi Arabia's orbit.

Unconditional support for Israel grew more effusive and hostility toward the Palestinians more inflexible. Breaking with decades of diplomatic protocol that aimed to save such moves for inclusion in a final Israeli-Palestinian peace deal, Trump announced in December 2017 that the U.S. embassy in Israel would move from Tel Aviv to Jerusalem. The decision explicitly recognized the latter as the capital of Israel, even though East Jerusalem, which is occupied by the Israeli military, has long been understood as the capital of a future Palestinian state. This move undercut the viability of the peace plan that Trump asked his son-in-law Jared Kushner to devise, in part by convincing the Palestinian side that Washington had dropped even the pretense (though it has long been a false one) of being a neutral arbiter in peace talks.

Then, in March 2019, Trump declared that the United States would recognize Israeli sovereignty in the Golan Heights, territory Israel captured from Syria in the 1967 Six-Day War. Israel's seizure of the territory is considered illegal under international law and, although Washington has for the most part tacitly acknowledged Israeli sovereignty there, official U.S. policy has always been to leave the final determination to a negotiated peace settlement. Trump's unilateral declaration undermined an important international norm of territorial integrity, which was made worse when the administration refused to criticize Israeli prime minister Benjamin Netanyahu's announcement in April 2019 that Israel would begin annexing illegal Israeli settlements in the occupied Palestinian West Bank, which would effectively kill the prospects of a two-state solution.

The administration's approach to Saudi Arabia has been almost slavishly deferential. Washington has been closely aligned with the Kingdom of Saudi Arabia since President Franklin D. Roosevelt met with King Abdul Aziz Ibn Saud aboard the USS *Quincy* in Great Bitter Lake, Egypt, in 1945. The relationship was built around Saudi Arabia's status as an oil juggernaut, which bestowed on Riyadh vast economic and geopolitical influence. During the Cold War, the U.S.-Saudi relationship deepened as Washington sought to forestall Soviet clout in this strategically vital region. Saudi-American cooperation reached a zenith during the 1990–1991 Desert Shield and Desert Storm operations, with Riyadh inviting the United States to build a major military base in Dhahran to support the campaign to evict Iraq from Kuwait.

The successful conclusion of Desert Storm, the end of the Cold War, and favorable changes in international oil markets should have diminished the value of Saudi Arabia to U.S. interests. The U.S. military, however, did not leave Saudi Arabia. Instead, the air base in Dhahran, along with others established in Kuwait and Bahrain, became the basis for an expanded and permanent American military footprint in the Middle East.

Despite the long track record of cooperation, the American military presence in Saudi Arabia soon became problematic. Osama bin Laden's outrage at the American presence in Saudi Arabia prompted his decision to focus al Qaeda's strategy on the United States, leading eventually to the attacks on the American embassies in Kenya and Tanzania in 1998, the attack on the USS *Cole* in Yemen in 2000, and the attacks on September 11, 2001. The tensions in Riyadh's relationship with Washington were compounded in the aftermath of September 11. Not only did the majority of the hijackers come from Saudi Arabia, but many experts believe that the kingdom has bankrolled the spread of extremist Islamic doctrine and anti-American militant groups for decades.[27] As Hillary Clinton put it in a leaked classified diplomatic cable when she was secretary of state, "donors in Saudi Arabia constitute the most significant source of funding to Sunni terrorist groups worldwide."[28]

Under other circumstances these facts might have put a serious damper on the U.S.-Saudi partnership. Thanks to the 2003 American invasion of Iraq, however, Iran's influence in the Middle East has grown steadily over the past decade, fueling new worries in both Washington and Riyadh about the stability of the region and Iranian threats to both Saudi and American interests. As a result, the United States has grown closer to the House of Saud.

For example, President Trump inherited the Obama administration's policy of providing military, intelligence, and diplomatic support for Saudi Arabia's war against Yemen, its impoverished neighbor to the south. The Saudi-led coalition began bombing and blockading Yemen following internal strife and the 2015 ouster of Yemen's authoritarian president Abd-Rabbu Mansour Hadi, a loyal Saudi client installed in 2012 with the help of Washington and Riyadh. The Saudi-led coalition was soon credibly accused of multiple war crimes as bombs fell on hospitals, weddings, and residential areas, and civilian casualties mounted.

The Saudis also imposed a devastating blockade which caused a massive food shortage. This smacked of using starvation as a weapon of war. By 2018, Yemen was the site of the world's most acute humanitarian crisis, with tens of thousands of civilian deaths and an estimated 8.4 million people on the verge of starvation—an entirely manmade catastrophe enabled by Washington's crucial support.[29]

At least in part, the Obama administration's rationale for backing the war in Yemen was to placate an aggrieved Saudi Arabia. Riyadh was opposed to the Iran nuclear deal and worried about the prospect of a U.S. strategic tilt toward Tehran. Fortunately for the Saudis, Trump vowed during the campaign to withdraw from the Iran nuclear deal. As president, he fulfilled that campaign promise—despite stiff resistance from his own cabinet, military leadership, and the intelligence community.

As already noted, the JCPOA is one of the most robust nonproliferation regimes ever negotiated, and the International Atomic Energy Agency, an independent UN body, as of the summer of 2019 had repeatedly confirmed Iran's full compliance with the terms of the deal. All the other parties to the agreement, including Russia, China, Germany, France, and the United Kingdom, affirmed the value of the deal and urged Washington to uphold it.

Trump's advisers—Secretary of State Rex Tillerson, Secretary of Defense James Mattis, National Security Advisor H. R. McMaster, Chair of the Joint Chiefs of Staff Gen. Joseph Dunford, and Director of National Intelligence Dan Coats, among others—all publicly voiced their opposition to Trump's determination to withdraw from the agreement. He had to reshuffle his cabinet, promote the hawkish Mike Pompeo from CIA director to secretary of state, and replace McMaster with former UN ambassador John Bolton, a longtime advocate of war with Iran, before he could back out of the JCPOA with at least some support from the principals in his own administration.

Trump announced the withdrawal in May 2018, accompanied by a promise to rigorously reimpose harsh economic sanctions on Iran. This move isolated the United States from the international community. A return to comprehensive sanctions guaranteed worsening relations with global powers, from America's European allies to China, particularly because the administration threatened to enforce the sanctions even if it meant penalizing foreign companies for doing legitimate business in Iran. European capitals actively sought to circumvent such secondary sanctions and protect European companies from U.S. penalties.

In a major escalation, the Trump administration had Canadian authorities arrest the chief financial officer of one of China's biggest technology companies for engaging in economic relations with Iran that are legal under Chinese and international law. China then retaliated by arresting two Canadians. U.S. relations with some of the most important countries in the world thus markedly deteriorated in service of a reckless and ill-considered Iran policy.

Meanwhile, a steady stream of antagonism toward Iran poured out of the Trump administration, primarily from Bolton and Pompeo, in language reminiscent of the Bush administration's propaganda campaign in the lead-up to the 2003 invasion of Iraq. Trump officials repeatedly invoked regime-change rhetoric and blustery talk of military action as the basis for an anti-Iran posture that is hard to justify given Iran's compliance with the JCPOA and the negligible threat the country poses to the United States.

The costs and risks of undermining the JCPOA are deeply worrying. Not only has it isolated the United States, pitting America against the major powers in Europe and Asia, but it also incentivizes Iran to unburden itself from the deal's strict limitations on its nuclear program. Under the deal, Iran agreed to significantly roll back its nuclear program and keep it under tight regulation and monitoring for the foreseeable future in return for the economic benefits that would come with sanctions relief. Trump chose to deny Iran those benefits, despite its compliance with the terms of the deal. But, as a European diplomat explained, "If you put too much pressure on Iran, at some stage it will resume its nuclear program. It increases the risk of them misbehaving."[30] And indeed, in July 2019, Tehran violated the deal for the first time, exceeding the limits on its uranium stockpile.[31] Iran intended the breach to pressure the remaining signatories to provide the promised sanctions relief.

But by giving in to the perverse incentives imposed by the Trump administration, Iran provided hawks in Washington with exactly the pretext they need to attack Iran under the same illegitimate preventive war doctrines that justified regime change in Iraq. But Iran is a much bigger, more cohesive, and more capable state than Iraq was in 2003. The Iraq war cost trillions of dollars, thousands of U.S. lives, and hundreds of thousands of civilian lives. It destabilized the Middle East, empowered Iran, and exacerbated the terrorist threat by orders of magnitude. Informed estimates suggest war with Iran would be 10 to 15 times worse.[32]

Unfortunately, the Trump administration's more hawkish comportment went beyond mere rhetorical posturing. Indeed, it tangibly increased the risk of war. According to the *Wall Street Journal*, Trump's National Security Council, led by John Bolton, asked the Pentagon to provide "military options to strike Iran," a request that "rattled" officials at the State and Defense departments. According to one official, "People were shocked. It was mind-boggling how cavalier they were about hitting Iran."[33] While the Pentagon has military options prepared for virtually every country, such formal requests often signal intent across executive branch agencies and indicate a president's interest in considering military action. In this particular case, it was not clear whether Trump knew about the request, but the president said in February 2019 that the United States will maintain a troop presence at military bases in Iraq in order to "watch Iran," a mission that had not been stated explicitly or authorized by Congress. "We're going to keep watching and we're going to keep seeing and if there's trouble," Trump said in an interview, "if somebody is looking to do nuclear weapons or other things, we're going to know it before they do."[34]

The danger of such rhetoric and bureaucratic maneuvers is chillingly illustrated by another reported exchange between national security officials in 2018. In a discussion about U.S. naval vessels in the Persian Gulf, President Trump argued for attacking and sinking Iranian boats that engage in provocations on the high seas. Administration officials talked him back, aware of what a perilous escalation that would be.[35]

Bolton took another bold step in January 2019 when he claimed that "we have little doubt that Iran's leadership is still strategically committed to achieving deliverable nuclear weapons," a claim for which there is no available evidence, and which directly contradicts the assessments of the U.S. intelligence community.[36] Bolton is well known for this kind of prevarication. According to interviews with former colleagues of his, Bolton routinely skews intelligence and "resists input that doesn't fit his biases."[37] According to a report in the *New York Times*, "Senior Pentagon officials are voicing deepening fears that . . . Bolton could precipitate a conflict with Iran."[38] When the administration announced in April 2019 that it would designate Iran's Islamic Revolutionary Guard Corps as a foreign terrorist organization—the first time the U.S. government has designated a branch of a foreign government as a terrorist group—it took another small step toward conflict. Senior Pentagon officials, including Chairman of the Joint Chiefs of Staff Gen. Joseph Dunford, as well as CIA officials, reportedly opposed the decision, according to the *Wall Street Journal*, on the grounds that "it could lead to a backlash against U.S. forces in the region" and damage relationships with U.S. allies "without inflicting the intended damage to the Iranian economy."[39]

Just days after this news, Sen. Rand Paul asked Secretary of State Pompeo during congressional testimony whether the administration felt that the 2001 Authorization for the Use of Military Force (AUMF), which authorized military action against the terrorist groups that perpetrated the 9/11 attacks, could also serve as legal authorization for attacking Iran. Pompeo refused to answer the legal question, but said that "there is no doubt there is a connection between the Islamic Republic of Iran and al-Qaeda, period, full-stop."[40] Both the Bush and Obama administrations stretched the 2001 AUMF to justify military action entirely unconnected to the original reason the legislation was passed. Pompeo's statement served as a worrying indication of the Trump administration's limitless interpretation of its authority to initiate a war against Iran without explicit authorization from Congress.

In May 2019, Bolton made a series of escalatory decisions on Iran policy, including hyping vague threats from raw intelligence (later contradicted by other officials), depicting a long-scheduled carrier deployment to the Gulf as a show of force intended for Iran, and evacuating nonessential personnel from the nearby U.S. embassy in Iraq. Speculation of impending military action, stoked quite deliberately by Iran hawks within the administration, eventually led President Trump to publicly declare his opposition to attacking Iran militarily. In June 2019, after a series of attacks on shipping in the strait of Hormuz, Iran shot down an unmanned American surveillance aircraft. Trump considered retaliatory strikes, but he ultimately opted for additional sanctions instead. Separately, there were reports of U.S. cyberattacks. And the administration announced the deployment of an additional 1,000 troops to the region.[41] The risk of an inadvertent, tit-for-tat escalation, however, is an inherent feature of the administration's overall approach.[42]

Meanwhile, in Syria, Trump doubled down on the Obama administration policy of aggressive air strikes, aiding local forces, such as Kurdish militias, to battle jihadists, and obliquely calling for the removal of President Bashar al-Assad from power. But Trump's approach has not been identical to Obama's. It has been more hard-line. Twice in the span of a single year, Trump took unilateral military action to bomb Syrian military assets, supposedly as punishment for the use of chemical weapons, although casualties from such attacks are a tiny fraction of the total in Syria's civil war. Since Congress never voted to authorize these military strikes, and since they did not preempt a direct threat to the United States, they were plainly illegal. They also lacked approval from the UN Security Council and thus ironically violated the very set of international norms cited to justify them.

The White House discontinued the Obama-era CIA program of aiding Syrian rebels but would later quadruple the number of U.S. troops there.[43] Although Trump himself seems to dislike having boots on the ground, his attempt to withdraw by February 2019 was essentially defeated by the national security bureaucracy, which managed to persuade Trump to leave a residual force of up to 1,000 U.S. troops in Syria.[44] That translates to another indefinite commitment of troops in yet another Middle Eastern country on dubious legal grounds and an even weaker strategic basis to pursue vague, possibly unachievable objectives superfluous to core U.S. security interests.[45] If that weren't bad enough, continued meddling in the chaos of civil war in Syria risks mission creep, which could more deeply entangle America in the quagmire.

In August 2017, under pressure from his national security team, particularly then secretary Mattis, Trump ordered a surge of about

4,000 additional U.S. forces to Afghanistan in direct contravention of his campaign promises to withdraw from the stalemated war.[46] The increase in troops was accompanied by an intensified U.S. bombing campaign that resulted in a spike in civilian casualties.[47] After 18 years of military occupation, counterinsurgency operations, and nation-building in Afghanistan, the U.S.-backed regime in Kabul is weak and unable to establish territorial control, and it maintains one of the world's worst records for corruption and human rights abuses. The Taliban hold more territory than at any time since 2001. Trump is clearly ambivalent about continuing the U.S. commitment in Afghanistan, but so far he has not managed to bring it to an end.

To its credit, the Trump administration has also quietly pursued peace talks with the Taliban. Presumably the hope is to secure a political settlement that will permit a U.S. withdrawal, though U.S. officials have pushed for a leave-behind force in any final peace deal. Not clear is whether the diplomatic overture will succeed so long as the United States insists on the survival of the regime in Kabul, which the Taliban view as illegitimate. At the same time, President Trump suspended $300 million in aid to Pakistan, which had received $14 billion in U.S. taxpayer money in 2002–2018. Such aid had flowed to Islamabad even though the Pakistani government had funneled support to insurgents fighting U.S. forces throughout the Bush and Obama administrations.[48] The United States should certainly not be providing billions of dollars to a corrupt regime that supports terrorist groups, but it is unlikely Pakistan will react to the suspension of aid by discontinuing its support for militants.[49]

Europe

Even as he has reinforced and expanded U.S. security commitments to Europe, Trump has managed to simultaneously undermine the transatlantic relationship in troubling ways. He has tactlessly berated European allies for not carrying their own weight in terms of national defense and deliberately made European leaders doubt the reliability of the American commitment without actually initiating a formal revision to it.[50] The president's protectionist impulses on trade have also made for a tense and distrustful relationship with Europe. Not only did Trump slap tariffs on European steel and aluminum imports, but, as noted previously, his administration has also sought to impose economic sanctions on European companies that do business in Iran, even though they are permitted to do so under their own laws. Worsening diplomatic relations with some of America's closest allies in Europe can hardly be chalked up as a foreign policy achievement, nor is it a sign of Trump's supposed commitment to restraint.

As a policy matter, the administration's reaffirmation of the American security commitment to Europe is consistent with primacy. Overall, U.S. troop deployments in Europe have increased, as have military exercises as far east as the Baltics and the Black Sea.[51] In December 2018, the Pentagon also was actively exploring the prospect of establishing a new U.S. military base in Poland.[52] In 2018, the United States led NATO in conducting the largest military exercises since the end of the Cold War.[53] Far from trying to dismantle NATO, as many of his critics have charged, Trump has called for broadening NATO's mandate to focus on challenging China.[54] Trump has even presided over the expansion of NATO, welcoming Montenegro as the 29th member in 2017. Further expansion is expected, with Macedonia taking steps to be the 30th member.[55] And the former Soviet republic of Georgia may not be far behind. In a 2017 visit to Tbilisi, Vice President Pence declared, in the presence of the Georgian prime minister, "We strongly support Georgia's aspiration to become a member of NATO."[56] In July 2019, after toying with the prospect of inviting Brazil into the NATO alliance, Trump officially designated Brazil as a major non-NATO ally, a privileged place in America's alliance politics.[57]

Bringing in new members to the antiquated Cold War–era military alliance is not new, but neither is it wise. Given the problems inherent in extended deterrence, particularly in far-flung locales that carry little intrinsic strategic value for the United States, these commitments undermine the credibility of Washington's threats and promises. Few Americans are eager to fight and die, or have their sons and daughters do so, for small, distant, or unfamiliar countries that they can't even find on a map. Resourcing these commitments is also burdensome for a cash-strapped electorate focused on domestic priorities and a federal government $22 trillion in debt.

Despite occasionally expressing sympathy with the need to draw down, rather than expand, America's overseas military commitments, President Trump has done the opposite. Indeed, he even went further than Obama, authorizing the delivery of lethal aid to Ukraine in its fight against Russian-backed separatists, a policy more likely to deepen and prolong the Ukraine-Russia standoff than to successfully roll back Russian aggression or deter it in the future. Trump's Department of Defense is even training Ukrainian military forces. This policy only increases the risk of a dangerous escalation with Russia for the sake of a country with whom the United States is not formally allied, a country far more important to Moscow's perceived interests than Uncle Sam's.[58]

In addition, despite the president's own obsequious rhetoric toward Russian president Vladimir Putin, the administration has explicitly identified Russia as a major geopolitical adversary that America must confront.[59] Suffice it to say, ramping up U.S. military activity in Eastern Europe while casting Russia as an enemy in official documents is likely to further damage U.S.-Russia relations and exacerbate the volatile flashpoints between the two powers. It's a recipe for deepening Russian feelings of insecurity and provoking more Russian counterbalancing efforts. As previously mentioned, the administration formally announced in February 2019 that the United States would withdraw from the 1987 INF Treaty, a major arms control treaty with Russia. Within days, Russian officials announced new plans to procure land-based missile systems of precisely the type banned by the INF, in a tit-for-tat dynamic that risks sparking a new arms race.[60] In the broader strategic context, hostility to both Russia and China risks pushing those two powers closer together—to the detriment of U.S. interests and at the expense of worthwhile bilateral cooperation on arms control, Syria, North Korea, and the rise of China.

U.S. foreign policy should better reflect the reality of the situation: Russia is nowhere close to the geopolitical threat it once was.

All Americans should take seriously Moscow's cyber operations against the United States, including those intended to sow division amid a contentious presidential campaign. Cybersecurity is an all-hands-on-deck enterprise. State and local governments have an obligation to protect the electoral process from tampering, and all citizens should be wary of misleading or demonstrably false stories—a problem that Trump and others in his administration have often made worse. But, even so, the Russian threat in the realm of information warfare has been exaggerated.[61]

In the more conventional domain of military power, Russia is hardly a direct security threat. Its GDP is valued at about $1.6 trillion, less than a 10th of the United States' and roughly equivalent to that of Spain and Portugal combined. The collective GDP of the European countries in NATO is $19 trillion, almost 12 times Russia's. Europe also vastly out-spends Russia on defense. Annual NATO-Europe defense spending is roughly $229 billion, compared with Russia's $66.3 billion. The mili-tary power Russia does possess is underwhelming as far as great powers go, with relatively limited power-projection capabilities and few strate-gic allies that can supplement Moscow's out-of-area ambitions. Added to these limitations are endemic corruption and unfavorable long-term demographic trends that will further sap the country's power potential. Clearly, Europe can handle whatever threat Russia might pose to the region, and the United States should adopt a less hostile posture toward Moscow.

East Asia

U.S. security policy in Asia has not fundamentally changed under President Trump. The United States is still treaty-bound to protect major East Asian allies like Japan, South Korea, and the Philippines, and it continues its role as guarantor of the status quo in Taiwan. America's forward presence remains robust, with more than 150,000 active-duty military personnel stationed at scores of military bases throughout the region and more than half of overall U.S. naval strength regularly pa-trolling the Pacific theater.

Most of the Trump administration's policy focus in East Asia has centered on two major issues, China and North Korea. Official national security policy documents identify the rise of China as a major threat that the United States must confront. Beijing's growing economic and military might, according to this view, threatens U.S. supremacy in the so-called liberal world order and encourages a more assertive Chinese foreign policy, to the detriment of global security and U.S. interests. Administration officials, including the president, reportedly view the threat from China through the lens of a best-selling book, *The Hundred-Year Marathon: China's Secret Strategy to Replace America as the Global Superpower,* by the Hudson Institute's Michael Pillsbury.[62] Steve Bannon claimed the book has served as the "intellectual architecture" of Trump's confrontational approach to Beijing.[63] China specialists have offered sharp criticisms of the book, however. "The evidence that Pillsbury supplies," according to the Harvard University scholar Alastair Iain Johnston, "does not sustain this narrative" that China has a secret plan to replace America; and to the extent that the book has influenced policymakers in the Trump administration, "it could delegitimize closer U.S.-China coordination" and "contribute to an inaccurate and insufficiently nuanced understanding of the complex motivations behind Chinese foreign policy."[64]

The threat from China has been increasingly overstated. Hawks point to Chinese maritime and territorial claims in the South China Sea and the Belt and Road Initiative (BRI), Beijing's ambitious plan for a set of intercontinental infrastructure projects to facilitate deeper trade relationships around the world. China's claims in the South China Sea are indeed expansive and contrary to an international legal ruling, but they hardly present a threat to U.S. national security.[65] Continually engaging in provocative freedom-of-navigation operations to confront Chinese naval vessels and challenge China's claims in the sea, as both the Obama and Trump administrations have done, only further militarizes the dispute while raising the risk of inadvertent escalation following some kind of clash on the high seas.

Hawks similarly depict the BRI as an aggressive anti-American Chinese initiative that ominously pulls numerous weaker countries into

China's geopolitical orbit. A congressionally appointed bipartisan commission recommended in 2018 that the United States challenge China's Belt and Road Initiative by providing "additional bilateral assistance for countries that are a target of or vulnerable to Chinese economic or diplomatic pressure."[66] Such a policy would lock America in a dangerous globe-spanning zero-sum competition with China with no end in sight. And it would be entirely unnecessary. Indeed, according to Deborah Brautigam of Johns Hopkins University's School of Advanced International Studies, certain elements of China's BRI "should be encouraged," as they "shift more of the risks" of various worthwhile investments "to Chinese investors." Brautigam points out that the fear of China's alleged "debt-trap diplomacy" is based on a single case in which Chinese companies secured a 99-year lease over a shipping port in Sri Lanka. "The idea that Chinese banks and companies are luring countries to borrow for unprofitable projects so that China can leverage these debts to extract concessions is now deeply embedded in discussions of China's BRI program," she writes. "Yet the evidence for this project being part of a Chinese master plan is thin."[67]

The logic of BRI is primarily commercial, not military or geostrategic. And too many in Washington assume that the reality of the initiative will match the grandiose ambition of its authors in Beijing. Just five years after it launched, the BRI is lagging behind its projected benchmarks and, while much of it will surely prove productive, has also redirected vast sums of Chinese capital to wasteful construction projects that are unlikely to provide a good return on investment. According to the International Monetary Fund's managing director Christine Lagarde, the ambitious global scale of the BRI itself makes "failed projects and the misuse of funds" more likely.[68] BRI projects are rife with cost overruns, cronyism, and corruption, partly because they are often initiated and managed according to the political incentives of Chinese Communist Party planners rather than purely economic calculations of supply, demand, and efficiency. Beijing's effort to encourage private investment in BRI projects has failed, suggesting that the initiative is less than economical and may prove a strategic blunder for China.[69] Many Asian countries are increasingly leery of China's BRI and suspicious of perceived efforts to expand Beijing's influence over them.[70] Such sentiments are likely to intensify with time, making the geostrategic challenge of BRI much less scary indeed.

In a major address in October 2018, Vice President Pence depicted China as a 21st-century opponent of virtually existential proportions, a successor to the Soviet Union that requires a comparably all-consuming whole-of-government global strategy to confront. He lamented China's authoritarianism, condemned Chinese efforts to "interfere in the domestic policy and politics of this country," and cited Pillsbury to allege, erroneously, that China's foreign policy "contradict[s] any peaceful or productive intentions of Beijing."[71]

Although maintaining an apparently cordial relationship with President Xi Jinping, Trump has been vehement in his condemnation of China, particularly on trade policy. Pence complained about the U.S. trade deficit with China and excoriated Chinese "tariffs, quotas, currency manipulation, forced technology transfer, intellectual property theft, and industrial subsidies" as such a threat as to require our own big government economic protectionism in response. The administration has imposed tariffs on $250 billion worth of Chinese goods as of May 2019, threatening to more than double that number unless Beijing makes major trade concessions.[72]

While China certainly does engage in some unfair trade practices, the Trump administration's narrow emphasis on this issue simultaneously embellishes the problem and obscures the tremendous value of the U.S.-China economic relationship, which is mutually beneficial. The total value of U.S. trade with China exceeded $635 billion in 2017, an enormous benefit to both countries and one of the most important bilateral trade relationships in the world.[73] In 2016 alone, Chinese enterprises invested more than $50 billion in the U.S. private sector, helping create more than 200,000 American jobs.[74] Deepening this economic relationship while trying to engage with Chinese efforts such as BRI or the Asian Infrastructure Investment Bank (AIIB) as a partner rather than a spoiler has a much better chance of improving Chinese behavior and cultivating a cooperative relationship with America's nearest peer competitor.

Trump's elective trade war with China has resulted in billions of dollars of losses for both countries, with the automotive, technology, and agricultural industries taking the biggest hit.[75] Ironically, though, even if this punitive approach succeeds in coercing China to change its economic policies according to U.S. demands, that wouldn't necessarily serve Trump's bottom line. For example, in trade negotiations, the White House has pressed China to agree to purchase more than $1 trillion worth of U.S. goods and services, but given the high cost of production in the United States, many companies would be forced "to open new factories in China and give Beijing bureaucrats more sway over the U.S. firms," according to the *Wall Street Journal*.[76] In particular, U.S. companies that manufacture semiconductor chips have concerns about product security and intellectual property theft.[77] In other words, the administration's concerns about supply chain vulnerabilities and trade imbalances could actually be exacerbated by its own negotiating position.

Moreover, China isn't the only one with unfair trade practices. In fact, the only country that receives more formal WTO complaints over trade policy violations than China is the United States.[78] And, historically, China does a better job than the United States of complying with the rules once complaints are made. This strongly suggests that engaging in skillful diplomacy with China to negotiate a compromise on trade policy would be fruitful. Certainly such an effort would be less harmful than instigating a trade war, which has not only provoked Chinese retaliation and brought mutual economic pain but aggravated overall U.S.-China tensions. Understanding Beijing's naval development and expansive claims in the South China Sea as borne out of a sense of military and economic insecurity helps to ease the often overwrought anxiety in Washington over China's rise.[79] Intellectual property theft and other shady trade practices are rather typical of up-and-coming great powers.[80] The United States certainly engaged in such behavior as it rose to economic and military prominence. But economic development tends to gradually undercut the utility of the worst of these habits and, thus, China can be expected to engage in them less as time goes on.

As a matter of security policy, this antagonistic approach and demonizing rhetoric risks sparking a bitter rivalry that America can neither win nor afford to wage. Hegemonic transitions, in which the distribution of power shifts from one dominant state to a rising challenger, tend to be dangerous and prone to conflict, often as a result of some tit-for-tat escalation on the periphery that each rival expects to win without direct military confrontation. Cautious, prudent, and flexible statecraft, as well as a willingness to make certain concessions, however, can overcome these inherent risks. Unfortunately, given the worsening Sino-American relationship, the intensifying mutual distrust, and the growing number of flashpoints between the two nations, the Trump administration's confrontational approach could become a self-fulfilling prophecy. He is making an enemy out of China before it acts like one and in the absence of a clear threat to U.S. national security.

Trump's critics in the foreign policy establishment consistently complain about his administration's disrespect for longstanding U.S. alliances. But there is little evidence of this in East Asia. Much to the contrary, the Trump administration has doubled down on America's alliances in the Pacific. In a clear attempt to challenge China's claims in the South China Sea, Secretary Pompeo announced while on a trip to the Philippines that "any armed attack on Philippine forces, aircraft, or public vessels in the South China Sea will trigger mutual defense obligations under Article IV of our mutual defense treaty."[81]

Before this, the U.S. commitment to defend Philippine claims in the South China Sea was ambiguous. The mutual defense treaty certainly obligates the United States to defend the Philippines if its territory is attacked, but pledging to defend Philippine vessels far off the coast and into international waters is a clear broadening of the commitment. By removing all doubt, the Trump administration not only acted in accordance with the general consensus in the foreign policy establishment, but also further insinuated America into a localized dispute on the other side of the planet with little national security value to the United States. What's worse is that the purported strategic logic of this expansive interpretation of the U.S.-Philippine mutual defense treaty is to deter, and even roll back, China's claims in the area, an objective that is highly unlikely to be achieved by the mere utterance of U.S. backing. It does, however, raise the risk of entrapment and inadvertent escalation.[82]

Trump's initial policies toward North Korea were broadly consistent with those of his predecessors. The administration worked with the UN Security Council and regional powers to intensify the economic pressure against Pyongyang, while the president repeatedly issued threats of unilateral preventive military action unless Kim Jong Un forfeited his nuclear capabilities.

This "maximum pressure" policy held until Kim, through a South Korean liaison, offered to meet with Trump face to face. Trump accepted the offer immediately, in contrast to his three predecessors who declined to meet directly with North Korea's Supreme Leader. Trump's hard-line posture toward Pyongyang changed dramatically in the course of these negotiations. His public statements went from over-the-top hostility to credulous praise of Kim Jong Un, ridiculed by critics as naive submissiveness. Upon returning home from the Singapore summit with Kim in June 2018, long before any substantive progress toward limiting Pyongyang's nuclear program could have been made, the president declared on Twitter, "There is no longer a Nuclear Threat from North Korea."[83] Months later, he would report that negotiations were going swimmingly, largely because of the rapport he had been able to establish with Kim. "We fell in love," he explained.[84]

Trump's détente with Pyongyang has indeed made some kind of disastrous war on the Korean peninsula less likely. That is a good thing. But the claim that negotiations are going well is harder to maintain. For starters, there appears to be a huge gap in how each side defines an acceptable deal. The Trump administration has emphasized the need for North Korea's "complete, verifiable, irreversible denuclearization" to secure any relief from economic sanctions. Kim, on the other hand, has communicated a more gradual step-by-step reciprocation of compromises and concessions. In the months after the Singapore summit, North Korea followed through on several promised confidence-building measures, including returning the remains of U.S. soldiers from the Korean War and suspending nuclear tests and tests of missiles that can reach the U.S. homeland. In September 2018, Kim signed on to a statement with South Korean president Moon Jae-in suggesting that further disarmament measures are on the table if the United States delivers on "corresponding measures."

Although Kim agreed to vague language about denuclearization in the joint communique signed at the Singapore Summit, his definition of denuclearization doesn't match the Trump administration's. The White House has repeatedly made clear that they expect North Korea to completely denuclearize in exchange for sanctions relief. Pyongyang, on the other hand, has clarified that, for them, complete "denuclearization" includes the removal of U.S. troops and military assets from South Korea (U.S. nuclear weapons were removed in 1992 and have not been returned). This gap in understanding the terms of negotiation can make for perilous uncertainty, causing each side to distrust the other or take drastic steps when the other side appears unwilling to play ball.

Comprehensive economic sanctions on North Korea are still in place. The Trump administration suspended military exercises. And some officials have reportedly entertained the possibility of revising the U.S. security commitment to South Korea and formally ending the Korean War in some kind of prospective grand bargain with the North.[85] Such a negotiating posture would be a significant break with past policy, though Trump's own national security officials have resisted it.

Africa

Trump's commitment to maintain U.S. global hegemony is so strong that it extends beyond containing Russia and China in their own spheres. It also includes a hubristic 21st-century version of the "Scramble for Africa," the European imperial contest on the continent in the late 19th and early 20th centuries. In December 2018, the president approved a new strategy for Africa described by National Security Advisor John Bolton as "the result of an intensive interagency process" that "reflects the core tenets of President Trump's foreign policy doctrine."[86] According to a *Wall Street Journal* report, this new strategy "is part of a broader effort . . . to fight for global supremacy with Russia and China."[87]

The strategy consists of three sets of policies. First, it calls for engaging African nations to advance U.S. trade and commercial ties on the continent. As Bolton explained, this effort is intended to support U.S. investment opportunities, expand Africa's middle class, and outcompete burgeoning Russian and Chinese influence there. The strategy calls for ensuring the "independence" of African nations. However, it appears intended to ensure that African nations are dependent on the United States instead of on Russia or China. Independence, per se, seems to have little to do with it.

For example, as part of the administration's supposedly new approach, Bolton described a sustained U.S. effort to reform the domestic legal and economic systems of an unspecified number of African countries to better reflect America's system and thereby facilitate greater U.S. economic access. First of all, that is arguably the most ambitious nation-building project America has pursued since the post–World War II reconstruction of Europe and Asia. The reality is that "reforming" African countries in this way is extremely difficult and prone to failure. Most such efforts end up simply reinforcing the illiberalism and corruption that plague many of these nations and looking more like the open-door policies of the 19th century than the Marshall Plan of post–World War II Europe.

Second, the strategy vastly expands America's overall military commitments in Africa. It aims to counter the "serious threat" from "radical Islamic terrorism and violent conflict."[88] Reviving the War on Terror with renewed focus in Africa is likely to generate endless opportunities for U.S. military intervention and new counterinsurgency campaigns that go well beyond a targeted effort to foil active terrorism plots against the United States. The U.S. military's posture in the Middle East since 9/11 provides ample evidence that this strategy is based on an inflated sense of the threat of international terrorism and a considerable overconfidence in the effectiveness of U.S. military force. It is, in short, a recipe for failure. Moreover, the commitment to counter the threat of "violent conflict" anywhere in a continent of 54 countries marks a stunning expansion of U.S. security responsibilities.[89]

Third, the strategy calls for an overhaul of U.S. aid to Africa. Rather than providing support to UN peacekeeping programs and humanitarian needs on the continent, for example, the Trump administration proposes that U.S. aid be redirected to purposes more closely aligned with perceived U.S. security interests. The Better Utilization of Investments Leading to Development Act, enacted in October 2018, was sold to President Trump as a vehicle for countering Chinese influence in developing countries.[90] More likely, it will translate into increased aid to corrupt governments that agree (at least superficially) to conform to Washington's preferences—whether that entails permitting U.S. military presence in-country, allowing the United States to train local security forces, or cracking down on groups that those regimes lump in with the alleged terrorist threat in Africa.

What Bolton describes is an expansion of America's existing posture in Africa. We already have hundreds of U.S. military facilities there; scores of training programs for local security forces in countries like Niger, Mali, and Cameroon; and an ongoing drone bombing campaign, with little in the way of Congressional authorization or oversight, in Libya, Somalia, and beyond.[91] This is anything but a retreat from the world, and it demonstrates no sense within the administration that the conventional approach is objectionable.

EXPLAINING TRUMP'S EMBRACE OF PRIMACY

Overall, Trump has mostly adhered to the primacy playbook. In the few areas where he has brought nontrivial change, it has mostly been for the worse. Even where significant policy changes have been implemented and warrant hope for progress, as on North Korea, incompetent management creates enormous risks. The most striking difference Trump brings to the presidency is not a specific policy change, but a style. He speaks off the cuff and often contradicts his own policies. He doesn't even feign the typical decorum of the office and routinely violates important norms rarely before transgressed so openly. Trump appears to have brought more change to U.S. foreign policy than he actually has, simply because he is such an outrageous personality who disregards the etiquette, protocols, and conventions that previous presidents observed.

Given the bracing challenge to traditional American foreign policy that Trump outlined during his campaign, why does so much of his foreign policy today look so similar to the policies of primacy from the past several decades? Why has he implemented his America First vision in a few cases but not in others?

One partial explanation is that, on several issues, Trump's position as a candidate actually reflected the broad primacy consensus rather than a radically new direction. Even in the few cases where Trump has shifted from the Obama administration stance—for example, the decision to pull out of the Iran nuclear deal—doing so was entirely consistent with standard Republican arguments, as well as his own predilection for gaining status and respect through combative confrontation. In short, Trump's America First vision has at times overlapped with the primacy playbook, and the result has been continuity at the grand strategic level.

The real challenge, then, is to explain why Trump has failed to move foreign policy in an America First direction on those issues he criticized so witheringly as a candidate. Though Trump's America First impulses can be clearly seen on the trade and immigration fronts, little has been done with respect to pulling American troops out of what Trump has repeatedly called "pointless wars" and "costly" nation-building projects. Nor has the United States made any substantial changes to its alliances in Europe or Asia, despite Trump's tough questioning of their value.

Expectations that Trump would make radical changes to American foreign policy have been based, at least implicitly, on the assumption that the president has the ability to make such changes. That assumption is understandable. In his famous 1973 book, historian Arthur Schlesinger Jr. coined the phrase "imperial presidency" to refer to the way in which powers granted to the president during crises and wars have tended to become permanent, amplified by the growth of the executive branch over time and by the advent of television, which gave the president even greater influence over the political agenda and public debates.[92] Since then, few topics have garnered as much consensus as this one; scholars widely agree the president's freedom of action on foreign affairs is vast and has grown steadily over time.[93]

Even without the steady accumulation of new legal authority, the White House enjoys significant advantages in the national security and foreign policy domain. Most fundamentally, perhaps, the president exercises authority over foreign policy thanks to his control of the executive branch and his constitutional role as commander in chief of the armed forces. In contrast, Congress is a large and unruly group of politicians. Often short on expertise and shirking direct responsibility for foreign policy, they typically lack the political will to challenge the White House on these matters.

In addition, the president, by virtue of the analytical and information capabilities of the executive branch, including the National Security Council and the intelligence services, inevitably has an advantage in foreign policy debates with members of Congress, most of whom are not experts in international security and have no independent means for accessing classified information. Finally, the president also enjoys a decided advantage in the marketplace of ideas; thanks to his bully pulpit, the president can set the news agenda and frame key foreign policy debates in ways favorable to his plans.[94]

In normal circumstances these advantages present little problem; presidential leadership provides a necessary unity of command and vision for foreign policy, ideally complemented by active oversight of foreign policy implementation by Congress. The problem arises when Congress abandons its constitutionally mandated roles and cedes new powers to the president. Scholars have documented a long and troubling list of abdications of congressional responsibility over time. On international trade and arms sales, for example, Congress has ceded the president wide latitude on paper and almost total authority in practice. Congress has also essentially abandoned its role in declaring war.

Perhaps the clearest sign of the trend is the occasional spasms of congressional activity to rein in the president. The 1973 War Powers Act, the 1976 National Emergencies Act, and the 1976 Arms Export Control Act, for example, were efforts to limit presidential power and rebalance the playing field, especially on foreign policy. None of them, however, has proven particularly effective at stemming the growth of executive power.[95]

The terrorist attacks of 9/11 provided the most recent boost to the imperial presidency. The USA PATRIOT Act, passed in October 2001, provided the executive branch expanded powers of surveillance, investigation, and detention. Even that wasn't enough for some. Vice President Cheney argued that the president needed additional powers to conduct surveillance and track terrorists. On the basis of memos drafted by Justice Department lawyer John Yoo, Cheney came up with a novel interpretation of almost unlimited executive authority that supposedly allowed the president unprecedented license to operate without oversight from Congress. At one point, Cheney defended the expansion of executive power after 9/11 by arguing that the War Powers Act had been an unconstitutional "infringement on the authority of the president."[96]

For much of the War on Terror, Congress had almost given up on the idea of limiting presidential authority to use force. The 2001 Authorization to Use Military Force, narrowly written to authorize the president to defeat al Qaeda and those responsible for the 9/11 attacks, remains the sole legal justification for American military intervention in most of the Middle East, Africa, and South Asia regardless of the current adversaries and objectives. A few members of Congress have raised the question of debating a new authorization, with limits and timelines. But 18 years into the War on Terror, hardly any such debate has occurred.[97]

The 2018 showdown between Trump and Congress over Saudi Arabia is the exception that proves the rule. After two failed attempts in the Senate to end American support for Saudi Arabia's intervention in Yemen, the Saudis' cold-blooded murder of journalist Jamal Khashoggi tipped the scales. Though the CIA concluded the killing had been ordered by Saudi Crown Prince Mohammed bin Salman, Trump voiced continued support for Saudi Arabia and the crown prince. As noted above, Trump argued in explicit zero-sum, transactional terms, that the partnership—and the profits from U.S. arms sales to Saudi Arabia—were too valuable to risk by withdrawing support for bombing Yemen.

In December 2018, the Senate finally voted, 56–41, to end American support to Saudi Arabia for its war in Yemen.[98] The vote marked the first time that the Senate had invoked the War Powers Act since it was passed, and it explicitly rebuked Trump's protective stance toward Saudi Arabia.

But while the vote provided a glimpse of the limits to the imperial presidency, it also showed just how difficult it is to impose effective limits.

As horrible as it was, the murder of Jamal Khashoggi should not have been necessary to understand the devastation wrought by Saudi Arabia's war in Yemen. Yemen has held the title of the world's worst humanitarian crisis almost since the war began in 2015. Thousands have died and millions face starvation and disease, thanks largely to an indiscriminate air campaign that UN investigators believe may amount to war crimes. For example, in August of 2018, a Saudi jet bombed a Yemeni school bus, killing 40 children.[99]

But not until the murder of Khashoggi, who happened to work for the *Washington Post*, was there finally enough momentum for the Senate to act decisively. Even then, the first Senate vote turned out to be largely symbolic. Then speaker Paul Ryan (R-WI) used a procedural maneuver to ensure the House wouldn't vote on any bill that might trigger the War Powers Act.[100] By April 2019, both chambers of Congress voted to end U.S. involvement in the war. Trump promptly vetoed the resolution.[101] Thus, the difficulty of getting enough members of both parties and both chambers to go against the president, especially during politically polarized times, clearly protects White House initiative—even when the president takes actions that upset most members of Congress.

Indeed, the cult of the presidency has not weakened since Trump took office. Writing in late 2018, James Goldgeier and Elizabeth Saunders argued:

> In reality, the problem goes well beyond Trump, and even beyond the well-documented trend of increasing presidential power. Constraints on the president—not just from Congress but also from the bureaucracy, allies, and international institutions—have been eroding for decades. Constraints are like muscles: once atrophied, they require bulking up before the competitor can get back in the game. Trump did not create the freedom of action he is now routinely displaying. He has merely revealed just how difficult it is to prevent it.[102]

The imperial presidency argument suggests that the combination of Trump's authoritarian tendencies, his nontraditional views, and the vastly expanded powers of the modern presidency should result in plenty of change. More specifically, the theory predicts the most change on issues where Trump has the freest hand: foreign policy.

Indeed, this argument provides a reasonably satisfying explanation for several of the major policy changes Trump has directed while in office. The best example is international trade. As already noted, Trump has made several major policy changes, reversing the efforts of previous administrations—withdrawing from the arduously negotiated TPP trade deal, restructuring the terms of NAFTA, and launching a trade war with China while also hitting American allies with tariffs. Thanks to prior congressional decisions that empower the White House on trade, Trump eagerly exercised unilateral action in each of these cases despite widespread concerns about his strategy. And though the new version of NAFTA, now known as the USMCA, will require ratification, there is little chance the Senate will undo Trump's handiwork.

The imperial presidency argument is less useful for explaining why Trump hasn't pushed for more change in other areas where he enjoys a relatively free hand. Why, for example, despite his public doubts about the wisdom of foreign military occupations, has Trump expanded the U.S. presence in Afghanistan, Syria, and the Middle East more broadly? And why, given Trump's personal antagonism toward many European allies, has U.S. policy toward Europe not shifted in a more America First direction? Observers have generated all sorts of theories. Here we consider four of the most convincing arguments: learning on the job, indifference and chaos in the White House, political calculations, and strategic consensus and structural inertia.

Learning on the Job

One popular attempt to explain continuity under Trump suggests that his initial positions on a range of issues were mostly just campaign rhetoric. Once confronted with a harsh dose of reality and the complexity of making big changes to foreign policy, Trump decided that the status quo was not quite as foolish as he had previously believed.[103] As Senate Majority Leader Mitch McConnell put it in 2017, "I think

President Trump is learning the job, and some of the things that were said during the campaign I think he now knows that's simply not the way things ought to be."[104]

On the surface this argument certainly makes sense. All presidents learn a great deal on the job, and Trump, as we have noted, entered the campaign with less foreign policy knowledge than most candidates and little understanding of the major debates in international security. He may have taken more radical positions on foreign policy because of a desire to win the election rather than because they reflected deeply held beliefs or careful consideration. Once elected, Trump was forced to learn quickly on the job, and his views shifted as he began to appreciate the nature of enduring national interests, the complexity of international relations, and the wisdom of established foreign policies. Trump himself acknowledged as much at one point after a conversation about North Korea's nuclear program with Chinese leader Xi Jinping. "After listening for 10 minutes, I realized it's not so easy. . . . I felt pretty strongly that they had a tremendous power" over North Korea. "But it's not what you would think."[105]

For someone with as little foreign policy background as Trump, it is tempting to imagine that this dynamic has shaped every decision he has made. And without access to discussions between Trump and his team, we can't say for sure how important Trump's recognition of new information and the complexities of international affairs may have been. Some observers credit Trump's decision not to make major demands on (or pull out of) NATO and other alliances to learning on the job.[106] Another potential example of this dynamic at work is Afghanistan. Although Trump acknowledged his initial doubts about the wisdom of keeping American forces there, he told the *Washington Post*, "We're there because virtually every expert that I have and speak to [says] if we don't go there, they're going to be fighting over here. And I've heard it over and over again."[107]

On the other hand, this explanation clearly falls flat when it comes to those positions that Trump has maintained from candidacy to the White House. Trump had no more experience with immigration, homeland security, or nuclear proliferation than with other issues; yet his positions on the border wall, travel ban, and pulling out of the Iran nuclear deal did not change after he took office. Beyond that, although Trump has admitted to the complexities of foreign policy on occasion, he much more commonly points out how intelligent and knowledgeable he is. More than once he has claimed to know more about the Islamic State than the generals.[108] According to the contemporaneous notes of a senior White House official following a meeting with national security officials, which were provided to the journalist Bob Woodward, Trump "lecture[d] and insult[ed] the entire group about how they didn't know anything when it came to defense or national security."[109] Confidence in his ability to discern the right path forward, in short, does not appear to be a problem for Trump, even when it runs contrary to the conventional wisdom. Indeed, Trump seems perfectly comfortable pressing forward with these policies, suggesting that we might not want to put too much stock in the learning-on-the-job theory as a general explanation for the shape of Trump's foreign policies.

Indifference and Chaos in the White House

Another perspective suggests that Trump's own indifference toward foreign policy, his chaotic approach to policymaking, and the dysfunctional nature of the Trump White House have combined to make the foreign policy process more turbulent and less predictable—while at the same time making major foreign policy change less likely. This argument begins with the assumption that Trump himself is not particularly interested in most foreign policy issues. The Mueller investigation has also served as a serious distraction, limiting the amount of time available for thinking about foreign policy. As a result, trade, immigration, and border security are the only areas where Trump has made sustained efforts to push the America First agenda. Much of American foreign policy is thus on cruise control, in the hands of status quo–oriented advisers and bureaucrats whose inclination is to implement and maintain, not to innovate and reshape.

The second pillar of this argument is that, to put it mildly, Trump's approach to running his presidency is unsystematic. Most administrations attempt to plot foreign policy campaigns through coordinated efforts on the legislative, bureaucratic, and communication fronts. Trump, in contrast, seems to make foreign policy decisions on impulse, without coordination, and sometimes without any communication whatsoever with his national security team.

Trump's tendency to tweet and make policy on the fly has made it more difficult for his administration to pursue a coherent approach to many issues. This *New York Times* description of a period in March 2018 serves as an excellent summary of Trump's approach:

> President Trump decamped to his oceanfront estate here on Friday after a head-spinning series of presidential decisions on national security, trade, and the budget that left the capital reeling and his advisers nervous about what comes next. The decisions attested to a president riled up by cable news and unbound. Mr. Trump appeared heedless of his staff, unconcerned about Washington decorum, or the latest stock market dive, and confident of his instincts. He seemed determined to set the agenda himself, even if that agenda looked like a White House in disarray.[110]

The result of Trump's foreign policymaking style is a sharp zigzagging from issue to issue, from position to position, without any obvious grounding in strategy. Amplifying the notion that Trump is indifferent to the substance of much foreign policy, he often appears to take public positions simply to get attention, score political points, or boost his own ego. Indeed, the growing number of occasions on which Trump has tweeted or made statements in direct response to what he sees on the Fox News network only strengthens this idea.[111] The cruise missile attacks against the Assad regime, for example, came after Trump saw pictures of the victims on television. As one observer noted, "Trump goes where the applause is loudest. If that means being a full-throated birther, fine! If that means inciting hysterics about Mexicans, game on! If that means hugging NATO or smiling at corporate cronyism, Trump's your man!"[112]

Finally, the indifference and chaos argument also highlights the historically high level of attrition among Trump's national security team. In December 2018, Secretary of Defense James Mattis resigned in protest after Trump's surprise announcement (made without consulting Mattis or any of his other foreign policy advisers) that the United States would be withdrawing its troops from Syria. Following Mattis's departure, Trump was working with an interim secretary of defense, his second secretary of state, and his third national security adviser. Given the importance of people and personal relationships to the process of making foreign policy, this turnover, which has been accompanied by a reshuffling of supporting staff, has only added to the difficulty of crafting and implementing foreign policy.[113]

The "White House in chaos" view is certainly consistent with the uneven progress of America First. Trump has long made immigration and trade his priorities, and those areas are the least affected by the chaos in the White House's policymaking process. Meanwhile, issues that Trump cares less about have tended to get less attention from him, slowing the progress of America First on those fronts—and making Trump's foreign policy more of a roller coaster ride as he jumps from issue to issue depending on the news cycle or whims of the moment.

Political Calculations

A more sanguine explanation, offered by Trump's supporters, is that his foreign policy moves simply reflect strategic political calculations of what is possible and how much risk is involved. After all, making major changes to American foreign policy is difficult from a policy and implementation perspective, and the process entails both geopolitical and domestic political risk. Trump and his team may have simply made choices that maximize the risk–reward ratio.[114]

This logic could explain why Trump has made bold moves on issues where he views himself as being on solid ground politically and where the potential downside costs are relatively low. On trade and immigration, for example, Trump has repeatedly said in public that he believes both issues are great for him politically.[115] Making and lobbying for big changes on those fronts thus carries little risk. In the worst-case scenario, he fails to get what he wants (e.g., funding for his border wall) and uses that as a political weapon against his opponents.

The same logic might explain why Trump has been much more cautious on other issues, such as the U.S. relationship with Russia, making major changes to NATO or other alliances, or withdrawing American forces from Afghanistan, Iraq, and Syria. In the case of Russia, Trump is fighting a Congress that wants to take a much harder line, raising the threat that Congress could derail other initiatives if Trump pushes too hard toward closer relations with Putin. In the cases of Afghanistan, Syria, and Iraq, Trump may be avoiding the risk of public outcry if withdrawal produces even short-term instability. Although Trump has made clear that he would prefer to bring troops home, he has also admitted that his advisers believe the risk of more terrorist attacks is high. Politically, this puts Trump in a difficult position. If he orders the troops home and another major attack occurs on U.S. soil, he will incur serious political damage.

Strategic Consensus and Structural Inertia

Finally, and perhaps most importantly, Trump has faced all the same strategic and structural constraints that have long served to keep American foreign policy moving in the same general direction. Seven decades spent pursuing primacy have imbued the status quo with tremendous inertia—difficult for even a determined president to change. University of Birmingham international relations professor Patrick Porter writes, "Trump is not a typical president. But on grand strategic questions, *tradition imposed constraints.*"[116]

The first of these constraints is the strategic consensus embraced by the foreign policy establishment. Throughout the Cold War, scholars and political leaders praised the bipartisan foreign policy consensus on the need for an ambitious strategy to contain the Soviet Union, to build and sustain a new international order, and to maintain the world's most capable military—the strategy we call primacy in this book. Politics, observers often noted during the Cold War, stopped at the water's edge. And most historians have agreed that consensus on these key objectives allowed the United States to marshal its strengths and mobilize allies effectively after World War II.

As successful as America's Cold War strategy may have been, seven decades of general agreement on foreign policy matters also produced a severe case of groupthink. The Washington, DC, foreign policy establishment—including current and former government officials, military leaders, and bureaucrats who have played key roles in helping oversee American foreign policy—overwhelmingly supports primacy. Barack Obama found the foreign policy establishment so single-minded and implacable, in fact, that he and his deputy national security advisor for strategic communications, Ben Rhodes, nicknamed it "The Blob."[117] The Blob is so effective in promoting primacy that it is often quite difficult to find opposing points of view, much less robust debate, about American foreign policy on Capitol Hill or in the White House.[118]

This remarkable level of strategic consensus props up primacy and pushes back against Trump's America First doctrine in at least three important ways. First, by dominating the marketplace of ideas—through think tanks, political talk shows, and other media—the establishment not only provides an intellectual defense for primacy but also prevents exposure to alternative ideas and arguments. And whenever it looks like presidents or the public are tiring of the game, primacy's publicists start cranking out books. As Obama's interest in primacy appeared to be waning near the end of his second term, a raft of books began to appear decrying Obama's retrenchment and raising alarms about the dangers of American retreat from global leadership.

One result of this dynamic is that, in 2016, nearly every presidential candidate other than Donald Trump articulated a foreign policy vision in complete alignment with the core pillars of primacy.[119] And though Donald Trump's foreign policy views lie outside the mainstream, he retains a good deal in common with primacy—likely more than he would in the absence of such consensus. His push for increased defense spending, attacking terrorist groups overseas, selling weapons abroad to increase American leverage over allies, and his aggressive approach to nuclear proliferation, all fit neatly under the primacy umbrella.

The second way in which the Blob constrains would-be foreign policy mavericks is by occupying all the major policymaking roles in government. As the famous saying goes, "people are policy," and the

Blob dominates the pool of people from which presidents must choose their national security team. To be sure, these professionals, the vast majority of whom have worked in the Pentagon, State Department, the U.S. military, or DC think tanks and universities for most of their careers, have impressive resumes and can draw on a wealth of experience to carry out the making of foreign policy. At the same time, however, they have been socialized by the strategic consensus as well as government agencies whose mandates are tied to maintenance of the status quo. Many Republican foreign policy professionals effectively took themselves out of the running for administration jobs by signing statements opposing Trump's candidacy. Meanwhile, many of the former senior military leaders who served in the Trump administration built their careers on the basis of operations justified entirely by primacy's core assumptions. Generals McMaster, Kelly, and Mattis, for example, spent most of their early careers focused on containing the Soviet Union and rose through the ranks by fighting terrorism in Afghanistan and elsewhere.

This dynamic is the source of the "adults in the room" argument, which holds that one of the most important constraints on America First has been the beliefs and actions of Trump's own appointees.[120] Given that the foreign policy establishment has no America First bench, Trump has had to make do with personnel who have more mainstream—or at least non–America First—views. The most dramatic evidence for this argument comes from a senior member of the Trump administration, who admitted in the anonymous op-ed mentioned in Chapter 3, that "many of the senior officials in [Trump's] own administration are working diligently from within to frustrate parts of his agenda and his worst inclinations."[121]

The result has been a great deal of internal opposition to Trump's preferred foreign policies. According to news reports, Trump's advisers have managed to talk Trump out of a long list of policy changes. In addition to pushing back on Trump's inclination to withdraw from NATO, Trump's national security team has repeatedly obstructed his efforts to pull U.S. troops from Afghanistan and Syria. Trump's cruise missile strikes in response to Syrian leader Bashar al-Assad's use of chemical weapons reportedly came only after Mattis and others had talked him out of simply trying to assassinate Assad.[122]

Other times, however, Trump has clearly overruled his team, in some cases replacing people with whom the disagreements had become too sharp. Secretary Tillerson and National Security Adviser McMaster left after failing to get on the same page with Trump. So did Gary Cohn, Trump's first chief economic adviser, whose cardinal sin was to be a strong advocate of free trade.[123] James Mattis apparently left on his own terms, but for the same reason: he did not share Trump's worldview.

The determining factors behind the amount of continuity or change seem to be Trump's priorities and bandwidth. Trump clearly wins despite pushback from his advisers when he really wants to—as he has done repeatedly on trade. But the Blob's pushback—especially on the War on Terror and more traditional areas of foreign policy, like the NATO alliance or competition with Russia—seems to limit how many battles Trump can wage and win over a given time frame. Combining the strategic-consensus argument with the White-House-in-chaos argument, Patrick Porter has argued, "Trump, with his inchoate worldview, was not a determined revisionist who could overcome these [Blob-imposed] obstacles, and, instead, on security issues, if not on tariffs and protectionism, quickly fell into line."[124]

Beyond pushback from the Blob, a second form of inertia is structural. Consider for a moment the incredible size of the U.S. foreign policy complex: the defense, intelligence, and diplomatic agencies employ millions of people at a cost of more than $1 trillion each year. Consider too how deeply committed Washington is to the business of maintaining international order: the United States is not only a permanent member of the UN Security Council (not to mention the largest funder of the UN); it is also a signatory to dozens of treaties and partnerships that commit the United States to providing for the security of more than 60 countries. The United States maintains over 800 military bases abroad and at any given time has hundreds of thousands of troops stationed abroad. Many thousands of these, of course, are actively engaged in the globe-straddling war on terrorism in the Middle East, Central Asia, Africa, and elsewhere.[125]

In short, the U.S. foreign policy complex is so vast, and the U.S. foreign policy establishment so deeply committed to the present course, that changing direction takes concerted effort. In the absence of direct and continual pressure to revise policies, the bureaucracy will continue on its course. From this perspective, transforming American grand strategy from primacy to something as radically different as Trump's America First vision represents a Herculean task.

FROM BAD TO WORSE? AMERICA FIRST AND TRUMP FOREIGN POLICY MOVING FORWARD

An assessment of Trump's foreign policy so far reveals all the long-standing weaknesses of American intervention and hyperactivity, plus a new raft of problems stemming from Trump's unique blend of transactionalism, Jacksonian militarism, status-seeking, and authoritarian impulses. Where Trump has not made serious efforts to influence foreign policy, the inertia of the system, both intellectual and bureaucratic, has helped keep American foreign policy on the same steady, if misguided, course of primacy. Where Trump has exerted the power of his office more directly, such as with trade and immigration, he has succeeded in changing the terms of public debate and begun to make major changes in policy.

These same tensions between the status quo and Trump's impulses may play an increasingly powerful role in influencing Trump's foreign policy as the pressures of the job intensify, and as the fallout from various investigations of the president and his associates become public and the 2020 election campaign picks up. This does not bode well, however, for the prospect of responsible, coherent, practicable policy changes grounded in a sophisticated strategic framework. An even bigger question is how these forces will play out over the medium to long term, after Trump leaves office and new administrations attempt to persuade the electorate and the Washington policy establishment to embrace a new path forward that reins in military intervention and privileges other forms of global engagement, including diplomacy and trade.

The constituency for such a new approach exists, and is growing; we explore it in the next chapter.

CHAPTER 5
The Evolution of American Internationalism and the Emergence of "Generation Restraint"

Well before Donald Trump's election, the foreign policy establishment was already worrying about softening public support for American leadership of the "liberal international order." As Ian Bremmer wrote in 2012, "In an age of austerity, Americans have less interest in helping manage turmoil in the Middle East, rivalries in East Asia, or humanitarian crises in Africa . . . "[1] In 2013, the Pew Research Council reported that for the first time since the question was initially asked by Gallup in 1964, a majority of the public—52 percent—agreed that the United States should "mind its own business internationally," up from just 30 percent in 2002 in the wake of 9/11. Also in 2013, a survey of the members of the Council on Foreign Relations, comprising primarily professionals working in the foreign policy establishment, found that 92 percent believed that, in recent years, "the American public has become less supportive of the U.S. taking an active role in world affairs." In 2014, the Chicago Council on Global Affairs also recorded a near-historic low, with just 58 percent saying the United States should take an "active part" in world affairs, a figure similar to the post–Vietnam War era low. A 2016 Pew study found that 70 percent of the public wanted the next president to focus more on domestic affairs, and just 17 percent wanted the president to focus more on foreign affairs.[2] (See Figure 5.1.)

Against this backdrop, Trump's election terrified the foreign policy establishment from both parties and provided rocket fuel for the

Figure 5.1

Support for international engagement

Panel A: Chicago Council on Global Affairs

Do you think it will be best for the future of the country if we take an active part in world affairs or if we stay out of world affairs? (% active part)

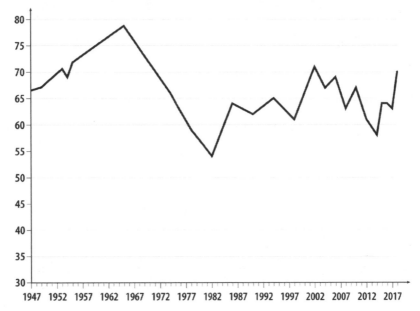

Source: Chicago Council on Global Affairs.

Panel B: Gallup Center and Pew Research Center

The U.S. should mind its own business internationally and let other countries get along the best they can on their own. (% disagree)

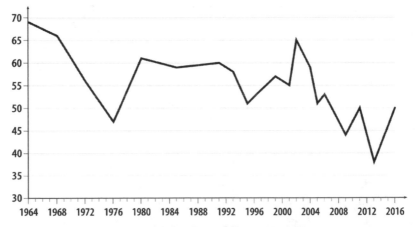

Sources: Gallup Organization, 1964–1993; Pew Research Center 1995–2016.

most pessimistic takes on these trends. Some policymakers continued to maintain that recent polls were only a blip and that the public's basic faith in international engagement remained unshaken. But the number of people who voted for Trump and his America First vision suggested to others that fundamental forces were at work undermining American internationalism. After all, as several scholars have noted, American internationalism emerged out of the "extraordinary circumstances" in which the United States found itself after World War II. As those circumstances have faded into history, and as Americans have become less confident in their leaders and the domestic benefits—especially the economic benefits—of global leadership, the foundations of internationalism may have eroded.[3] Writing in the *New York Times*, Brookings Institution scholar Robert Kagan stated these concerns bluntly: "President Trump may not enjoy majority support these days, but there's good reason to believe his 'America First' approach to the world does. . . . The old consensus about America's role as upholder of global security has collapsed in both parties."[4]

We argue in this chapter that the foreign policy establishment is right to be worried, but not for the reasons typically offered. The declining support for international engagement is not just a blip; it is a signal of a permanent shift in preferences for how the United States engages the world. To be sure, recent short-term fluctuations in the polls mostly reflect the impact of current events, especially public dissatisfaction with endless and unproductive conflicts in the Greater Middle East and, more recently, with Trump's own foreign policy. Over the long run, however, attitudes have shifted because of seismic changes in our nation and our world: the end of the Cold War, the relative decline of American global economic power as other countries rise, declining public confidence in the United States and its institutions, and the increasing rejection of the military-centric nature of American foreign policy. These dynamics are not irreversible, but they have great inertia, and most of them lie beyond the ability of policymakers and politicians to alter. As a result, they will continue to help shape public attitudes well into the future.

At the same time, however, these trends do not signal the death of American internationalism. They signify widespread support neither for isolationism nor for America First. Poll after poll reveals that most

Americans continue to reject Trump's positions on the most essential elements of his doctrine, including immigration, international trade, and his approach to dealing with both allies and adversaries. Although dissatisfaction with the status quo provided a window of opportunity for Trump to criticize traditional elements of foreign policy, the polls reveal that the actual policies spawned by his brand of nationalism, militarism, protectionism, and xenophobia have failed to resonate with a majority of Americans.[5]

Overlooked in the debate is what has really been going on over many decades: an intergenerational process of attitude change. Support for internationalism is not changing because all Americans are changing their minds; it is evolving because, since the end of World War II, successive generations of Americans have come of age during conditions that made them less apt to embrace expansive foreign policy goals and the frequent use of military force. As a result, younger Americans are the most likely to question the traditional approach to foreign policy. At the same time, younger Americans are the most likely to reject Trump's America First policies, and they remain supportive of most forms of peaceful international engagement.

Unlike Donald Trump, these attitude shifts will be permanent fixtures of American politics. Just as older Americans have remained more supportive of American global leadership and more hawkish throughout their lives, so too are younger Americans likely to retain their preferences over the coming decades. Happily, as we will illustrate below, these generational attitude shifts are harbingers not of isolationism, but of a more prudent internationalism. Absent major domestic political and economic turnarounds or devastating international crises, the demographic math will produce an electorate increasingly ready to embrace a more restrained foreign policy focused on peace, free trade, and shared international leadership.

Shifting Patterns of Internationalism

As Figure 5.1 shows, public support for international engagement appears quite stable over the sweep of history and the fluctuations merely a function of temporary—and understandable—public reactions to events. After the Vietnam War, for example, the public's appetite for international engagement waned, only to rise again after the war's effects eventually wore off. Similarly, public support for international engagement spiked after 9/11 in response to the threat posed by al Qaeda, but it eventually drifted back toward the historical average.

From this perspective a simple explanation for the low points during 2013 and 2014 is war fatigue.[6] In its 2012 report, the Chicago Council on Global Affairs had already noted, "The declining enthusiasm for an activist role appears to be related in part to views of the wars in Iraq and Afghanistan."[7] Although both wars began with majority support, by 2005, a majority had come to believe the war in Iraq was a mistake. Afghanistan, always a more popular war, has also lost favor with the public. The percentage who think the war in Afghanistan was a mistake climbed steadily after 2003, peaking at 48 percent in 2014; various polls also find that, since 2010, a majority has opposed continuing the war.[8] Thus, with almost 7,000 U.S. military personnel killed and roughly 1 million wounded, and trillions of dollars spent killing terrorists and "exerting influence" in the Greater Middle East and elsewhere, most observers acknowledge that Americans want to spend more time focusing on domestic concerns. But just because people are tired of the lack of progress and messiness and cost of intervention in the Middle East doesn't mean that Americans have turned their backs on the fundamental pillars of American foreign policy. For example, both Pew and the Chicago Council recorded higher levels of public support for international engagement after the emergence of the Islamic State as a major threat in late 2014.

War fatigue explains much of the recent opinion trends, and without question, public attitudes have displayed a remarkable level of stability over many decades. But what these "topline" figures do not reveal is the slow but steady shifts in attitudes that have been taking place across generational cohorts. As Figure 5.2 shows, public support for international engagement looks very different when we break out attitudes toward international engagement by generation.

Figure 5.2

American support for international engagement by generation

Do you think it will be best for the future of the country it we take an active part in world affairs or if we stay out of world affairs? (% active part)

Panel A: Silent, Greatest, and Lost Generation trends

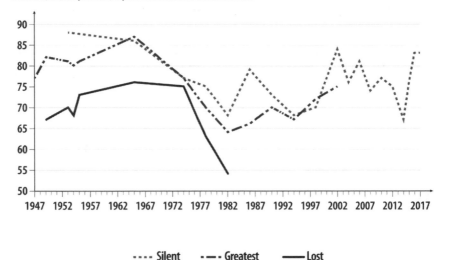

Panel B: Baby Boomer, Generation X, and Millennial trends

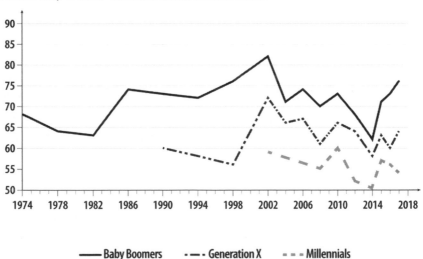

Source: A. Trevor Thrall et al., "The Clash of Generations? Intergenerational Change and American Foreign Policy Views," Chicago Council on Global Affairs, June 2018.

Americans became more supportive of international engagement from the Lost Generation (born 1893–1908) through the Greatest Generation (born 1909–1928) to the Silent Generation (born 1929–1945). Since then, support for international engagement has declined through the Baby Boomers (born 1946–1964) and Generation X (born 1965–1980); the lowest support for international engagement recorded today is among Millennials (born 1981–1996). And though the temporary effects of events are clear from Figure 5.2, as the attitudes of each generation fluctuate up and down over time, what is critical to notice is that the generation gaps have not disappeared. Each generation has started from a very different baseline of support for international engagement, and that baseline has served as a sort of anchor over time regardless of the ups and downs that reflect current events.

The size of the gaps varies from generation to generation, but the cumulative effect since World War II is significant. In the 2017 Chicago Council poll, for example, 78 percent of the Silent Generation responded that the United States should take an active role in world affairs compared with just 51 percent of Millennials. That makes the average member of the Silent Generation *over 50 percent more likely* to support global engagement than the typical Millennial. As members of the Silent Generation and the Baby Boomers die off (at a rate of roughly 2 million per year), they are being replaced by younger Americans (now including Generation Z, those born from 1997 onward) with different views, slowly but steadily reshaping the electorate.

At first glance this trend appears to support the theory that American internationalism is losing steam. A closer examination of the data, however, makes clear that reports of its death have been greatly exaggerated. The differences in Figure 5.2 are dramatic, but the meaning of people's answers to the survey question is less clear. The question itself is incredibly vague. What does "taking an active part in world affairs" or "staying out" really mean? How are respondents interpreting those phrases? How do we know that all respondents think they mean the same thing or are responding to the same current events—either in a given survey year or over time?

Because of concerns about this very issue, the Chicago Council on Global Affairs in 2014 added an open-ended question to its survey, asking people to explain their answers to the active part/stay out question. Unsurprisingly, perhaps, the responses showed that people had a wide range of rationales for both wanting to be engaged with the world and wanting to stay out of world affairs. Those who answered "stay out" usually did so out of unhappiness with a specific element of American foreign policy rather than a desire for true isolationism. The most popular reasons had to do with a desire to focus more on domestic issues, a desire for the United States to be more selective in its engagement abroad, and a sense that certain military engagements had been ineffective. The Chicago Council thus concluded, correctly, that providing a "stay out" answer did not signal an automatic preference for isolationism.[9]

In turn, the Chicago Council's analysis suggests that the generation gaps on the active part/stay out question are also more likely due to specific underlying causes rather than a growing desire for isolationism (that is, for actual disengagement from world affairs) among young Americans. Indeed, a growing body of academic research gives us good reason to suspect that the general question about global engagement is at root driven by more specific impulses. Thanks in particular to the work of political scientist Eugene Wittkopf, most scholars agree that people's support for "cooperative internationalism"—that is, diplomacy and working with other countries through international institutions—is relatively distinct from their support for the use of coercion and especially military force, also known as "militant internationalism."[10] In other words, people are not so much isolationist versus internationalist; rather, they tend to have preferred modes of engagement. Taking our cue from Wittkopf's observations, we can tell a much more revealing story about shifting public attitudes through an analysis of three major aspects of American foreign policy: (1) the use of military force, (2) international cooperation, and (3) free trade.

When we use that lens, the results are clear: the evolution of American internationalism is not a general movement toward isolationism.

Instead, it reflects a new balance of preferences between militant and cooperative approaches to engagement. Younger generations remain just as supportive of international cooperation and free trade as older generations, but they are significantly less supportive of U.S. military power and the use of military force.

Shrinking Support for the Use of Military Force

Table 5.1 shows that younger Americans, especially Millennials, are typically the least supportive of using military force across a wide range of hypothetical scenarios. Of course, in some cases a majority of younger Americans do support the use of force—typically when the threat is most directly aimed at the United States or in situations involving humanitarian intervention.

Given the relative lack of enthusiasm for the use of force, it follows that younger people are also less confident in the utility of military power in general. While 62 percent of the Silent Generation believe U.S. military superiority is an effective foreign policy tool, just 35 percent of Millennials do.[11] And as Figure 5.3 shows, except for the short post-9/11 burst, the majority of Millennials do not see maintaining superior U.S. military power worldwide as a "very important" foreign policy goal, also in stark contrast to older Americans.

Finally, it makes sense that those who are least supportive of the use of military force would be the least supportive of higher defense spending. And indeed, as Figure 5.4 shows, younger Americans are the least supportive of increasing the Pentagon's budget. Once again, the trend is most pronounced among Millennials. In the 2017 Chicago Council survey, Millennials were the only generation in which more respondents supported cutting defense spending than expanding it, by a nine-percentage-point margin, 35 percent to 26 percent. Generation X favored expanding over cutting by 34 percent to 25 percent, while Baby Boomers supported expanding over cutting by 44 percent to 19 percent, and among the Silent Generation, 48 percent favored expanding spending and just 14 percent favored cutting spending.

Table 5.1

Support for the use of military force

(% supporting)

Survey question	Silent	Baby Boomer	Generation X	Millennial
Conducting airstrikes against Syrian president Bashar al-Assad's regime	59	49	48	35
The use of U.S. troops if North Korea invaded South Korea	72	68	60	54
Conducting airstrikes against violent Islamic extremist groups	79	74	65	62
Using U.S. troops if China initiates a military conflict with Japan over disputed islands	48	44	39	33
The use of U.S. troops if Russia invades a NATO ally like Latvia, Lithuania, or Estonia	56	53	52	49
Using U.S. troops to deal with humanitarian crises	70	68	68	65
Using U.S. troops to fight against violent Islamic extremist groups in Iraq and Syria	65	64	64	60
Conducting airstrikes against North Korea's nuclear production facilities	41	42	44	36
Using U.S. troops if Russia invades the rest of Ukraine	41	39	35	38
Using U.S. troops to stop or prevent a government from using chemical or biological weapons against its own people	74	76	73	73
Sending combat troops into Syria to fight violent Islamic extremist groups	39	36	48	41
Sending combat troops into Syria to forcibly remove Syrian president Bashar al-Assad from power	24	32	23	30
Sending U.S. troops to destroy North Korea's nuclear facilities	19	27	31	28

Source: 2017 Chicago Council Survey.

Figure 5.3

Support for maintaining superior military power worldwide

Below is a list of foreign policy goals that the United States might have. For each one, please select whether you think that it should be a very important foreign policy goal of the United States, a somewhat important foreign policy goal, or not an important goal at all: Maintaining superior military power worldwide. (% very important)

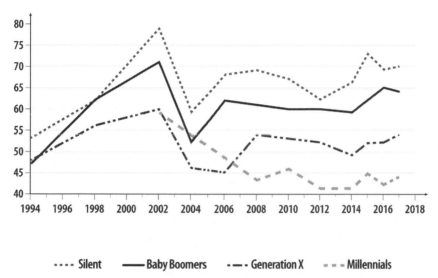

Source: A. Trevor Thrall et al., "The Clash of Generations? Intergenerational Change and American Foreign Policy Views," Chicago Council on Global Affairs, June 2018.

Steady Support across Generations for International Cooperation and Free Trade

Turning to support for international cooperation and trade, we see a very different story. Relative to older Americans, Millennials exhibit greater confidence in diplomacy, economic strength, and cooperation. A 2015 Pew survey, for example, found that 75 percent of Americans ages 18–29 believed good diplomacy was the "best way to ensure peace," compared with 19 percent who believed military strength was the answer. In contrast, among Americans 65 and older good diplomacy was the choice of 47 percent, while military strength was the answer for 39 percent.[12] Millennials are also the most likely to answer that a country's economic strength is more important in determining a nation's power and influence.[13]

Figure 5.4

Support for expanded defense spending

Below is a list of present federal government programs. For each, please select whether you feel it should be expanded, cut back, or kept about the same: Defense spending. (% expand)

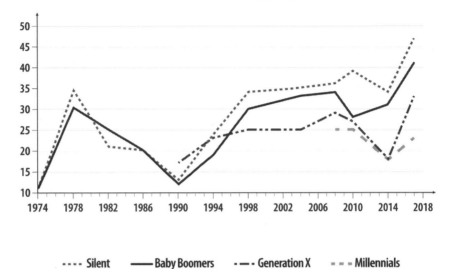

---- Silent   —— Baby Boomers   · — · Generation X   ▪ ▪ ▪ Millennials

Source: A. Trevor Thrall et al., "The Clash of Generations? Intergenerational Change and American Foreign Policy Views," Chicago Council on Global Affairs, June 2018.

When it comes to international cooperation, research has shown that Millennials are at least as, if not somewhat more, supportive of all forms of cooperation, from formal treaties to participation in the International Criminal Court to strengthening the United Nations.[14] As Table 5.2 shows, for example, the 2017 Chicago Council survey found no drop-off among younger Americans in support for participation in the Paris climate change agreement or the Iran nuclear deal. Figure 5.5 reveals the same pattern with respect to support for existing U.S. alliances such as NATO.[15]

Support for free trade has also remained steady over the generations. Younger Americans display the same, if not greater, levels of support for globalization and free trade relative to older Americans. As Figures 5.6 and 5.7 show, though Millennials are somewhat less likely to think that international trade has been good for creating jobs in the United States, no significant difference appears on the questions of whether trade has been good for the U.S. economy or for consumers; a strong majority

Table 5.2

Participation in international agreements

(% support U.S. participation)

Survey question	Silent	Baby Boomer	Generation X	Millennial
The Paris Agreement that calls for countries to collectively reduce their emissions of greenhouse gases	76	69	69	74
The agreement that lifts some international economic sanctions against Iran in exchange for strict limits on its nuclear program for at least the next decade	63	56	62	62

Source: A. Trevor Thrall et al., "The Clash of Generations? Intergenerational Change and American Foreign Policy Views," Chicago Council on Global Affairs, June 2018.

Figure 5.5

Attitudes toward NATO commitment

Do you feel we should increase our commitment to NATO, keep our commitment to what it is now, decrease our commitment to NATO, or withdraw from NATO entirely? (% increase + maintain)

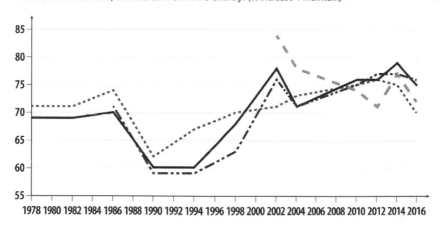

Source: A. Trevor Thrall et al., "The Clash of Generations? Intergenerational Change and American Foreign Policy Views," Chicago Council on Global Affairs, June 2018.

Figure 5.6
Attitudes toward international trade

Overall, do you think international trade is good or bad for the United States? (% good)

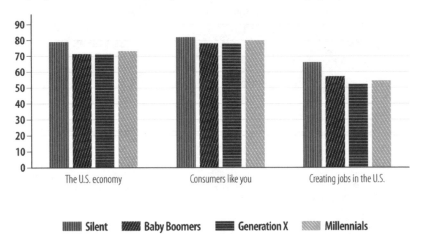

Source: A. Trevor Thrall et al., "The Clash of Generations? Intergenerational Change and American Foreign Policy Views," Chicago Council on Global Affairs, June 2018.

Figure 5.7
Views on globalization

Turning to something else, do you believe that globalization, especially the increasing connections of our economy with others around the world, is mostly good or mostly bad for the United States? (% mostly good)

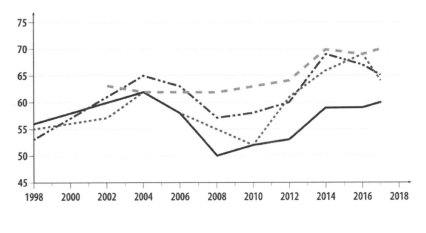

Source: A. Trevor Thrall et al., "The Clash of Generations? Intergenerational Change and American Foreign Policy Views," Chicago Council on Global Affairs, June 2018.

Figure 5.8
Support for free trade agreements

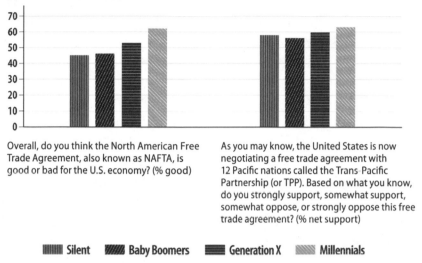

Overall, do you think the North American Free Trade Agreement, also known as NAFTA, is good or bad for the U.S. economy? (% good)

As you may know, the United States is now negotiating a free trade agreement with 12 Pacific nations called the Trans-Pacific Partnership (or TPP). Based on what you know, do you strongly support, somewhat support, somewhat oppose, or strongly oppose this free trade agreement? (% net support)

▓ Silent   ▓ Baby Boomers   ▓ Generation X   ▓ Millennials

Source: A. Trevor Thrall et al., "The Clash of Generations? Intergenerational Change and American Foreign Policy Views," Chicago Council on Global Affairs, June 2018.

of younger Americans believes that international trade is good for the United States. More generally, Millennials are the most likely to respond that globalization has been "mostly good" for the American economy, and as Figure 5.8 shows, they are the most supportive of trade deals like NAFTA and the TPP.

EXPLAINING THE RISE OF "GENERATION RESTRAINT"

Having documented the presence of generation gaps in foreign policy attitudes, the next critical step is to explain them. If, as some suggest, Americans remain committed to the expansive goals and traditional tactics of U.S. foreign policy, then perhaps the polls are simply showing the impact of aging and current events. If so, then as Millennials and Generation Z reach maturity, they will take an "internationalist turn" and exhibit the same levels and patterns of support for foreign policy as their elders. From this perspective, nothing has changed and there is no reason to expect the future electorate's attitudes to diverge from the foreign policy establishment's preferred course. The weight of the available evidence, however, suggests that this view is wrong. A more plausible explanation is that changing historical circumstances— including the relative decline of America's global power, decades of unpopular military actions abroad, and the end of the Cold War—have combined to impart very different worldviews to younger Americans. And these beliefs, once embraced, are very resistant to change.

The argument that people's views on foreign policy will change as they get older is plausible on the surface. Public opinion researchers have documented a wide range of attitudes and behaviors that change in a fairly predictable way as people get older. People become more risk averse as they get older, more attentive to public affairs, and more likely to vote. The most relevant point here is that people tend to pay more attention to public affairs as they get older. This tendency could help explain the internationalism gap between younger and older Americans through the following logic: As the youngest generation, Millennials are less knowledgeable about global affairs and disinterested in foreign policy. But as they age, they will become more interested in and better informed about foreign affairs. As people age, they also become parents and take on leadership positions in society and may feel a deeper sense of responsibility for the nation. Thus, as people age, they may be more likely to realize the value of American leadership abroad.

The reality, however, is that younger people have not always been less internationalist than their elders. As panel A of Figure 5.2 illustrates, public support for international engagement grew from the Lost Generation (those born between 1893 and 1908) to the Greatest Generation (those born between 1909 and 1927) and peaked with the Silent Generation (those born between 1928 and 1945). Not until after the Silent Generation were younger generations less supportive of international engagement.

Furthermore, the aging argument is a poor fit for the specific pattern of shifting attitudes we have just outlined. According to the logic of the aging-effects hypothesis, younger Americans should be less supportive of international cooperation, trade, and the use of military force, as well as less likely to want to "take an active part" in world affairs more generally. But as we have shown, younger Americans are already just as supportive of most forms of international engagement as their elders. To salvage the aging-effects story, we would have to argue that aging somehow affects only people's attitudes toward the use of military force and the generic "active part" question without having any impact on people's attitudes toward international cooperation and trade. And given that younger generations were more supportive of international engagement than older generations until World War II, this inability to explain the data is a death blow to the aging argument.

A better potential explanation for attitude shifts is demographic and social change. Given the large-scale changes to the composition of the American polity since World War II, older generations and younger generations may simply be so different that they hold different views. Thanks to increased immigration, rising education rates, and shifting political currents, America's population looks very different today than it did in the 1940s. To the extent that those changes are linked to attitudes on foreign affairs, they should help explain the trends we see.

What complicates the story is that not all of the changes point in the same direction when it comes to support for international engagement. On the one hand, being white has typically correlated with somewhat higher support for international engagement, which should have a damping effect on younger American's support for international engagement because the country has become much less white over time. On the other hand, education is even more heavily correlated with support for international engagement, and here the arrow points the other way. Younger Americans are far more likely to have finished high school and completed at least some college than those in the Silent Generation. Past research indicates this should make younger Americans more supportive of international engagement, other things being equal. On balance, then, demographic changes seem more likely to have made younger Americans more supportive of international engagement.

The most important impact that demographic changes have on younger people's preferences concerns how, not whether, to engage the world. A great deal of research backs up what is pretty obvious to even the casual observer: conservative ideology is closely correlated with support for militant internationalism and skepticism about international cooperation, while liberal ideology is most closely associated with support for international cooperation and opposition to the use of military force.[16] Since World War II, each generation since the Silent Generation has tilted a bit further toward the liberal side of the spectrum. In the 2017 Chicago Council survey, people self-identifying as conservative outnumbered those identifying as liberal by 24 percentage points among the Silent Generation, by 13 points among Baby Boomers, and by 8 points among Generation X. Among Millennials, however, those identifying as liberals outnumbered conservatives by 5 percentage points. This trend clearly suggests a better explanation for the decline in confidence and comfort with the role of military force in American foreign policy than aging effects. Because younger Americans are more likely to be liberal than their elders, they are also more likely to embrace international cooperation while rejecting militant forms of global engagement.

Ideological change, however, is not the only explanation for the trends at work. The generation gaps persist even when we control for political party. As Figures 5.9 through 5.12 show, Republican and

Figure 5.9
Preferences for the U.S. role in world affairs, by generation and party

Do you think it will be best for the future of the country if we take an active part in world affairs or if we stay out of world affairs? (% active part)

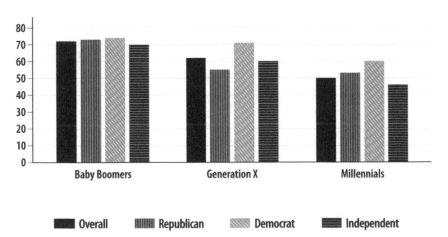

Source: A. Trevor Thrall et al., "The Clash of Generations? Intergenerational Change and American Foreign Policy Views," Chicago Council on Global Affairs, June 2018.

Figure 5.10

Support for maintaining U.S. military superiority, by generation and party

How effective do you think each of the following approaches are to achieving the foreign policy goals of the United States? (% very effective)

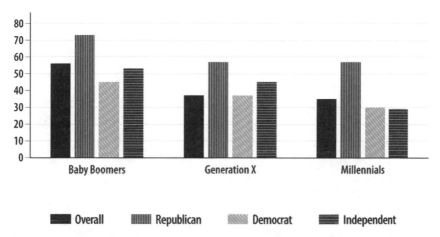

Source: A. Trevor Thrall et al., "The Clash of Generations? Intergenerational Change and American Foreign Policy Views," Chicago Council on Global Affairs, June 2018.

Figure 5.11

Support for maintaining existing alliances, by generation and party

How effective do you think each of the following approaches are to achieving the foreign policy goals of the United States? (% very effective)

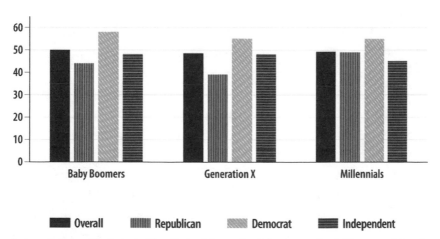

Source: A. Trevor Thrall et al., "The Clash of Generations? Intergenerational Change and American Foreign Policy Views," Chicago Council on Global Affairs, June 2018.

Figure 5.12

Support for globalization, by generation and party

Turning to something else, do you believe that globalization, especially the increasing connections of our economy with others around the world, is mostly good or mostly bad for the United States? (% mostly good)

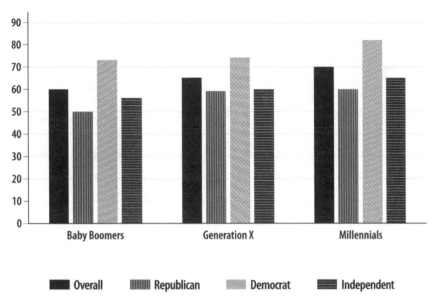

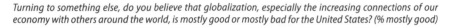

Source: A. Trevor Thrall et al., "The Clash of Generations? Intergenerational Change and American Foreign Policy Views," Chicago Council on Global Affairs, June 2018.

Democratic Millennials alike are less interested in taking an active part in world affairs than the elders in their own parties, while both Republican and Democratic Millennials remain as supportive of international cooperation and free trade as their fellow partisans.

These results make clear that ideological change itself is not enough to explain everything we see going on with American attitudes over many decades. The best explanation is what academics call political socialization—that is, the enduring influence of events experienced during a person's formative years. At the heart of this explanation is the "critical period," a concept first offered by the influential sociologist Karl Mannheim nearly 70 years ago. The hypothesis holds that the state of the world and transformative events that occur during young adulthood produce outsized and permanent effects on people's attitudes.[17]

Thanks to technological, political, and social change, as well as to crises, wars, globalization, and the end of the Cold War, each new American generation has come of age in a world that looks very different from the one its parents and grandparents confronted. And because young people are at their most impressionable as they come of age, their experiences during late adolescence and early adulthood produce changes in their baseline attitudes about a host of cultural, social, and political issues. In this way each generation's way of thinking about the world is distinguished from that of its predecessors. This argument explains why the Lost Generation, which came of age during World War I and the Great Depression, had a more skeptical view of military force and U.S. adventures abroad compared with members of the Silent Generation, whose critical period was influenced by the decisive victory of World War II and a time of unequaled U.S. economic and political hegemony. The critical-period framework also provides insight into why Millennials, who grew up during the Great Recession and unsuccessful War on Terror, express preferences so similar to those of the Lost Generation.

Today's younger Americans have spent their formative years and early adulthood witnessing lengthy, unsuccessful wars and military intervention in Iraq, Afghanistan, and elsewhere. They did not experience the heady aftermath of World War II, when the United States enjoyed incredible economic and political dominance. And with the oldest of them born in 1981, Millennials weren't all that aware of the role military strength played in the successful containment strategy of the Cold War. If they were aware, they'd have also noticed that the United States rarely used military force after the Vietnam debacle and still won the Cold War in 1991. Simply put, to young Americans, war has looked like a poor approach. As a result, they do not share their elders' confidence in America's ability to use military force to pursue national interests effectively.

Younger Americans these days also see the world as a less dangerous place than do older Americans. As Table 5.3 shows, Millennials

Table 5.3

Perceptions of threat

Below is a list of possible threats to the vital interest of the United States in the next 10 years. For each one, please select whether you see this as a critical threat, an important but not critical threat, or not an important threat at all (% critical threat)

	Silent	Baby Boomer	Generation X	Millennial
International terrorism	81	80	73	66
Cyberattacks on U.S. computer networks	80	81	74	66
North Korea's nuclear program	84	82	75	64
Possibility of any new countries, friendly or unfriendly, acquiring nuclear weapons	65	66	60	54
Climate change	41	41	43	52
Russian influence in American elections	44	42	41	43
Military power of Russia	40	40	37	38
Political instability in the Middle East	55	53	41	34
Development of China as a world power	39	40	36	30
Large numbers of immigrants and refugees coming into the U.S.	41	41	40	29

Source: A. Trevor Thrall et al., "The Clash of Generations? Intergenerational Change and American Foreign Policy Views," Chicago Council on Global Affairs, June 2018.

simply worry less about most potential threats, whether the issue is North Korean or Iranian nuclear weapons, international terrorism, or cyberconflict. This attitude may follow from their lack of confidence in the utility of military force: if you don't trust the hammer, maybe nothing looks like a nail.

At a more fundamental level, younger Americans have also become increasingly less likely to express belief in American exceptionalism. Just half of Millennials responded that the United States is the "greatest country in the world," compared with three-quarters of Baby Boomers and the Silent Generation. Four years ago, the American National Election Study similarly found that although 79 percent of the Silent Generation consider their American identity to be extremely important, only 45 percent of Millennials do.[18] As a generation less wrapped up in the flag than their elders, Millennials are more likely to cast a jaundiced eye toward the United States unilaterally flexing its military muscle across the globe.

AMERICA FIRST? NO THANKS. AMERICAN ATTITUDES TOWARD THE TRUMP DOCTRINE

The discussion so far makes clear that the pessimists' worst-case scenario—a national retreat into isolationism—is off the mark. Decades of survey data reveal that the primary change afoot is in public preferences for how, not whether, to engage the world. Nonetheless, Trump's assault on free trade, his inconsistent treatment of allies, his relentless attacks on immigrants, and his generally callous rhetoric toward many traditional foreign policy practices are reasonably seen as worrisome. Has Trump amplified whatever cracks do exist in support for traditional American foreign policy?

Actually, despite Trump's bluster and bravado, the fears of the pessimists have not come to pass. So far during the Trump administration, we have seen an extraordinary level of backlash to Trump and his America First vision. Not only have his signature policies actually become less popular since he took office, but Trump's rhetoric has also spawned greater support—at least temporarily—for almost every aspect of international engagement, from free trade to the use of American troops abroad.

Trump's trade wars with China, his imposition of tariffs on allies such as Canada, and his criticism of NAFTA as "the worst deal ever made" may have energized his base, but Trump's course on trade has not been popular overall.[19] A 2018 Chicago Council survey found historically high support for free trade, with 82 percent agreeing that free trade was good for the American economy, which represented an unprecedented jump of 15 percentage points since Trump won the Republican nomination in 2016.[20] And though Trump subjected NAFTA to withering criticism for years before renegotiating it, a June 2018 survey found that 63 percent of Americans believed the agreement was good for the U.S. economy, up 10 percentage points from 2017 and a record high for NAFTA support.[21] Even the TPP, which Trump summarily pulled out of after taking office, now receives support from a majority of Americans—with 61 percent answering that the United States should participate in it.[22]

Trump is also clearly in the minority camp when it comes to immigration, another key pillar of the America First vision. Trump began his presidential campaign in 2015 complaining of Mexican immigrants: "They're bringing drugs. They're bringing crime. They're rapists."[23] Since taking office, Trump has made reducing and controlling immigration a central part of his political agenda, repeatedly emphasizing the threat from both legal and illegal immigrants, and even shutting down the government in December 2018 over his failure to convince Congress to provide him funding for a border wall.

But most Americans simply don't share the president's dim view of immigrants. According to the June 2018 Chicago Council on Global Affairs poll, just 39 percent of Americans see immigrants and refugees as a critical threat to the vital interests of the United States.[24] On the other hand, Gallup found that 71 percent say immigration is a good thing for the country today.[25] And poll after poll finds that a majority of Americans think that even illegal immigrants should have the opportunity to stay in the United States—68 percent in a recent Quinnipiac poll say they should be able to apply for citizenship.[26] Relatedly, Trump faces the same political headwinds in the debate over how to handle the "Dreamers," children brought to the United States by undocumented immigrants, many of whom have lived almost their whole lives here. Seventy-nine percent of Americans think the Dreamers should be allowed to stay and become citizens.[27] In short, the majority of Americans have rejected this pillar of the America First agenda; just 40 percent approved of Trump's handling of immigration as of November 2018.[28]

Unsurprisingly then, most Americans have never been keen on Trump's favorite construction project. Despite his nonstop efforts to frame the southern border wall as a critical security issue, support for building it has rarely nudged above 40 percent since the month after

Trump took office. A January 2019 Quinnipiac poll found that Americans oppose building a wall on the Mexican border by 55–41 percent.[29]

The only areas in which Trump has found somewhat more support are issues on which his America First sensibilities align with public perceptions of security threats. During the campaign, Trump argued that refugees fleeing the civil war in Syria should not be allowed to enter the United States because terrorists might hide among them. Trump's position received majority support. Two-thirds of Americans supported preventing Syrian refugees from coming to the United States in a June 2017 poll.[30] And though poll results have varied widely, a majority of Americans seem to approve of Trump's "travel ban" temporarily restricting visa applicants from six Muslim-majority countries to those who can show a close family relationship. As of this writing, the most recent poll on this question by Morning Consult/Politico in July 2017 found that 60 percent approved the travel ban.[31]

CONCLUSION

American internationalism is not dead, but it is changing, and for the better. The foreign policy establishment's defenders are right that current events explain a lot of the fluctuations in public attitudes on foreign affairs, but they are wrong to assume that nothing fundamental is changing. Those who have argued that something is going on, on the other hand, are correct but have drawn the wrong conclusions about what that is.

American support for international engagement is not disappearing; it is evolving toward a more decided preference for peaceful international cooperation. Our analysis suggests that the United States is undergoing an inexorable shift. Older, more hawkish Americans comfortable with expansive foreign policy goals and ambitious American leadership are being replaced by younger Americans who are less certain about the righteousness of American primacy and more restrained in their approach to wielding American military power in pursuit of the country's national interests.

For those who worried about what Trump's election meant for the public's foreign policy attitudes, the polls provide a degree of solace. Despite all the advantages conferred by his office and the bully pulpit, Donald Trump has utterly failed to increase support for his America First vision. In fact, Americans are now more supportive of international cooperation, free trade, and general engagement with the world than when Trump took office. Though much of this recent movement is likely a short-term "Trump effect," at the very least the polls make clear that Trump has not created a new wave of America First adherents.

At the same time, the reality that *any* support exists in the United States for the illiberal, counterproductive, and dangerous policies Trump espouses should signal to political leaders of all stripes that public support for prudent foreign policy is not a given. It also reveals that traditional justifications for American foreign policy no longer command as much support as they once did. To ensure that Trump's combination of nativism and isolationism does not become the doctrine of the future, the United States will need other leaders to articulate a new foreign policy vision that acknowledges public concerns while doing a better job of explaining how and why the nation must engage the rest of the world.

This task will not be an easy one. Globalization, automation, populism, and other powerful trends that are reshaping both international and domestic politics will not relent any time soon. To the extent that these forces help explain both Trump's success and public attitudes, we should expect continued debate and division over the future of American foreign policy. Americans worried about economic competition from other nations or concerned about terrorism, immigration, and the influence of other cultures on their way of life may continue to look to leaders like Trump for answers. The next and concluding chapter explains how responsible politicians can address these issues.

CONCLUSION
Toward a More Prudent American Grand Strategy

The Trump presidency was destined, it seems, to operate under a cloud of suspicion. From the start, controversy surrounded Donald Trump and his campaign. The special counsel investigation by Robert Mueller into the Trump campaign and possible connections with Russian assets has led not only to credible allegations of unlawful conduct by Trump himself, but also to dozens of criminal indictments or convictions of Trump associates, including former campaign manager Paul Manafort, former National Security Advisor Michael Flynn, and long-time personal attorney Michael Cohen. Although the Mueller report did not accuse Trump himself of breaking the law, a number of investigations relating to Trump and his family remain ongoing. Rarely has a presidency been as plagued with the prospect of impeachment as this one. Trump's inexperience, his capricious management style, and his disdain for orderly interagency processes have only added to the storm of chaos and impropriety that has typified his administration.

In its conduct of foreign policy, the Trump administration has been impulsive, ad hoc, and incompetent. When the president has been able to wrench the debate toward his worldview, the result has been a mixture of backlash, false starts, and foolish policies. Other times, the broken and outdated grand strategy of primacy has continued apace, though with considerably less strategic coherence and greater resistance from both allies and adversaries. The reputation of the United States has plunged since Trump's election, making the successful pursuit of U.S. interests, however they are defined, much more difficult. In this dynamic and crowded international arena, resistance to U.S. power and influence is growing, and America's capacity for overcoming this resistance is diminishing.

Here, we conclude by prescribing a more restrained grand strategy that eschews the policy of managing world order through force and coercion, calling instead for relinquishing America's global military commitments and focusing on promoting U.S. security and prosperity through trade, cooperation, and diplomacy.

THE CASE FOR DOING SOMETHING DIFFERENT

Donald Trump's frontal assault on the foreign policy community shocked their senses and wounded their pride. Whereas he called U.S. foreign policy a disaster, most of its architects believe it has worked pretty well. The world under American primacy has grown safer, richer, and freer, they point out, and that benefits the United States. Meanwhile, as the primacists see it, the costs of maintaining the current system—a loosely liberal order under American leadership—are not onerous and, in their view, are clearly outweighed by the benefits. Trying something different, they say, would be unwise. We should ignore calls for the United States to change direction and focus instead on making primacy work better—including by explaining its benefits more clearly to the American people.[1]

This book documents the many reasons these arguments don't hold water and why a more concerted marketing campaign is unlikely to work. Americans, particularly younger Americans who have reached adulthood in the post-9/11 global war on terrorism, doubt that American military dominance has delivered safety and security. They are eager to continue and even expand America's engagement with the rest of the world, but skeptical that such engagement must be primarily military in nature.

The members of the U.S. foreign policy community are correct on one point, however, though not for the reasons they think. The world has,

indeed, changed—and mostly for the better. People around the world
are living longer, healthier, and more fulfilling lives. The benefits are
not limited solely to those living in advanced economies; living standards have improved even for the world's poorest. Organized, state-on-
state conflict, meanwhile, has nearly disappeared. To be sure, pockets
of chaos and violence persist. Civil war and persecution of religious and
ethnic minorities have occurred on nearly every continent within the
past quarter century, from Rwanda, Bosnia-Herzegovina, and Kosovo in
the 1990s, to Somalia, Syria, and Yemen in the mid to late 2010s. These
tragedies notwithstanding, the general human condition has improved
during the period of American military dominance. And the one cata-
clysm that world leaders feared most, a third world war, has not occurred.

That does not mean, however, that American military power is
responsible for all this progress.[2] Relative peace between the great powers since 1945 also coincides with the emergence of nuclear weapons.
And an entire generation of international relations scholars has a ready
explanation for why that is. The threat and use of force in a world with
nuclear weapons simply cannot play the role it once did in international
politics.[3] States with a reliable nuclear arsenal, one that is impervious
to a debilitating surprise attack, don't "need to worry very much about
their sovereignty or independence," according to Harvard University's
Stephen Walt. "A handful of survivable weapons makes it very unlikely
that another state will attack you directly or try to invade and take
over your country."[4] Unsurprisingly, the principal victors of World
War II—the United States, the Soviet Union, Great Britain, France, and
China—all acquired nuclear weapons within a few decades of the war's
end and have demonstrated little interest in giving them up.

These great powers also secured for themselves a privileged place
in the dominant multilateral institution of the postwar era, the United
Nations. That body affirmed the importance of sovereign equality and
explicitly proscribed the use of force except in self-defense. That doesn't
mean interstate war has ended. But the occasional transgressions—from
the Soviet Union's invasion of Afghanistan to America's overthrow of
Saddam Hussein's Iraq—have inevitably generated criticism and recrim-
ination from the international community.

Last, global trade has thrived within the international system that emerged after World War II, and globalization accelerated further after the fall of the Berlin Wall. Francis Fukuyama went too far in positing the "end of history."[5] But he correctly predicted that international economics would trend toward greater openness and interdependence, and away from the closed trading blocs that characterized the colonial era of the 18th and 19th centuries or the contest between East and West (i.e., communism and capitalism) during the Cold War. Today, for the most part, government officials aim to preserve and expand global trade, both because such trade is economically beneficial and because it is broadly conducive to peace. The belief that global trade depends on U.S. military might is widespread, but unsubstantiated.[6] At the very least, America's current commitments and force posture far exceed what is necessary to secure a global commons safe enough for buyers and sellers to engage in mutually beneficial trade.[7]

Policymakers in Washington, DC, and throughout the American foreign policy establishment see U.S. power as the linchpin of the global order and the United States itself as an indispensable nation. The truth is that many countries benefit from the relative peace and prosperity that prevails today and thus have a powerful incentive to preserve it. U.S. leaders should capitalize on a unique opportunity to lock in those gains and build a more resilient global order, one that is not overly dependent on a single powerful state.

An additional reason to undertake such a transition is this: while the United States is powerful, it is not all-powerful. The U.S. military is strong but not omnipotent. Many critical problems are simply not susceptible to military solutions. And maintaining the ability to easily fight and win wars single-handedly against determined adversaries—through what the Pentagon calls "overmatch"—will only grow more costly and difficult over time.

Defenders of primacy regularly decry the crisis of America's diminishing military power and exhort their fellow Americans to support the cuts to domestic spending and tolerate the higher taxes that would be required to pay for a military budget approaching $1 trillion. Considerable evidence indicates that the public will to sustain such a massive military buildup simply doesn't exist and cannot be easily mobilized. Most Americans don't know how much they are already paying for the U.S. military, both in absolute terms and relative to other major rivals such as China and Russia, but a mere one in four thinks we should be spending more.[8]

REIMAGINING U.S. FOREIGN POLICY

American foreign policy had a much better track record during the Cold War than it has had since. The most important reason was the clarifying effect of superpower competition with the Soviet Union. The organizing principle of containment served as both motivation and restraint on American actions, and it helped ensure a level of coherence and consistency in foreign policy. Though American foreign policy during the Cold War was not perfect, since then the lack of a clear strategy and the absence of effective constraints on Washington's adventurism have produced a dismal record. America's post–Cold War foreign policy has done too much, at too great a cost, for too little return.[9]

The debate over the organizing principles that should guide American foreign policy once Trump leaves office is already under way. On the right, establishment conservatives like former Ohio governor John Kasich and several conservative academics have sharply criticized Trump's foreign policy. They have issued calls for the United States to renounce Trump's unilateralist approach to foreign policy and to reaffirm America's commitment to active global leadership, not only on security issues but on human rights and the promotion of liberal values as well.[10]

On the left, resistance to Trump's America First agenda is often accompanied by calls for a renewed commitment to use U.S. power to promote a liberal human rights agenda and to challenge corrupt authoritarian capitalism around the world.[11] But among progressives, there has also been a growing sentiment that the United States has relied too much on military force over the past several decades. In a speech at Westminster College in 2017, Sen. Bernie Sanders (I-VT) called on Americans to confront the fact that "American intervention and the use of American military power has produced unintended consequences which have caused incalculable harm."[12] In a related vein, writer Peter Beinart has made a strong case for bringing the War on Terror to an end and substantially reducing America's overseas military presence.[13]

Bridging much of the left and right, however, is perhaps the most popular candidate for a new guiding principle in U.S. foreign policy: the fear of a rising China. Observers across the political spectrum argue that the United States should once again use containment as the model, this time assigning China the role of superpower nemesis.[14]

Although the temptation to replay America's greatest hits is understandable, the Cold War is a poor guide to grand strategy in the 21st century. China is not the Soviet Union, and the conditions of today's international system are not those of the post–World War II era. Unlike the Soviet Union, China has not declared its intention to destroy the United States or capitalism or to overturn democratic governments around the world. Debate over China's exact intentions will persist, but there are good reasons to believe that China's best strategy is to continue working within the same global system that helped it grow rich and prosper over the past several decades. Any efforts by China to add to its territory through conquest of its neighbors would not only incur the direct costs of war but also raise the threat of confrontation with the United States and others. In addition, such a move would risk negative economic consequences either from sanctions or simply by destabilizing trade in the Pacific.

Furthermore, despite its still-growing and impressive economic and military might, China does not represent a direct security threat to the United States. China's neighbors should be wary of its growth. But the risk of war between China and the United States would be vanishingly low even if China's intentions were ambitious, mostly because of geography and nuclear weapons. Even in the extreme worst-case and highly unlikely scenario in which China forcibly reabsorbed Taiwan, little would change for the United States. Moreover, aggressive efforts to deny Chinese influence in its own neighborhood will make cooperating with China on other important matters—including trade—more difficult.[15]

In the wake of World War II, America's allies were bankrupt and the international system lacked robust institutions to support commerce and cooperation. Today, in contrast, America's allies are wealthy and powerful; the international system of free trade, as well as the plethora of UN and related international organizations, is quite robust and enjoys widespread acceptance. The United States has long relied on buttressing its Asian allies, such as Taiwan, South Korea, and Japan, against potential threats from China. But all of them now have economies capable of supporting competent militaries, and they are also trading partners of great importance to China. Unlike during the Cold War, when little trade took place between the American and Soviet bloc nations, China's largest trading partner is the United States, followed by its various Asian neighbors. As a result, a Cold War–level mobilization effort is not necessary for the United States to defend the liberal international order, nor to protect the "free world" from the Chinese threat.

So, where *should* the debate over U.S. foreign policy go? Restraint has gradually gained traction in the academic community. And more recently, fatigue from almost two decades of costly post-9/11 wars has generated public support for a less interventionist foreign policy.[16] At times, Trump appeared to have tapped into this discontent. Over the course of his campaign, he adopted positions that enthused his base—including promises to end wars and nation-building and to extract more value from U.S. alliances—but were deeply unpopular with the foreign policy establishment. The fact that he won in November 2016 signaled that the politics of foreign policy was undergoing a possibly permanent shift. Positions that would have once rendered a candidate for high office unelectable might even have helped Trump win.

The danger today is that reactions to Trump will cause another shift—but in the wrong direction. To the extent that both Democrats and Republicans oppose Trump, many have also become more hawkish in their opposition to his perceived (but largely imaginary) retrenchment. And, despite the evidence we've presented in this book, his detractors are likely to erroneously associate him with isolationism and retreat, rendering sensible adjustments to U.S. foreign policy increasingly unwelcome. "Traditionalists" would create a false dichotomy, explains the University of Birmingham's Patrick Porter, "between primacy or 'global leadership' on one hand and inward-looking isolation on the other." The "advocates of primacy," Porter notes, "brand today's realists who call for retrenchment as Trumpian," in the hope that even a tenuous association with Trump's many other unpopular policy positions and unpleasant character traits will forever discredit anything other than their approach to the world.[17] This book rejects that false binary choice in favor a third option: restraint.

Embracing Restraint

The United States should embrace a foreign policy of restraint grounded in three core principles. The first principle concerns the scope of American ambitions. The United States should reject the myths of primacy and the hyperactive foreign policy it has promoted. The United States is not the indispensable nation. Nor is it insecure. Nor is it capable of micromanaging the world's affairs efficiently and effectively from Washington, DC. The United States should instead pursue a more modest foreign policy agenda that facilitates global trade and focuses more narrowly on the physical security of the homeland, while worrying less about trying to control the world.

The United States enjoys so many geographic, economic, and military advantages that it does not need to do much to ensure its own security. Civil wars and unrest in the Middle East, for example, may be troublesome, or even harmful to American interests like the stability of oil prices or the spread of democracy, but they do not threaten American national security much, if at all. U.S. troops should not be sent to try to pick winners in these internecine fights, nor should they be expected to remain in those places for years or decades to build nations in our image.

Similarly, U.S. security doesn't depend upon alliances. To be sure, countries friendly to the United States continue to feel threatened by predatory or potentially hostile neighbors. It is important to remember, however, that the primary Cold War motivation to create alliances was to disarm the military threat posed by a Soviet Union that most believed had ambitious goals of dominating Europe and threatening the existence of the United States. Without such a justification today, the United States gains little from its alliances and instead puts itself at risk of having to cope with crises and to fight wars on behalf of other nations.

Rethinking and reforming the U.S. alliance system is therefore of primary importance. A considerable share of U.S. military spending goes to protecting allies from harm. And Donald Trump is not the first to acknowledge this point. In 1963, President John F. Kennedy insisted that the United States "cannot continue to pay for the military protection of Europe while the NATO states are not paying their fair share. . . . We have been very generous to Europe and it is now time for us to look out for ourselves" and "consider very hard the narrower interests of the United States."[18] Nearly every administration since has acknowledged the problem of allied burden-sharing in both Europe and Asia.

Primacists fear that without U.S. security commitments, allies will take insufficient steps to defend themselves from harm, choosing instead to capitulate to regional rivals like China or Russia. But restructuring, and even rescinding, America's Cold War–era alliances to reflect modern realities would not ineluctably portend those allies' domination by neighboring powers. With proper encouragement, our formerly weak and fragile allies could become capable and empowered partners. A regional descent into arms races and insecurity spirals is by no means the most likely scenario. When common security challenges emerge, the United States can always work with others to address them. We need not be permanently locked into alliances to do so.

Although terrorist groups like al Qaeda and the Islamic State remain a concern, the terrorist threat cannot serve as a guiding principle for foreign policy. Not only is the eradication of terrorism impossible in a practical sense, but over time terrorist threats have proven less significant than many believed immediately after the attacks of 9/11.[19] Moreover, the War on Terror has illustrated that continuous military intervention is not the answer. Instead, the United States should address the threat of terrorism by continuing to improve its homeland security measures, maintaining vigilance on the intelligence front, and using diplomacy and other tools to discourage conflict and the use of violence as an instrument of politics wherever possible.

Contrary to what some critics of restraint argue, doing less in foreign policy does not mean retreat or isolationism. It simply means that the United States should recognize—and take advantage of the fact—that it does not need to fight most wars or meddle in the internal affairs of other nations or worry about who owns which oil fields in the Middle East or which island in the South China Sea. Restraint means realizing that although caring about such things is easy, most things that happen in the world just don't have a significant impact on the security of the United States or the well-being of American citizens. Restraint means appreciating that, when the United States does intervene in the affairs of other nations, our ability to manage outcomes is very limited, often contested bitterly, and usually expensive.

The second principle undergirding restraint concerns the means that America uses to achieve its foreign policy goals. The primary tools of American engagement should be diplomacy, commerce, and cooperation—rather than military force. War and intervention have played a disproportionately large role in U.S. foreign policy since World War II. Looking back on the Cold War, Kenneth Waltz notes that "in the roughly thirty years following 1946, the United States used military means in one way or another to intervene in the affairs of other countries about twice as often as did the Soviet Union."[20] In the post–Cold War era, U.S. military action has been even more ubiquitous. The Congressional Research Service lists more than 200 instances of the use of U.S. armed forces abroad since 1989.[21]

Although the United States will always need a strong military for deterrence and self-defense, the use of force should be a last resort. The current American addiction to military intervention reflects both the desire to manage the world's affairs and the belief that war or the threat of it is the best way to do that. In fact, the military is a notoriously blunt instrument. America's use of force to spread democracy, fight terrorism, and build nations abroad has shown that the liberal application of military force can make small conflicts bigger, create new enemies, and drag the United States further into unwinnable situations.

Adopting the principle of restraint—that is, restraining the impulse to use force—may require Washington to accept that the United States can't always get the results it wants. Nor will the dividends always come quickly. Diplomacy is a slow business in the best of times, and, as we have seen in cases like Syria, diplomacy cannot always prevent or resolve conflicts. But, as the Syrian case also shows, military intervention was not a reasonable option for the United States. The Syrian civil war did not represent a direct threat to the United States, certainly not one that justified risking American lives, and the underlying problems in Syria were simply not susceptible to resolution through U.S. military action. Indeed, limited meddling on behalf of all sides in Syria exacerbated and prolonged the fighting. The only responsible answer is to encourage negotiations among the various factions in the hope of eventually producing a durable peace.

More importantly, diplomacy, commerce, and cooperation are the most direct paths to achieving most of what Americans want from foreign policy: good relations with friendly nations, increasing levels of mutually beneficial trade, and the ability to work multilaterally to set global standards and solve global problems. While advocates of primacy argue that a global U.S. military presence is necessary to protect world markets, for example, the trade policies of the United States and international cooperation among nations are actually far more important. Trade will carry on uninterrupted if the United States pulls its military out of South Korea, but not if the United States pulls out of the World Trade Organization and abandons all of its free trade agreements.

Diplomacy is also the best first step when dealing with contentious issues and "rogue nations." President Obama's negotiation of the JCPOA was a good example of how diplomacy can resolve problems that might otherwise look like candidates for the use of force. Rather than bombing or invading Iran, as many Iran hawks had advocated since the early 2000s, the Obama administration combined global economic sanctions with multilateral diplomacy, producing an agreement that halted, and rolled back, Iran's nuclear program. The contrast between this approach and the Bush administration's approach to Iraq in 2003 is stark and instructive: no lives were lost, either American or Iranian. The United States did not spend billions of dollars on a military campaign. There was no decade-long occupation by American troops, no Iranian civil war following regime change, and no explosion of terrorism.

A successful foreign policy of restraint will require a much greater commitment to diplomacy than has been the case under Trump.

The United States should upgrade its diplomatic infrastructure and capabilities. That will mean taking some of the excess funds in the Pentagon's budget and devoting them to training and employing experienced diplomats to do the hard work of nimble and intelligent statecraft. The State Department must be rebuilt and revitalized after the demoralizing "reorganization" it suffered under Rex Tillerson's watch and the indifference to diplomacy—bordering on disdain—that Trump and his team have displayed thus far. America should seek multilateral support for most major international undertakings, especially those involving the potential use of economic sanctions or military force.

The third principle is to realign our foreign policy with the liberal values and norms of behavior traditionally espoused by U.S. political leaders. Primacy has eroded America's moral authority and undermined the normative, rules-based character of the international system. It is difficult to make the case that U.S. military power upholds the liberal order while it is being used to help Saudi Arabia, arguably the world's most regressive authoritarian regime, commit war crimes in Yemen. America's hardline policy against Iran is justified in part by the latter's illiberal regime and support for terrorist proxies, but Washington elects to support numerous dictatorships that routinely back their own violent militants. The United States has repeatedly used force in the name of "humanitarian intervention" to stop thuggish regimes from slaughtering their own people, despite lending its support to equally reprehensible governments that commit comparable crimes against humanity.

The basic liberal principles that underpin today's international institutions and legal regimes are laudable and worthwhile. But in its zeal to police world order, America has weakened the most important conventions of this post–World War II system: territorial integrity, nonintervention, and nonaggression. In a notable 1986 ruling, the International Court of Justice held that the United States violated these very principles of international law by supporting the Contra rebels against the government of Nicaragua and by mining Nicaraguan harbors in covert CIA operations. The United States dismissed the legitimacy of the court and refused to pay the reparations the court granted to Nicaragua—just the type of response permitted under the logic of exceptionalism and one deeply at odds with the internationalist tradition heralded by defenders of the "liberal, rules-based international order." Even in cases where the United States has worked within the system, it has often disregarded the system's constraints. In 2011, the UN Security Council approved a U.S.-led NATO military operation to impose a no-fly zone to protect Libyan people from the Qaddafi regime's suppression of armed rebels. But the coalition almost immediately exceeded the UN mandate and pursued regime change instead.

Assuming the role of global cop and enforcer of the liberal world order seems to necessitate violating the very rules and norms that we command others to follow. When President Obama condemned Russia's annexation of Crimea on the grounds that international law prohibits redrawing territorial borders "at the barrel of a gun," much of the rest of the world balked: the United States did exactly that in the 1999 Kosovo war. In 1974, Turkey invaded and annexed a large portion of Cyprus and went on to ethnically cleanse the area of its inhabitants, but Washington never brought itself to condemn the transgressions of a NATO ally. Israel too has annexed and occupied territory in violation of international law while receiving significant support from the United States. Obama's secretary of state John Kerry castigated Russia's territorial grab this way: "You just don't in the 21st century behave in 19th century fashion by invading another country on completely trumped up pretext."[22] With the illegal invasion of Iraq still ripe in the collective consciousness, Kerry's assertion was hardly persuasive. Such tone-deaf hypocrisy perverts the so-called liberal order and undermines the legitimacy of U.S. power.[23]

The goal of a world order constrained by international rules and norms and infused with liberal principles is not advanced by a foreign policy that routinely contradicts those values. As the most powerful country in the world, the United States has outsized influence over the character of the international system. More than those of any other single nation, its actions determine the basis of international norms. A grand strategy of restraint carries the benefit of being more consistent with both the U.S. Constitution and the UN Charter. A less interventionist foreign policy is not only appropriate given the essentially benign security environment we currently inhabit but would also resurrect our international image and revive the old American tradition of serving as an example for other countries to emulate, rather than a ruffian to obey.

★★★★★

A foreign policy of restraint grounded in these three principles— setting modest, achievable objectives; privileging diplomacy and cooperative global engagement through trade, over threats; and modeling the behavior we expect others to follow—will benefit the United States in several ways. First and most obviously, a more restrained foreign policy will reduce the negative side effects of America's hubris. Foreign policy elites protested when Trump labeled their handiwork a "disaster," but he was more right than wrong. The human costs of the past two decades of military intervention have been staggering on all sides. The financial burden has also been enormous: the cost of the War on Terror alone could be as high as $6 trillion. Diminished public confidence in U.S. foreign policy at home and growing anti-Americanism around the world have been another cost of a hyperactive America.

Second, forgoing the unilateral use of military force and intervening less often will increase America's diplomatic flexibility and enhance America's moral capital, boosting the effectiveness of its efforts to foster prosperity and peace. Nations like Switzerland and Canada play an important role in international diplomacy because other states know they have no intention of using military force to coerce others. The United States, by contrast, has frequently encountered resistance.

The United States does not have to adopt a neutral stance in international affairs. It can and should oppose human rights violations, wars, and terrorism; and its diplomacy should reflect that. Nor does it have to abandon all forms of coercion. Multilateral economic sanctions—or the threat of them—have at times proven to be effective tools of diplomacy. But, on balance, the track record of military and economic coercion in international politics is not a good one, especially when the negotiations center on issues of great importance to the target country. In such cases, threats of military force are more likely to result in escalation and further violence than to produce the end we seek.

Many observers, of course, believe just the opposite: that taking military force "off the table" will hamstring any efforts at diplomacy. Why would Iran or North Korea, for example, be willing to negotiate with the United States about their nuclear programs if there were not some sort of threat at the end of the line? This logic makes sense in the abstract, but the number of cases to which it applies is more limited than many contend. Why did Iran and North Korea seek nuclear weapons? A large part of the answer was their fear of the United States. If the United States had a deeper commitment to diplomacy and cooperation, potential adversaries would have less need for a nuclear deterrent.

The third benefit of restraint is that a less expansive foreign policy agenda will allow the United States to reduce military spending significantly. These savings can be put to the urgent task of rebuilding the United States and restoring some semblance of fiscal responsibility. An enormous chunk of America's defense spending goes to support a military big enough to intervene abroad on a regular basis; to the ongoing support of campaigns in Syria, Afghanistan, Iraq, and elsewhere; and to the upkeep of hundreds of military bases all around the world. Right-sizing and optimizing the force structure for self-defense, ending the military side of the War on Terror, and pulling back from bases America does not need for its own security could produce savings of hundreds of billions of dollars each year without any reduction in American security.

Reforms are also needed to make the foreign policy process more transparent to Congress and to the public. Democratic theory holds that the free press and the marketplace of ideas help democracies make better policy by subjecting the arguments of political leaders and the performance of government institutions and policies to scrutiny and debate. Presidents and the Pentagon, on the other hand, often prefer secrecy so they don't have to explain what they're doing, or why, or be held accountable for things that go wrong. That approach to foreign policy should be anathema to a democracy. When the Pentagon and the White House refuse to tell the American people how many troops they have abroad or what their mission is, as has been the case in Syria to name just one example, we clearly have a problem.

Finally, a restrained foreign policy will align better with the classical liberal values of the nation's founding, help curb excessive government power at home, and improve public confidence in American moral leadership. The founders wisely noted the connection between America's foreign policy and the health of American democracy at home. Playing the role of global hegemon and using military force to pursue national "interests" abroad undermine the argument for following liberal norms. At the same time, this pursuit of primacy has fueled the unhealthy growth of presidential power, which in turn has further promoted American tendencies for intervention and meddling abroad while continually threatening civil liberties at home.

Power does not check itself, in either the international domain or the domestic. The shift from primacy to restraint will therefore require not merely a change in the conception of the U.S. role in the world, but a restoration of America's constitutional principles. Congress needs to rein in the unilateral powers of the executive branch by reasserting its Article I authority to determine the nation's involvement in foreign conflicts. Too often presidents have waged war and conducted military operations short of war without gaining clear authorization to do so. This practice not only cuts against the separation of powers set out in the Constitution but also prevents the people's representatives from ensuring the nation's foreign policy reflects public preferences.

What Trump's presidency proves, however, is that even a commander in chief who is averse to the imperial responsibilities of primacy will not readily shirk them. "Once a state has enjoyed the perquisites of a great power, it will find it difficult to adjust to a smaller and less privileged role," the political scientist Robert Jervis once wrote. "As the state and its citizens become accustomed to influence, wealth, and deference they develop a sense of entitlement and great ability. Few tasks are seen as beyond reach; retrenchment is felt to be an abdication of responsibility."[24]

Donald Trump's ascendance to the highest office in the nation is perhaps the most compelling illustration of the hazards of vesting the presidency with so much unbridled power. We share many of the concerns voiced by the foreign policy establishment about what President Trump might do to U.S. foreign policy and how detrimental that could be to the stability of the international system. But any world order that depends for its survival on the whims of a single person in a single branch of government in a single country is simply untenable. Trump seems to have come along at the tail end of America's "unipolar moment." The relative decline in U.S. power is yet more reason to revise our grand strategy to accommodate changing conditions in an increasingly multipolar world.

The solution is restraint. Who will be its champion?

NOTES

Introduction

1. Shane Goldmacher, "White House on Edge as 100-Day Judgment Nears," *Politico*, April 4, 2017.

2. Tim Hains, "Trump: NATO Is Obsolete and Expensive, 'Doesn't Have the Right Countries in It for Terrorism,'" *RealClearPolitics*, March 27, 2016.

3. "Full Transcript: Third 2016 Presidential Debate," *Politico*, October 20, 2016.

4. Jeremy Stahl, "What Trump Was Saying about Russia at Key Moments in the Manafort Saga," Slate, November 2, 2017.

5. Stahl, "What Trump Was Saying."

6. Richard N. Haass, "The Isolationist Temptation," *Wall Street Journal*, August 5, 2018.

7. Hal Brands, "U.S. Grand Strategy in an Age of Nationalism: Fortress America and Its Alternatives," *Washington Quarterly* 40, no. 1 (Spring 2017): 73–94.

8. Colin Kahl and Hal Brands, "Trump's Grand Strategic Train Wreck," *Foreign Policy*, January 31, 2017.

9. Thomas Wright, "The Foreign Crises Awaiting Trump," *The Atlantic*, January 20, 2017.

10. G. John Ikenberry, "The End of Liberal International Order?" *International Affairs* 94, no. 1 (2018): 7–23.

11. Eliot Cohen, "How Trump Is Ending the American Era," *The Atlantic*, October 2017.

12. Peter Baker, "Trump Commits United States to Defending NATO Nations," *New York Times*, June 9, 2017.

13. White House, "Remarks by President Trump to the People of Poland," July 6, 2017.

14. Elliott Abrams, "The Strike at Syria," *The Weekly Standard*, April 7, 2017.

15. Ian Bremmer (@ianbremmer), "Among US political establishment, attacks on Assad the most popular action Trump has taken to date as President," Twitter, April 6, 2017, 7:42 p.m., https://twitter.com/ianbremmer/status/850176828971114496.

16. "Transcript: Donald Trump's Foreign Policy Speech," *New York Times*, April 27, 2016.

17. Michael Anton, "The Trump Doctrine," *Foreign Policy*, April 20, 2019.

18. "Trump's Trade War," *Frontline*, PBS, May 7, 2019, https://www.pbs .org/wgbh/frontline/film/trumps-trade-war/.

19. Karl Rove, "Political Death by 1,000 Tweets," *Wall Street Journal*, June 7, 2017.

20. Philip Rucker, Robert Costa, and Ashley Parker, "Who's Afraid of Trump? Not Enough Republicans—At Least for Now," *Washington Post*, June 27, 2017.

21. Steve Holland and Jeff Mason, "Embroiled in Controversies, Trump Seeks Boost on Foreign Trip," Reuters, May 17, 2017; and John Wagner, Robert Costa, and Ashley Parker, "Trump Considers Major Changes amid Escalating Russia Crisis," *Washington Post*, May 27, 2017.

22. Patrick Radden Keefe, "McMaster and Commander," *New Yorker*, April 30, 2018.

23. Hains, "Trump: NATO Is Obsolete and Expensive."

24. Gerard Baker, Carol E. Lee, and Michael C. Bender, "Trump Says He Offered China Better Trade Terms in Exchange for Help on North Korea," *Wall Street Journal*, April 12, 2017.

25. Karen DeYoung and Greg Jaffe, "For Some Foreign Diplomats, the Trump White House Is a Troubling Enigma," *Washington Post*, October 9, 2017.

26. Bob Corker (@SenBobCorker), "It's a shame the White House has become an adult day care center. Someone obviously missed their shift this morning," Twitter, October 8, 2017, 8:13 a.m., https://twitter.com /senbobcorker/status/917045348820049920?lang=en.

27. Jonathan Martin and Mark Landler, "Bob Corker Says Trump's Recklessness Threatens 'World War III,'" *New York Times*, October 8, 2017.

28. Martin and Landler, "Corker Says Trump's Recklessness Threatens 'World War III.'"

29. Jenna Johnson, "Donald Trump Says He Will Accept Results of Election—'If I Win,'" *Washington Post*, October 20, 2016.

30. "11 Times Trump Threatened Clinton with Prison," CNN.com, November 15, 2017.

31. "Harper's Index," *Harper's Magazine*, December 2017, https://harpers .org/archive/2017/12/266578/.

32. John Glaser, "The Malady of Excessive Interventionism," *Cato at Liberty* (blog), December 5, 2017.

33. International Monetary Fund, "IMF DataMapper: World Economic Outlook—GDP based on PPP, Share of World," October 2018.

34. John Quincy Adams, *Address Delivered at the Request of the Committee of Arrangements for Celebrating the Anniversary of Independence, at the City of Washington on the Fourth of July 1821*, https://www.libertarianism.org/essays/address-delivered -request-committee-arrangements-celebrating-anniversary-independence.

Chapter 1

1. George Washington, "Washington's Farewell Address," September 17, 1796, The Avalon Project, Yale Law School.

2. John Quincy Adams, *Address Delivered at the Request of the Committee of Arrangements for Celebrating the Anniversary of Independence, at the City of Washington on the Fourth of July 1821*, https://www.libertarianism.org/essays/address-delivered -request-committee-arrangements-celebrating-anniversary-independence.

3. Woodrow Wilson, "Wilson's War Message to Congress" (April 2, 1917), World War I Document Archive, Brigham Young University.

4. Quoted in Walter McDougall, *Promised Land, Crusader State: The American Encounter with the World since 1776* (New York: Houghton Mifflin, 1997), p. 131.

5. Dwight D. Eisenhower, "Military-Industrial Complex Speech" (January 17, 1961), The Avalon Project, Yale Law School.

6. Greg Schneider and Renae Merle, "Reagan's Defense Buildup Bridged Military Eras: Huge Budgets Brought Life Back to Industry," *Washington Post*, June 9, 2004.

7. See, for example, Ted Galen Carpenter, *Gullible Superpower: U.S. Support for Bogus Foreign Democratic Movements* (Washington: Cato Institute, 2019), pp. 33–50; and Steve Coll, *Ghost Wars: The Secret History of the CIA, Afghanistan, and bin Laden, from the Soviet Invasion to September 10, 2001* (New York: Penguin Press, 2004).

8. Jeffrey Engel, *When the World Seemed New: George H. W. Bush and the End of the Cold War* (New York: Houghton Mifflin Harcourt, 2017), p. 391.

9. Shane Harris and Matthew M. Aid, "Exclusive: CIA Files Prove America Helped Saddam as He Gassed Iran," *Foreign Policy*, August 26, 2013, https:// foreignpolicy.com/2013/08/26/exclusive-cia-files-prove-america-helped -saddam-as-he-gassed-iran/; C. J. Shivers, "The Secret Casualties of Iraq's Abandoned Chemical Weapons," *New York Times*, October 14, 2014; and Adam Chadwick and Mike Schuster, "U.S. Links to Saddam during Iran-Iraq War," NPR.org, September 22, 2005.

10. Engel, *When the World Seemed New*, p. 393.

11. Hal Brands, *Making the Unipolar Moment: U.S. Foreign Policy and the Rise of the Post–Cold War Order* (Ithaca, NY: Cornell University Press, 2016), p. 308.

12. "George H. W. Bush Proclaims a Cure for the Vietnam Syndrome, 1 March 1991," Voice and Vision, http://vandvreader.org/george-h-w-bush -proclaims-a-cure-for-the-vietnam-syndrome-01-march-1991/.

13. Engel, *When the World Seemed New*, p. 405.

14. Patrick E. Tyler, "U.S. Strategy Plan Calls for Insuring No Rivals Develop," *New York Times*, March 8, 1992. See also "Excerpts from Pentagon's Plan: 'Prevent the Re-Emergence of a New Rival,'" *New York Times*, March 8, 1992.

15. Samuel Huntington, "Why International Primacy Matters," *International Security* (Spring 1993): 83.

16. Charles Krauthammer, "The Unipolar Moment," *Foreign Affairs* 70, no. 1 (Winter 1990/91): 23–33.

17. Patrick E. Tyler, "Pentagon Drops Goal of Blocking New Superpowers," *New York Times*, May 24, 1992. The full text of the document has since been declassified and is available online: National Security Council, "Defense Planning Guidance, FY 1994–1999," April 16, 1992, https://www.archives .gov/files/declassification/iscap/pdf/2008-003-doc1.pdf.

18. Quoted in Andrew J. Bacevich, *America's War for the Greater Middle East: A Military History* (New York: Random House, 2016), p. 156.

19. Bacevich, *America's War for the Greater Middle East*, p. 160.

20. Bacevich, *America's War for the Greater Middle East*, p. 143.

21. Colin Powell, *My American Journey* (New York: Random House, 1995), p. 576.

22. Quoted in Elaine Sciolino, "Madeleine Albright's Audition," *New York Times*, September 22, 1996.

23. William Kristol and Robert Kagan, "Toward a Neo-Reaganite Foreign Policy," *Foreign Affairs* 75, no. 4 (July/August 1996): 23, 31.

24. Engel, *When the World Seemed New*, p. 477.

25. Engel, *When the World Seemed New*, p. 76.

26. Engel, *When the World Seemed New*, p. 76.

27. Quoted in Engel, *When the World Seemed New*, p. 77.

28. Engel, *When the World Seemed New*, p. 77.

29. Joshua R. Itzkowitz Shifrinson, "Deal or No Deal? The End of the Cold War and the U.S. Offer to Limit NATO Expansion," *International Security* 40, no. 4 (Spring 2016): 7–44.

30. Derek Chollet and James Goldgeier, *America between the Wars: From 11/9 to 9/11* (New York: Public Affairs, 2008), p. 122.

31. George H. W. Bush, "Remarks to the Citizens in Mainz, Federal Republic of Germany" (May 31, 1989), American Presidency Project, UC Santa Barbara, https://www.presidency.ucsb.edu/node/262786.

32. Chollet and Goldgeier, *America between the Wars*, p. 125.

33. Anthony Lake, "Remarks to the Chicago Council on Foreign Relations," Chicago, IL, May 24, 1996.

34. William J. Clinton, "Commencement Address at the United States Military Academy in West Point, New York" (May 31, 1997) American Presidency Project, UC Santa Barbara, http://www.presidency.ucsb.edu/ws/index.php?pid=54210.

35. Chollet and Goldgeier, *America between the Wars*, p. 123.

36. Chollet and Goldgeier, *America between the Wars*, p. 134.

37. Madeleine K. Albright, "Statement at North Atlantic Council Ministerial Meeting," Sintra, Portugal, May 29, 1997.

38. Eric Schmitt, "Senate Approves Expansion of NATO by Vote of 80 to 19; Clinton Pleased by Decision," *New York Times*, May 1, 1998.

39. Chollet and Goldgeier, *America between the Wars*, pp. 122, 135.

40. George F. Kennan, "A Fateful Error," *New York Times*, February 5, 1997, cited in Chollet and Goldgeier, *America between the Wars*, p. 124.

41. Barbara Conry, "New Problems for NATO: Potential Conflicts Involving Czech Republic, Hungary, and Poland," in *NATO Enlargement: Illusions and Reality*, ed. Ted Galen Carpenter and Barbara Conry (Washington: Cato Institute, 2001), pp. 88–95.

42. Richard Haass, *A World in Disarray: American Foreign Policy and the Crisis of the Old Order* (New York: Penguin, 2017), pp. 95–96.

43. Michael O'Hanlon, *Beyond NATO: A New Security Architecture for Eastern Europe* (Washington: Brookings Institution Press, 2017), p. 2.

44. Engel, *When the World Seemed New*, p. 192.

45. Lake quoted in Chollet and Goldgeier, *America between the Wars*, pp. 135–36.

46. Chollet and Goldgeier, *America between the Wars*, p. 138.

47. Quoted in Chollet and Goldgeier, *America between the Wars,* p. 259.

48. Bacevich, *America's War for the Greater Middle East*, p. 204. The 9/11 commission repeated the conclusion that "Saudi Hezbollah" was to blame. "Evidence of Iranian involvement is strong," the report stated, but allowed "there are also signs that al Qaeda played some role." *The 9/11 Commission Report* (Final Report of the National Commission on Terrorist Attacks upon the United States), Official Government Edition (Washington: Government Printing Office, 2004), p. 60.

49. Chollet and Goldgeier, *America between the Wars*, pp. 186, 264.

50. *The 9/11 Commission Report*, pp. 48–49.

51. U.S. Commission on National Security in the 21st Century (The Hart-Rudman Commission), *New World Coming: American Security in the 21st Century: Major Themes and Implications*, The Phase I Report on the Emerging Global Security Environment for the First Quarter of the 21st Century (Washington: The Commission, 1999), p. 4.

52. *The 9/11 Commission Report*, p. 311.

53. "Text: President Bush Addresses the Nation," *Washington Post*, September 20, 2001.

54. Elliott Abrams et al., "Letter to President Clinton on Iraq," Project for the New American Century, January 26, 1998, https://web.archive.org /web/20130112203258/http://www.newamericancentury.org/iraqclinton letter.htm.

55. William Kristol and Robert Kagan, "Bombing Iraq Isn't Enough," *New York Times*, January 30, 1998; William Kristol and Robert Kagan, "A 'Great Victory' for Iraq," *Washington Post*, February 26, 1998; and Elliott Abrams et al., "Letter to Newt Gingrich and Trent Lott on Iraq," Project for the New American Century, May 29, 1998, https://web.archive.org/web/20130109214724 /http://www.newamericancentury.org/iraqletter1998.htm.

56. "Text: Cheney on Bin Laden Tape," *Washington Post*, December 9, 2001.

57. "Terrorism: Discovery That 11 September 2001 Hijacker Mohammed Atta Did Not Travel to the Czech Republic on 31 May 2000," Central Intelligence Agency, National Security Archive, December 8, 2001, https://www .documentcloud.org/documents/368985-2001-12-08-terrorism-discovery -that-11-september.html.

58. "Transcript for September 14," *Meet the Press*, NBC News, September 14, 2003.

59. "Full Text of Colin Powell's Speech," *The Guardian*, February 5, 2003.

60. John Brennan, "The October '02 National Intelligence Estimate," The Dark Side: Analysis, *Frontline*, PBS.

61. Paul Pillar, "The October '02 National Intelligence Estimate," The Dark Side: Analysis, *Frontline*, PBS.

62. Committee on Government Reform, Minority Staff, Special Investigation Division, "Iraq on the Record: The Bush Administration's Public Statements on Iraq," U.S. House of Representatives, March 16, 2004.

63. Select Committee on Intelligence, "Report on Postwar Findings about Iraq's WMD Programs and Links to Terrorism and How They Compare with Prewar Assessments," U.S. Senate, 109th Cong., 2nd sess., September 8, 2006.

64. Kenneth Pollack, *The Threatening Storm: The Case for Invading Iraq* (New York: Random House, 2002), p. 397.

65. See, for example, William A. Niskanen, "U.S. Should Refrain from Attacking Iraq," *Chicago Sun-Times*, December 7, 2001; Ted Galen Carpenter, "Overthrow Saddam? Be Careful What You Wish For," Cato Commentary, January 14, 2002; and Gene Healy, "The Wrong Place, the Wrong Time, the Wrong War," *Liberty*, January 2003, p. 29.

66. Emphasis in original. The advertisement is available online; see http://mearsheimer.uchicago.edu/pdfs/P0012.pdf.

67. See PolitiFact.com, "Media Polls on the Iraq War between 2003 and 2007."

68. U.S. Department of Defense, "Casualty Status," March 6, 2019.

69. Daniel Trotta, "Iraq War Costs U.S. More Than $2 Trillion: Study," Reuters, March 14, 2013.

70. Philip Bump, "15 Years after the Iraq War Began, the Death Toll Is Still Murky," *Washington Post*, March 20, 2018.

71. Neta C. Crawford, "Civilian Death and Injury in the Iraq War, 2003–2013," Costs of War Project, Watson Institute for International and Public Affairs, Brown University, March 2013.

72. Michael J. Mazarr, *Leap of Faith: Hubris, Negligence, and America's Greatest Foreign Policy Tragedy* (New York: Public Affairs, 2019), p. 4.

73. George F. Will, "Let America Plunge toward Our Fast-Unfolding Future," *Washington Post*, June 21, 2017, quoted in Mazarr, *Leap of Faith*, p. 5. On Will's earlier support for the war and his transformation to Iraq war skeptic, see Daniel Larison, "George Will and the Iraq War Dead-Enders," *American Conservative*, November 14, 2014.

74. Quoted in Trotta, "Iraq War Costs U.S. More Than $2 Trillion."

75. "Transcript: Obama's Speech against the Iraq War" (October 2, 2002), NPR.org, January 20, 2009.

76. Mark Leibovich, "The Speech that Made Obama," *New York Times*, July 27, 2016.

77. Ben Rhodes, *The World as It Is: A Memoir of the Obama White House* (New York: Random House, 2018), p. 7.

78. "Transcript: Donald Trump's Foreign Policy Speech," *New York Times*, April 27, 2016.

Chapter 2

1. See, for example, Stephen G. Brooks and William C. Wohlforth, *America Abroad: The United States' Global Role in the 21st Century* (New York: Oxford University Press, 2017); Stephen G. Brooks, G. John Ikenberry, and William C. Wohlforth, "Don't Come Home, America: The Case against Retrenchment," *International Security* 37 no. 3 (2012): 7–51; Daniel Egel et al., *Estimating the Value of Overseas Security Commitments* (Santa Monica, CA: RAND Corporation, 2016); and G. John Ikenberry, *Liberal Leviathan: The Origins, Crisis and Transformation of the American World Order* (Princeton, NJ: Princeton University Press, 2011).

2. William Kristol and Robert Kagan, "Toward a Neo-Reaganite Foreign Policy," *Foreign Affairs* 75, no. 4 (July/August 1996).

3. Michael Mandelbaum, *The Case for Goliath: How America Acts as the World's Government in the 21st Century* (New York: Public Affairs, 2005), p. 188.

4. "American Umpire: Trailer and Press Release," film by James Shelley and Elizabeth Cobbs, blog post, Small Wars Journal, 2016.

5. Madeleine K. Albright, interview by Matt Lauer, *Today*, NBC, February 19, 1998.

6. John Mearsheimer, *The Tragedy of Great Power Politics* (New York: W. W. Norton & Company, 2001), p. 41.

7. Quoted in David Boaz, *The Libertarian Reader: Classic and Contemporary Writings from Lao-Tzu to Milton Friedman* (New York: Free Press, 1997; 2015), p. 412.

8. George Washington, "Washington's Farewell Address," September 17, 1796, The Avalon Project, Yale Law School.

9. Eric A. Nordlinger, *Isolationism Reconfigured: American Foreign Policy for a New Century* (Princeton, NJ: Princeton University Press, 1995), p. 6.

10. Hal Brands, *American Grand Strategy in the Age of Trump* (Washington: Brookings Institution Press, 2018), p. 43.

11. Bret Stephens, *America in Retreat: The New Isolationism and the Coming Global Disorder* (New York: Sentinel, 2015), p. 102.

12. When candidate Donald Trump suggested that he would welcome the addition of countries such as Japan and South Korea, the reaction was strong and swift.

13. Stephen M. Walt, *The Hell of Good Intentions: America's Foreign Policy Elite and the Decline of U.S. Primacy* (New York: Farrar, Straus and Giroux, 2018), pp. 280, 281.

14. John Mueller, *Atomic Obsession: Nuclear Alarmism from Hiroshima to al-Qaeda* (New York: Oxford University Press, 2010), p. 158.

15. Robert Kagan, "Trump's America Does Not Care," *Washington Post*, June 14, 2018.

16. See Benjamin Herscovitch, "A Balanced Threat Assessment of China's South China Sea Policy," Cato Institute Policy Analysis no. 820, August 28, 2017.

17. G. John Ikenberry, "The Future of the Liberal World Order: Internationalism after America," *Foreign Affairs* 90, no. 3 (May/June 2011): 56.

18. G. John Ikenberry, "Why the Liberal Order Will Survive," *Ethics and International Affairs* 32, no. 1 (2018): 17–29.

19. Robert Kagan, "Things Will Not Be Okay," *Washington Post*, July 12, 2018.

20. Brands, *American Grand Strategy*, p. 170.

21. Frank Ninkovich, "Trumpism, History, and the Future of U.S. Foreign Relations," in *Chaos in the Liberal Order: The Trump Presidency and International Politics in the Twenty-First Century*, ed. Robert Jervis, Francis J. Gavin, Joshua Rovner, and Diane N. Labrosse (New York: Columbia University Press, 2018), p. 407.

22. See Ikenberry, *Liberal Leviathan*, pp. 342–48.

23. Ikenberry, "Why the Liberal Order Will Survive."

24. The Union of International Associations maintains a list of international organizations and associations.

25. Stephen G. Brooks, G. John Ikenberry, and William C. Wohlforth, "Lean Forward: In Defense of American Engagement," *Foreign Affairs* 92, no. 1 (January/February 2013).

26. Daniel Drezner, "Bucks for the Bang? Assessing the Economic Returns to Military Primacy," in *A Dangerous World? Threat Perception and U.S. National Security*, eds. Christopher A. Preble and John Mueller (Washington: Cato Institute, 2014), pp. 197, 207.

27. Walt, *The Hell of Good Intentions*, pp. 166–67.

28. Gary Clyde Hufbauer and Paul L. Grieco, "The Payoff from Globalization," *Washington Post*, June 7, 2005. See Peterson Institute for International Economics, https://piie.com/commentary/op-eds/payoff-globalization.

29. Francis J. Gavin, *Gold, Dollars, and Power: The Politics of International Monetary Relations, 1958–1971* (Chapel Hill: University of North Carolina Press, 2004), p. 12, cited in Benjamin H. Friedman et al., "Correspondence: Debating American Engagement: The Future of U.S. Grand Strategy," *International Security* 38, no. 2 (Fall 2013): 191.

30. See Michael Mastanduno, "System Maker and Privilege Taker: U.S. Power and the International Political Economy," *World Politics* 61, no. 1 (January 2009): 121–54.

31. Eugene Gholz, Daryl G. Press, and Harvey M. Sapolsky, "Come Home, America: The Strategy of Restraint in the Face of Temptation," *International Security* 21, no. 4 (Spring 1997): 44–45.

32. Friedman et al., "Correspondence: Debating American Engagement," p. 191.

33. Data from WhiteHouse.gov, Office of Management and Budget, Historical Tables, "Table 6.1—Composition of Outlays: 1940–2024."

34. WhiteHouse.gov, "Table 6.1—Composition of Outlays: 1940–2024."

35. Eric Edelman et al., *Providing for the Common Defense: The Assessment and Recommendations of the National Defense Strategy Commission* (Washington: United States Institute of Peace, November 2018), pp. xii, 11, 19.

36. Jon Kyl and Roger Zakheim, "If Anything, America's Defense Budget Is Too Small," *Politico Magazine*, January 15, 2019, https://www.politico.com /magazine/story/2019/01/15/trump-2019-national-defense-commission -strategy-224016.

37. Estimated national defense outlays in 2018 were $643.2 billion; 5 percent, year-over-year real growth would produce a Pentagon budget of $971.9 billion by 2024. See WhiteHouse.gov, "Table 6.1—Composition of Outlays: 1940–2023"; and Taxpayers for Common Sense, "Pentagon Inflation Calculations," https://www .taxpayer.net/wp-content/uploads/2018/11/Pentagon-Inflation-Calculations.png.

38. Congressional Budget Office, "Trends in Spending by the Department of Defense for Operation and Maintenance," January 5, 2017. See also Steven Kosiak, "Is the U.S. Military Getting Smaller and Older? And How Much Should We Care?," Center for a New American Security, March 14, 2017.

39. Edelman et al., *Providing for the Common Defense*, p. 63.

40. Frank Newport, "The Military's Positive Image and the Defense Budget," Gallup.com, April 1, 2019.

41. "Summary of the 2018 National Defense Strategy of the United States of America: Sharpening the American Military's Competitive Edge," Department of Defense, January 2018, pp. 3, 6.

42. International Institute for Strategic Studies, *The Military Balance 2018* (Washington: IISS, 2018), p. 19.

43. John Halpin, Brian Katulis, Peter Juul, Karl Agne, Jim Gerstein, and Nisha Jain, "America Adrift: How the U.S. Foreign Policy Debate Misses What Voters Really Want," Center for American Progress, May 5, 2019.

44. Quoted in Walt, *The Hell of Good Intentions*, p. 38.

45. Andrew Bacevich, "Trump Loves Winning, but American Generals Have Forgotten How," Huffington Post, November 29, 2016, https://www .huffpost.com/entry/trump-loves-winning-but-american-generals-have-forgotten -how_b_583d87b2e4b04b66c01bb1e3.

46. Pew Research Center, "Greatest Threats around the World," August 1, 2017.

47. See, for example, Chaim Kaufmann, "Threat Inflation and the Failure of the Marketplace of Ideas: The Selling of the Iraq War," in *American Foreign Policy and the Politics of Fear: Threat Inflation since 9/11*, ed. A. Trevor Thrall and Jane K. Cramer (New York: Routledge, 2009), pp. 97–116; and Benjamin H. Friedman, "Alarums and Excursions: Explaining Threat Inflation in U.S. Foreign Policy," in *A Dangerous World? Threat Perception and U.S. National Security*, ed. Christopher A. Preble and John Mueller (Washington: Cato Institute, 2014), pp. 281–303.

48. See Christopher Preble, "Meet the Organization Pushing Regime Change in Iran—and Its Willing American Accomplices," The National

Interest (Online), July 15, 2018, https://nationalinterest.org/blog/skeptics /meet-organization-pushing-regime-change-iran%E2%80%94and-its-willing -american-accomplices; and Christopher Preble, "Here's How the Road to Iraq Is Repeating Itself with Iran," *The National Interest* (Online), July 5, 2018, https://nationalinterest.org/blog/skeptics/heres-how-road-iraq-repeating -itself-iran-25097.

49. Ivo H. Daalder and James G. Stavridis, "NATO's Victory in Libya: The Right Way to Run an Intervention," *Foreign Affairs* 91, no. 2 (March/ April 2012); and Hillary Clinton, quoted in Corbett Daly, "Clinton on Qaddafi: 'We Came, We Saw, He Died,'" *CBS News*, October 20, 2011.

50. Alan Kuperman, "A Model Humanitarian Intervention? Reassessing NATO's Libya Campaign," *International Security* 38, no. 1 (Summer 2013): 105–36.

51. "President Obama: Libya Aftermath 'Worst Mistake' of Presidency," BBC, April 11, 2016.

52. Jeffrey Goldberg, "The Obama Doctrine," *The Atlantic*, April 2016.

53. A 2018 survey of adults in eight Arab countries (Egypt, Iraq, Jordan, Lebanon, Palestine, Saudi Arabia, Tunisia, and the United Arab Emirates), plus Iran and Turkey, found the United States and Iran at the bottom of the favorability list. Attitudes toward the United States were particularly low (single digits) in Egypt and Iraq. See Zogby Research Services, "Middle East Public Opinion," November 2018. These findings are consistent with global trends, which have seen a marked decline in favorability ratings for the United States, and for Donald Trump in particular. See Richard Wike et al., "Trump's International Ratings Remain Low, Especially among Key Allies," Pew Research Center, October 1, 2018, http://www.pewglobal.org/2018/10/01/americas -international-image-continues-to-suffer/.

54. Researcher Christopher Claassen found that support for democracy was declining in places that lacked strong democratic traditions. See Christopher Claassen, "Support for Democracy Is Declining—but Not in the U.S. or Other Western Democracies," Monkey Cage, *Washington Post*, July 5, 2018.

55. On the Powell doctrine and its precursor, the Weinberger doctrine, as useful guides to U.S. foreign policy, see Ian Bremmer, *Superpower: Three Choices for America's Role in the World* (New York: Portfolio/Penguin, 2015), pp. 90–91, 98–99. The original Weinberger doctrine was spelled out in his "Uses of Military Power," speech before the National Press Club, Washington, DC, November 28, 1984, reprinted in Caspar W. Weinberger, *Fighting for Peace: Seven Critical Years in the Pentagon* (New York: Warner Books, 1990), pp. 433–48.

56. MJ Lee, "How Donald Trump Blasted George W. Bush in SC—and Still Won," CNN.com, February 21, 2016.

57. Pew Research Center, "Public Sees U.S. Power Declining as Support for Global Engagement Slips," December 3, 2013.

58. Pew Research Center, "Public Uncertain, Divided over America's Place in the World," May 5, 2016.

59. On the rise of the rest, see Fareed Zakaria, *The Post-American World: Release 2.0* (New York: Norton, 2011).

60. Patrick Porter, "A World Imagined: Nostalgia and Liberal Order," Cato Institute Policy Analysis no. 843, June 5, 2018.

61. Bruce Jentleson, "The Liberal Order Isn't Coming Back: What Next?," *Democracy: A Journal of Ideas* no. 48 (Spring 2018).

62. Richard Lough, "Germany's Merkel Calls for a European Union Military," Reuters, November 13, 2018.

63. Steven Pinker, *The Better Angels of Our Nature: Why Violence Has Declined* (New York: Viking Books, 2011).

CHAPTER 3

1. Benjamin Friedman and Justin Logan, "Why Washington Doesn't Debate Grand Strategy," *Strategic Studies Quarterly* 10, no. 4 (Winter 2016): 14–45.

2. Abby Phillip, "O'Reilly Told Trump That Putin Is a Killer. Trump's Reply: 'You Think Our Country Is So Innocent?,'" *Washington Post*, February 4, 2017.

3. Richard N. Haass, "The Isolationist Temptation," *Wall Street Journal*, August 5, 2016.

4. Thomas Wright, "Trump's 19th Century Foreign Policy," *Politico Magazine*, January 20, 2016.

5. Stephen Wertheim, "Quit Calling Donald Trump an Isolationist. He's Worse Than That," *Washington Post*, February 17, 2017.

6. Bob Woodward, *Fear: Trump in the White House*, (New York: Simon & Schuster, 2018), p. 309–10.

7. Robert Kagan, "Trump's America Does Not Care," *Washington Post*, June 14, 2018.

8. Hal Brands and Peter Feaver, "Saving Realism from the So-Called Realists," *Commentary*, August 2017.

9. Daniel Drezner, "So When Will Realists Endorse Donald Trump?" *Washington Post*, February 1, 2016.

10. Charlie Laderman and Brendan Simms, *Donald Trump: The Making of a World View* (London: Endeavour Press Ltd., 2017), p. 24.

11. Randall Schweller, "Why Trump Now: A Third-Image Explanation," in *Chaos in the Liberal Order: The Trump Presidency and International Politics in the*

Twenty-First Century, ed. Robert Jervis, Francis J. Gavin, Joshua Rovner, and Diane Labrosse (New York: Columbia University Press, 2018), p. 23.

12. Brian Rathbun, "The Rarity of Realpolitik: What Bismarck's Rationality Reveals about International Politics," *International Security* 43, no. 1 (Summer 2018): 7–55.

13. Edward Hallett Carr, *The Twenty Years' Crisis, 1919–1939: An Introduction to the Study of International Relations* (London: Macmillan, 1946), p. 8.

14. Hans Morgenthau, *Politics among Nations*, 5th ed. rev. (New York: Alfred A. Knopf, 1978), p. 4.

15. Rathbun, "The Rarity of Realpolitik," p. 10.

16. David Leonhardt and Stuart A. Thompson, "Trump's Lies," *New York Times*, updated December 14, 2017.

17. Woodward, *Fear*, p. 209.

18. Glenn Kessler, "Not Just Misleading. Not Merely False. A Lie," *Washington Post*, August 22, 2018.

19. Glenn Kessler, Salvador Rizzo, and Meg Kelly, "President Trump Has Made More than 10,000 False or Misleading Claims," *Washington Post*, April 29, 2019.

20. Colbert I. King, "Trump Is a Bald-Faced Liar," *Washington Post*, June 22, 2018; Bella DePaulo, "I Study Liars. I've Never Seen One Like President Trump," *Washington Post*, December 8, 2017; and Susan B. Glasser, "It's True: Trump Is Lying More, and He's Doing It on Purpose," *New Yorker*, August 3, 2018.

21. Woodward, *Fear*, p. 211.

22. Laderman and Simms, *The Making of a World View*, pp. 76–77.

23. Benji Sarlin and Liz Johnstone, "What Is Donald Trump's Position on Libya?" NBC News, June 5, 2016; and Kevin Robillard, "Trump: Hillary's Killed 'Hundreds of Thousands,'" *Politico*, December 13, 2015.

24. Donald Trump (@realDonaldTrump), "President Obama, do not attack Syria. There is no upside and tremendous downside. Save your "powder" for another (and more important) day," Twitter, September 7, 2013, 6:21 a.m., https://twitter.com/realdonaldtrump/status/376334423069032448; and Donald Trump (@realDonaldTrump), "Obama wants to unilaterally put a no-fly zone in Syria to protect Al Qaeda Islamists http://thebea.st/143tmfM Syria is NOT our problem," Twitter, May 29, 2013, 11:58 a.m., https://twitter.com/realdonaldtrump/status/339818069641801728.

25. Donald Trump (@realDonaldTrump), "The only reason President Obama wants to attack Syria is to save face over his very dumb RED LINE statement. Do NOT attack Syria,fix U.S.A.," Twitter, September 5, 2013, 4:13 a.m., https://twitter.com/realDonaldTrump/status/375577511473983488.

26. Donald Trump (@realDonaldTrump), "The President must get Congressional approval before attacking Syria-big mistake if he does not," Twitter, August 30, 2013, 4:02 p.m., https://twitter.com/realDonaldTrump /status/373581528405905408; and Donald Trump (@realDonaldTrump), "@walaa_3ssaf No, dopey, I would not go into Syria, but if I did it would be by surprise and not blurted all over the media like fools," Twitter, August 29, 2013, 5:09 a.m., https://twitter.com/realdonaldtrump/status/373054743742275584.

27. Donald Trump (@realDonaldTrump), "Russia vows to shoot down any and all missiles fired at Syria. Get ready Russia, because they will be coming, nice and new and "smart!" You shouldn't be partners with a Gas Killing Animal who kills his people and enjoys it," Twitter, April 11, 2018, 3:57 a.m., https://twitter.com/realDonaldTrump/status/984022625440747520.

28. Nicole Gaouette and Jill Disis, "Trump Dismisses Running Mate Pence's Syria View," CNN.com, October 10, 2016.

29. Kevin Liptak and Dan Merica, "Trump Says NATO No Longer 'Obsolete,'" CNN.com, April 12, 2017.

30. Tessa Berenson, "'NATO Is Much Stronger Now': Trump Claims Victory after Contentious Summit," Time.com, July 12, 2018.

31. Carrie Johnson, "2016 RNC Delegate: Trump Directed Change to Party Platform on Ukraine Support," NPR.org, December 4, 2017.

32. White House, "Presidential Executive Order on Buy American and Hire American," April 18, 2017.

33. Miriam Jordan, "Making President Trump's Bed: A Housekeeper without Papers," New York Times, December 6, 2018; Ryan Teague Beckwith, "Donald Trump Paid $1.4 Million in a Dispute over Undocumented Workers," Time.com, November 28, 2017; and Michelle Ye Hee Lee, "How Many Trump Products Were Made Overseas? Here's the Complete List," Washington Post, August 26, 2016.

34. David E. Sanger and William J. Broad, "Once 'No Longer a Nuclear Threat,' North Korea Now in Standoff with US," New York Times, August 10, 2018.

35. Courtney Kube and Carol E. Lee, "North Korea Is Still Making Nukes, and the Trump Admin Is Taking a Harder Line," NBC News, September 10, 2018.

36. Joshua Green, Devil's Bargain: Steve Bannon, Donald Trump, and the Storming of the Presidency (New York: Penguin Press), p. 208. Trump doesn't read. See Chris Cillizza, "The Trump Book Club Is Exactly What You Would Think It Would Be," CNN.com, May 7, 2018; Adam Frisk, "Donald Trump 'Incapable of Reading a Book, Much Less Writing One,' Says 'The Art of the Deal' Co-Author," Global News, July 5, 2018; and Jane Mayer, "Donald Trump's Ghostwriter Tells All," New Yorker, July 25, 2016.

37. John Cassidy, "There Is No Trump Doctrine, Only Contradictions and Bluster," *New Yorker*, September 21, 2017.

38. Thomas Otte, "The Waning of the Postwar Order," in *Chaos in the Liberal Order: The Trump Presidency and International Politics in the Twenty-First Century*, ed. Robert Jervis, Francis J. Gavin, Joshua Rovner, and Diane Labrosse (New York: Columbia University Press, 2018), p. 165.

39. Rebecca Friedman Lissner and Micah Zenko, "There Is No Trump Doctrine, and There Will Never Be One," *Foreign Policy*, July 21, 2017.

40. American Psychiatric Association, *The Principles of Medical Ethics: With Annotations Especially Applicable to Psychiatry, 2013 Edition* (American Psychiatric Association: Arlington, VA, 2013), pg. 9.

41. See Judith L. Herman and Robert Jay Lifton, "'Protect Us from This Dangerous President,' 2 Psychiatrists Say," Letter to the Editor, *New York Times*, March 8, 2017; and Nigel Barber, "Does Trump Suffer from Narcissistic Personality Disorder?," *Psychology Today*, August 10, 2016.

42. Morgan Gstalter, "Trump Again Labels Himself a 'Very Stable Genius,'" The Hill, July 12, 2018.

43. Dominic Rushe, "'I'm Really Rich': Donald Trump Claims $9bn Fortune during Campaign Launch," *The Guardian*, June 16, 2015.

44. Abby Ohlheiser, "Welp, Trump Just Dunked on Rosie O'Donnell on Twitter," *Washington Post*, May 11, 2017.

45. Terrence Dopp, "Trump Calls Omarosa a 'Dog' and a 'Crazed, Crying Lowlife,'" Bloomberg.com, August 14, 2018.

46. Igor Bobic, "Trump Invites His Employees to Praise Him during Cabinet Meeting," Huffington Post, June 12, 2017.

47. Laderman and Simms, *The Making of a World View*, pp. 29–30.

48. Josh Rogin, "In Debate, Trump's Lack of Nuclear Knowledge on Display," *Washington Post*, September 28, 2016.

49. Linda Qui, "Trump Falsely Claims GDP Growth Is Higher Than Unemployment 'for the First Time in 100 Years,'" *New York Times*, September 10, 2018.

50. David Nakamura, "'People Actually Laughed at a President': At U.N. Speech, Trump Suffers the Fate He Always Feared," *Washington Post*, September 25, 2018.

51. Donald Trump (@realDonaldTrump), "The concept of global warming was created by and for the Chinese in order to make U.S. manufacturing non-competitive," Twitter, November 6, 2012, 11:15 a.m., https://twitter.com/realdonaldtrump/status/265895292191248385.

52. Nolan D. McCaskill, "Trump Accuses Cruz's Father of Helping JFK's Assassin," *Politico*, May 3, 2016.

53. Heidi M. Przybyla, "DOJ Confirms No Evidence Supporting Trump Claim Obama Wiretapped Him," *USA Today*, September 2, 2017.

54. Adam Entous and Ronan Farrow, "The Conspiracy Memo about Obama Aides That Circulated in the Trump White House," *New Yorker*, August 23, 2018.

55. David Wright and Tal Kopan, "Cruz Unloads with Epic Takedown of 'Pathological Liar,' 'Narcissist' Donald Trump," CNN.com, May 3, 2016.

56. Rebecca Savransky, "Graham Accuses Media of Painting Trump as a 'Kook,' but Once Used Same Attack Himself," The Hill, November 30, 2017.

57. "Transcript of Mitt Romney's Speech on Donald Trump," *New York Times*, March 3, 2016.

58. Woodward, *Fear*, p. 235.

59. Woodward, *Fear*, p. 263.

60. Woodward, *Fear*, p. 286.

61. Woodward, *Fear*, p. 346.

62. Manu Raju, "Elizabeth Warren: Time to Use 25th Amendment to Remove Trump from Office," CNN.com, September 6, 2018.

63. Adam Goldman and Michael S. Schmidt, "Rod Rosenstein Suggested Secretly Recording Trump and Discussed 25th Amendment," *New York Times*, September 21, 2018; and Anonymous, "I Am Part of the Resistance Inside the Trump Administration," *New York Times*, September 5, 2018.

64. Philip Rucker and Karoun Demirjian, "Trump Attacks Corker, Who Responds by Calling the White House 'Adult Day Care,'" *Washington Post*, October 8, 2017.

65. Rucker and Demirjian, "Trump Attacks Corker."

66. Danielle Allen, "President Trump's Foreign Policy Is Perfectly Coherent," *Washington Post*, July 23, 2018.

67. Laderman and Simms, *The Making of a World View*, p. 90.

68. Transcript courtesy of Bloomberg Government, "Trump's Optimistic News Conference after Meeting with Kim Jong Un, Annotated," *Washington Post*, June 12, 2018.

69. Davide Furceri et al., "Macroeconomic Consequences of Tariffs," NBER Working Paper no. 25402, December 2018.

70. Woodward, *Fear*, p. 138.

71. Chad P. Brown, "For Trump, It Was a Summer of Tariffs and More Tariffs. Here's Where Things Stand," *Washington Post*, September 13, 2018.

72. Michael Hirtzer and Tom Polansek, "Trade Wars Cost U.S., China Billions of Dollars Each in 2018," Reuters, December 28, 2018.

73. Chad P. Brown and Eva (Yiwen) Zhang, "First Tariffs, Then Subsidies: Soybeans Illustrate Trump's Wrongfooted Approach on Trade," Peterson Institute for International Economics, July 30, 2018; Ana Swanson, "Trump Gives Farmers $16 Billion in Aid Amid Prolonged China Trade War," *New York Times*, May 23, 2019. https://www.nytimes.com/2019/05/23/us/politics/farm-aid-package.html

74. Bob Pisani, "Trump's Trade War Has Cost the S&P 10% This Year, JP Morgan Estimates," CNBC.com, December 7, 2018.

75. Maggie Fitzgerald, "This Chart from Goldman Sachs Shows Tariffs Are Raising Prices for Consumers and It Could Get Worse," CNBC.com, May 13, 2019.

76. Kate Gibson, "Trump's China Tariffs Hike Will Cost Average U.S. Family $831 a Year," CBS News, May 23, 2019.

77. Donald Trump (@realDonaldTrump), "When a country (USA) is losing many billions of dollars on trade with virtually every country it does business with, trade wars are good, and easy to win. Example, when we are down $100 billion with a certain country and they get cute, don't trade anymore-we win big. It's easy," Twitter, March 2, 2018, 2:50 a.m., https://twitter.com/realdonaldtrump/status/969525362580484098.

78. Woodward, *Fear*, p. 208.

79. Woodward, *Fear*, p. 221.

80. Idrees Ali, "Cost of One of Those 'Expensive' U.S.–South Korea Military Exercises? $14 Million," Reuters, July 6, 2018; and Mark Landler, "For Trump, Power and Values Matter Less than Dollars and Cents," *New York Times*, June 13, 2018.

81. Justin Sink, "Poland Offers 'Fort Trump' as Name If U.S. Builds Military Base," Bloomberg.com, September 18, 2018.

82. Christina Arabia and William Hartung, "Trends in Major U.S. Arms Sales in 2018: The Trump Record—Rhetoric Versus Reality," *Security Assistance Monitor*, Center for International Policy, April 2019.

83. Peter Baker, "In Trump's Saudi Bargain, the Bottom Line Proudly Wins Out," *New York Times*, October 14, 2018.

84. See Glenn Kessler, "Trump's $110 Billion in Arms Sales to Saudi Arabia: Still Fake," *Washington Post*, October 11, 2018; and Steve Herman (@W7VOA), "'You're talking about 500,000 jobs' lost in America if US cancels military equipment deals with Saudi Arabia, says @POTUS. 'They'll go to Russia. They'll go to China,'" Twitter, October 13, 2018, 1:28 p.m., https://twitter.com/w7voa/status/1051208033769070592?s=11.

85. Walter Russel Mead, *Special Providence: American Foreign Policy and How It Changed the World* (New York: Knopf, 2001).

86. Susan B. Glasser, "The Man Who Put Andrew Jackson in Trump's Oval Office," *Politico Magazine*, January 22, 2018.

87. Mead, *Special Providence*, p. 224.

88. Mead, *Special Providence*, p. 249.

89. Mead, *Special Providence*, p. 240.

90. Mead, *Special Providence*, p. 224.

91. Mead, *Special Providence*, p. 225.

92. Mean, *Special Providence*, p. 259.

93. Mead, *Special Providence*, p. 237.

94. Mead, *Special Providence*, p. 244.

95. Mead, *Special Providence*, p. 225.

96. Mead, *Special Providence*, p. 246.

97. Charlie Savage, "Trump Poised to Lift Ban on C.I.A. 'Black Site' Prisons," *New York Times*, January 25, 2017; and "Trump on Beating ISIS: 'You Have to Take Out Their Families,'" Fox News, December 2, 2015.

98. Woodward, *Fear*, pp. 146–47.

99. Michael Kranish and Marc Fisher, *Trump Revealed: An American Journey of Ambition, Ego, Money, and Power* (New York: Simon & Schuster, 2016), p. 260.

100. Mead, *Special Providence*, p. 255.

101. Mead, *Special Providence*, p. 235.

102. Michael Barbaro, "What Drives Donald Trump? Fear of Losing Status, Tapes Show," *New York Times*, October 25, 2016.

103. Veronica Stracqualursi, "Michael Cohen Testifies that Trump Paid for Portrait with Trump Foundation Funds," CNN News, updated February 27, 2019.

104. Laderman and Simms, *The Making of a World View*, p. 27.

105. Laderman and Simms, *The Making of a World View*, p. 32.

106. Laderman and Simms, *The Making of a World View*, p. 34.

107. Laderman and Simms, *The Making of a World View*, p. 39.

108. Laderman and Simms, *The Making of a World View*, p. 43.

109. Laderman and Simms, *The Making of a World View*, p. 46.

119. Laderman and Simms, *The Making of a World View*, pp. 47–49.

111. Laderman and Simms, *The Making of a World View*, p. 67.

112. Laderman and Simms, *The Making of a World View*, p. 71.

113. Laderman and Simms, *The Making of a World View*, p. 75.

114. Laderman and Simms, *The Making of a World View*, p. 86.

115. Laderman and Simms, *The Making of a World View*, p. 91.

116. Laderman and Simms, *The Making of a World View*, p. 93.

117. "Transcript: Donald Trump Interview with Bob Woodward and Robert Costa," *Washington Post*, April 2, 2016.

118. "Full Text: Donald Trump 2016 RNC Draft Speech Transcript," *Politico*, July 21, 2016.

119. Reinhard Wolf, "Donald Trump's Status-Driven Foreign Policy," *Survival* 59, no. 5 (October–November 2017): 99–116.

120. David Nakamura and John Hudson, "Trump, Once Fiery on Twitter, Warms to Old-Fashioned Mash Notes from Kim Jong Un," *Washington Post*, January 3, 2019.

121. Alan Cowell, "Fort Trump? Poland Makes a Play for a U.S. Military Base," *New York Times*, September 19, 2018.

122. Matt Alt, "Donald and Shinzo's Excellent Adventure," *New Yorker*, November 7, 2017.

123. Fareed Zakaria, "Trump Just Became President," CNN.com, April 7, 2017.

124. Walter Russell Mead, "In Striking Syria, Trump Made All the Right Calls," *Wall Street Journal*, April 7, 2017.

125. Richard Ned Lebow, *Why Nations Fight* (Cambridge, UK: Cambridge University Press, 2010).

126. Woodward, *Fear*, p. 216.

127. Woodward, *Fear*, p. 249.

128. Aaron Blake, "Trump Keeps Throwing Around the Word 'Treason'— Which May Not Be a Great Idea," *Washington Post*, May 15, 2018.

129. Blake, "Trump Keeps Throwing Around the Word 'Treason.'"

130. Avery Anapol, "Trump Demands NYT Turn Anonymous Source over to Government 'for National Security Purposes,'" The Hill, September 5, 2018.

131. Felicia Sonmez, "Trump Suggests That Protesting Should Be Illegal," *Washington Post*, September 5, 2018.

132. "Nadler Speaks after House Judiciary Committee Votes to Hold Barr in Contempt," MSNBC.com, May 8, 2019.

133. Steven Levitsky and Daniel Ziblatt, *How Democracies Die* (New York: Crown Publishing, 2018).

134. Michael S. Schmidt and Maggie Haberman, "Trump Wanted to Order Justice Dept. to Prosecute Comey and Clinton," *New York Times*, November 20, 2018.

135. Michael M. Grynbaum, "Trump Renews Pledge to 'Take a Strong Look' at Libel Laws," *New York Times*, January 10, 2018.

136. See Martha Cottam et al., *Introduction to Political Psychology* (Mahwah, NJ: Lawrence Erlbaum Associates, Inc., 2004), pp. 23–30.

137. See "Regime Type, Foreign Policy, and International Relations," in *The International Studies Encyclopedia*, ed. Robert A. Denemark and Renée Marlin-Bennett (Hoboken, NJ: Wiley-Blackwell, 2010); and Stephen Krazner, ed., *International Regimes* (Ithaca, NY: Cornell University Press, 1983).

138. Jeffrey Bader and Jonathan D. Pollack, "Time to Restrict the President's Power to Wage Nuclear War," *New York Times*, September 12, 2017; and Lisbeth Gronlund, David Wright, and Steve Fetter, "How to Limit Presidential Authority to Order the Use of Nuclear Weapons," *Bulletin of the Atomic Scientists*, January 23, 2018.

139. Ionut Popescu, "Trump Doesn't Need a Grand Strategy," *Foreign Affairs*, May 21, 2018.

140. See Robert Jervis, *Perception and Misperception in International Politics* (Princeton, NJ: Princeton University Press, 1976); and Christopher J. Fettweis, *Psychology of a Superpower: Security and Dominance in U.S. Foreign Policy* (New York: Columbia University Press, 2018).

CHAPTER 4

1. Gardiner Harris, "Pompeo Questions the Value of International Groups Like U.N. and E.U.," *New York Times*, December 4, 2018.

2. "State of the Union 2019: Transcript," CNN Politics, February 6, 2019.

3. Lara Seligman, "U.S. Military Targets Growing Russian and Chinese Influence in Latin America," *Foreign Policy*, November 19, 2018.

4. Mark Stevenson, "US Pledges $10.6B Aid for Central America, Southern Mexico," Associated Press, December 18, 2018.

5. White House, *National Security Strategy of the United States of America*, December 2017.

6. White House, *National Security Strategy*.

7. Alex Nowrasteh, "Trump's Wall Will Not Stop Terrorism," *New York Daily News*, December 18, 2018.

8. David Bier, "Trump Just Doesn't Understand the Border: Here Are the Facts," *New York Daily News*, January 8, 2019.

9. See Alex Nowrasteh, "President Trump Again Orders Troops to the Border," *Cato at Liberty* (blog), October 25, 2018.

10. Bess Levin, "Will Trump Invade Venezuela to Score Political Points?" *Vanity Fair*, September 26, 2018.

11. "President Says Venezuela Could Be 'Quickly Toppled,'" Time.com, September 26, 2018.

12. Ernesto Londoño and Nicholas Casey, "Trump Administration Discussed Coup Plans with Rebel Venezuelan Officers," *New York Times*, September 8, 2018.

13. Justin Sink and Jonathan Levin, "Trump Orders Sanctions on Venezuela Gold to Pressure Maduro," Bloomberg.com, November 1, 2018; and John Hudson and Lena H. Sun, "Trump Administration Prepares to Add Venezuela to List of State Sponsors of Terrorism," *Washington Post*, November 19, 2018.

14. Emily Tamkin, "When It Comes to Venezuela, Trump Follows in Obama Footsteps," *Foreign Policy*, June 1, 2017.

15. Juan Forero, "Documents Show C.I.A. Knew of a Coup Plot in Venezuela," *New York Times*, December 4, 2004; and Christopher Marquis, "Bush Officials Met with Venezuelans Who Ousted Leader," *New York Times*, April 16, 2002.

16. Josh Rogin, "Bolton Promises to Confront Latin America's 'Troika of Tyranny,'" *Washington Post*, November 1, 2018.

17. Peter Baker and Edward Wong, "Intervening against Venezuela's Strongman, Trump Belies 'America First,'" *New York Times*, January 24, 2019.

18. Peter Baker and Edward Wong, "On Venezuela, Rubio Assumes U.S. Role of Ouster in Chief," *New York Times*, January 26, 2019.

19. Jonathan Allen, "Bolton: 'All Options Are on the Table' for Trump in Venezuela," NBC News, January 28, 2019.

20. Kyle Rempfer and Todd South, "There Are Mounting Signs of Military Planning for Venezuela," *Military Times*, March 15, 2019.

21. Rempfer and South, "There Are Mounting Signs."

22. "Latin America Widens Trade Relations in the Time of Trump," *Latin Finance*, June 5, 2018.

23. Adam Taylor, "Trump Makes His First Presidential Visit to Latin America—a Region Where He Is Very Unpopular," *Washington Post*, November 30, 2018; and Elizabeth Keating, "Outlook Grim in Latin America for Relations under Trump," Gallup.com, January 24, 2018.

24. Jennifer Wilson and Micah Zenko, "Donald Trump Is Dropping Bombs at Unprecedented Levels," *Foreign Policy*, August 9, 2017.

25. Julian Borger, "US Air Wars under Trump: Increasingly Indiscriminate, Increasingly Opaque," *The Guardian*, January 23, 2018.

26. Spencer Ackerman, "Trump Ramped Up Drone Strikes in America's Shadow Wars," *Daily Beast*, November 25, 2018.

27. Scott Shane, "Saudis and Extremism: 'Both the Arsonists and the Firefighters,'" *New York Times*, August 25, 2016.

28. Wikileaks.org, "Terrorist Finance: Action Request for Senior Level Engagement on Terrorism Finance," Cable 09STATE131801_a, December 30, 2009.

29. Palko Karasz, "85,000 Children in Yemen May Have Died of Starvation," *New York Times*, November 21, 2018; and Pamela Falk, "8.4M Yemenis Depend on Emergency Food Aid, Says U.N. Report," CBS News, December 16, 2018.

30. Laura Rozen, "On Iran, US Allies Fear 'Maximum Pressure' Could Provoke Escalation," Al-Monitor, December 12, 2018.

31. Jon Gambrell and Amir Vahdat, "Iran Breaches Uranium Stockpile Limit Set by Nuclear Deal," Associated Press, July 1, 2019.

32. Lawrence Wilkerson, "I Helped Sell the False Choice of War Once. It's Happening Again," *New York Times*, February 5, 2018.

33. Dion Nissenbaum, "White House Sought Options to Strike Iran," *Wall Street Journal*, January 13, 2019.

34. Eric Schmitt and Alissa J. Rubin, "Trump Calls for Keeping Troops in Iraq to Watch Iran, Possibly Upending ISIS Fight," *New York Times*, February 3, 2019.

35. Jonathan Swan, "Inside the Oval: How Trump Tormented Mattis," Axios, January 13, 2019.

36. Elise Labott, "Bolton Reassures a Nervous Israel about Trump's Syria Plan," *Politico*, January 6, 2019.

37. Sebastian Rotella, "John Bolton Skewed Intelligence, Say People Who Worked with Him," *ProPublica*, March 30, 2018.

38. Eric Schmitt and Mark Landler, "Pentagon Officials Fear Bolton's Actions Increase Risk of Clash with Iran," *New York Times*, January 13, 2019.

39. Michael R. Gordon, Warren P. Strobel, and Nancy A. Youssef, "U.S. to Designate Iranian Guard Corps as a Foreign Terror Group," *Wall Street Journal*, April 5, 2019.

40. Nahal Toosi, "Rand Paul to Pompeo: You Do Not Have 'Permission' for War with Iran," *Politico*, April 10, 2019.

41. Erin Cunningham, John Hudson, and Missy Ryan, "'We Were Cocked and Loaded': Trump's Account of Iran Attack Plan Facing Scrutiny," *Washington Post*, June 21, 2019.

42. Julian E. Barnes and Eric Schmitt, "White House Reviews Military Plans against Iran, in Echoes of Iraq War," *New York Times*, May 13, 2019; Adam Rawnsley and Betsy Woodruff, "Trump Admin Inflated Iran Intel, U.S. Officials Say," *Daily Beast*, updated May 8, 2019; Maggie Haberman, Mark Landler, and Eric Schmitt, "Trump Tells Pentagon Chief He Does Not Want War with Iran," *New York Times*, May 16, 2019.

43. John Ismay, "US Says 2,000 Troops in Syria, a Fourfold Increase," *New York Times*, December 6, 2017.

44. Dion Nissenbaum and Nancy A. Youssef, "U.S. Military Now Preparing to Leave as Many as 1,000 Troops in Syria," *Wall Street Journal*, March 17, 2019; and Lara Seligman, "How John Bolton Won the Beltway Battle over Syria," *Foreign Policy*, February 22, 2019; and Seth Harp, "Is the Trump Administration Pivoting the Fight in Syria toward a War with Iran?" *New Yorker*, November 26, 2018.

45. Liz Sly, "America's Hidden War in Syria," *Washington Post*, December 14, 2018; and Karen DeYoung, "Trump Agrees to an Indefinite Military Effort and New Diplomatic Push in Syria, U.S. Officials Say," *Washington Post*, September 6, 2018.

46. David Nakamura and Abby Phillip, "Trump Announces New Strategy for Afghanistan That Calls for a Troop Increase," *Washington Post*, August 21, 2017.

47. David Ponniah, "Counting the Cost of Trump's Air War in Afghanistan," BBC News, June 7, 2018.

48. Emily Sullivan, "U.S. Cuts $300 Million in Aid to Pakistan; Says It's Failing to Fight Militants," NPR.org, September 2, 2018; and Phil Stewart and Idrees Ali, "Exclusive: Pentagon Cancels Aid to Pakistan over Record on Militants," Reuters, September 1, 2018.

49. Sahar Khan, "Double Game: Why Pakistan Supports Militants and Resists U.S. Pressure to Stop," Cato Institute Policy Analysis no. 849, September 20, 2018.

50. John Hudson et al., "U.S. Assessing Cost of Keeping Troops in Germany as Trump Battles with Europe," *Washington Post*, June 29, 2018; and Anita Kumar and Franco Ordonez, "Europeans Leaders Worry Trump Wants to Fulfill Promise to Bring American Troops Home," McClatchy News, July 6, 2018.

51. Damien Sharkov, "US Will Send 1,500 More Troops to Germany, Despite Trump's NATO Stance," *Newsweek*, September 8, 2018.

52. John Vandiver, "US Base in Poland Gets Serious Look as Talks Advance, Mattis Says," *Stars and Stripes*, November 14, 2018.

53. Ralph Klem, "Military Exercises as Geopolitical Messaging in the NATO-Russia Dynamic: Reassurance, Deterrence, and (In)stability," *Texas National Security Review* 2, no. 1 (November 2018); and Leonid Ragozin, "How NATO Is Preparing for the New Cold War," Bloomberg.com, November 20, 2018.

54. Robbie Gramer, "Trump Wants NATO's Eyes on China," *Foreign Policy*, March 20, 2019.

55. Aaron Mehta, "Macedonia Takes a Big Step to Becoming NATO's 30th Member," *Defense News*, October 1, 2018.

56. White House, "Remarks by the Vice President and Georgian Prime Minister in a Joint Press Conference," August 1, 2017.

57. Brett Samuels, "Trump Officially Designates Brazil a Non-NATO Ally," The Hill, July 31, 2019.

58. Terri Moon Cronk, "U.S. Troops Training Ukrainian Soldiers, Mattis Says," DoD News, Defense Media Activity, February 2, 2018.

59. White House, *National Security Strategy*.

60. "INF Nuclear Treaty: Russia Plans New Missile Systems after Pullout," BBC News, February 5, 2019.

61. Masha Gessen, "Russian Interference in the 2016 Election: A Cacophony, not a Conspiracy," *New Yorker*, November 3, 2017; and Morning Edition, "Journalists Argue Russian Interference Has Been Exaggerated," NPR.org, March 1, 2018.

62. Michael Pillsbury, *The Hundred-Year Marathon: China's Secret Strategy to Replace America as the Global Superpower* (New York: St. Martin's Griffin, 2015).

63. Alan Rappeport, "A China Hawk Gains Prominence as Trump Confronts Xi on Trade," *New York Times*, November 30, 2018.

64. Alastair Iain Johnston, "Shaky Foundations: The Intellectual Architecture of Trump's China Policy," *Survival* 61, no. 2 (April-May 2019), pp. 189, 199.

65. Benjamin Herscovitch, "A Balanced Threat Assessment of China's South China Sea Policy," Cato Institute Policy Analysis no. 820, August 28, 2017.

66. Tanner Greer, "One Belt, One Road, One Big Mistake," *Foreign Policy*, December 6, 2018.

67. Deborah Brautigam "Misdiagnosing the Chinese Infrastructure Push," *American Interest*, April 4, 2019.

68. Christine Lagarde, "Belt and Road Initiative: Strategies to Deliver in the Next Phase," IMF-PBC Conference, Beijing, April 12, 2018, https://www .imf.org/en/News/Articles/2018/04/11/sp041218-belt-and-road-initiative -strategies-to-deliver-in-the-next-phase.

69. Greer, "One Belt."

70. Jack Kim and Simon Lewis, "Southeast Asia Wary of China's Belt and Road Project, Skeptical of U.S.: Survey," Reuters, January 6, 2019.

71. White House, "Remarks by Vice President Pence on the Administration's Policy toward China," October 4, 2018.

72. Arren Kimbel-Sannit and Doug Palmer, "Companies Plead with Trump against New China Tariffs," *Politico*, June 16, 2019.

73. Bill Chappell, "Trump Hits China with Tariffs on $50 Billion of Goods; China Says It Will Retaliate," NPR.org, June 15, 2018.

74. Chas W. Freeman Jr., "China in the Post-American World," remarks to Le Cercle, Washington, DC, November 29, 2018.

75. Michael Hirtzer and Tom Polansek, "Trade Wars Cost U.S., China Billions of Dollars Each in 2018," Reuters, December 28, 2018.

76. Bob Davis, "U.S. Chip Makers Fear Trap in a Trade Deal with China," *Wall Street Journal*, March 18, 2019.

77. Davis, "U.S. Chip Makers Fear Trap."

78. James Bacchus, Simon Lester, and Huan Zhu, "Disciplining China's Trade Practices at the WTO: How WTO Complaints Can Help Make China More Market-Oriented," Cato Institute Policy Analysis no. 856, November 15, 2018.

79. Jennifer Lind and Daryl G. Press, "Markets or Mercantilism? How China Secures Its Energy Supplies," *International Security* 42, no. 4 (Spring 2018): 170–204.

80. Katherine C. Epstein, "To Understand China, Look to America's History," *Wall Street Journal*, March 19, 2019; and Deirdre Nansen McCloskey, "Quit Worrying and Learn to Love Trade with China," *Reason*, April 2019.

81. Zack Cooper, "The U.S. Quietly Made a Big Splash about the South China Sea," *Washington Post*, March 19, 2019.

82. Doug Bandow, "The Philippines 'Mutual' Defense Treaty Isn't Really Mutual at All," *National Interest*, April 7, 2019.

83. Veronica Stracqualursi and Stephen Collinson, "Trump Declares North Korea 'No Longer a Nuclear Threat,'" CNN.com, June 13, 2018.

84. "Trump on Kim Jong-un: 'We Fell in Love,'" BBC News, September 30, 2018.

85. Alex Ward, "Exclusive: Trump Promised Kim Jong Un He'd Sign an Agreement to End the Korean War," *Vox*, August 29, 2018.

86. John Bolton, "The Trump Administration's New Africa Strategy," remarks at Heritage Foundation, Washington, December 13, 2018.

87. Dion Nissenbaum, "U.S. to Africa: Pick Either US or China and Russia, Not Both," *Wall Street Journal*, December 13, 2018.

88. Bolton, "The Trump Administration's New Africa Strategy."

89. Bolton, "The Trump Administration's New Africa Strategy."

90. See David Pilling and James Politi, "U.S. Senate Passes $60 bn Foreign Development Bill," *Financial Times*, October 3, 2018; and Adva Saldinger, "A New U.S. Development Finance Agency Takes Flight," Devex, October 4, 2018.

91. Nick Turse, "U.S. Military Says It Has a 'Light Footprint' in Africa. These Documents Show a Vast Network of Bases," *The Intercept*, December 1, 2018.

92. Arthur M. Schlesinger Jr., *The Imperial Presidency* (New York: Houghton Mifflin Company, 2004).

93. See, for example, Gene Healy, *The Cult of the Presidency: America's Dangerous Devotion to Executive Power* (Washington: Cato Institute, 2009); Julian E. Zelizer, "The Conservative Embrace of Presidential Power," *Boston University Law Review* 88, no. 2 (2008): 499; Terry M. Moe and William G. Howell, "The Presidential Power of Unilateral Action," *Journal of Law, Economics, and Organization* 15, no. 1 (1999): 132–79; and Charlie Savage, *Takeover: The Return of the Imperial Presidency and the Subversion of American Democracy* (New York: Little, Brown, 2007).

94. Chaim Kaufmann has done an excellent case study illustrating the president's many advantages in foreign policy. See Chaim Kaufmann, "Threat Inflation and the Failure of the Marketplace of Ideas: The Selling of the Iraq War," *International Security* 29, no. 1 (2004): 5–48.

95. Alan Greenblatt, "Why the War Powers Act Doesn't Work," NPR.org, June 16, 2011; and A. Trevor Thrall and Caroline Dorminey, "Risky Business: The Role of Arms Sales in U.S. Foreign Policy," Cato Institute Policy Analysis no. 836, March 13, 2018.

96. Nina Totenberg, "Cheney: A VP with Unprecedented Power," NPR.org, January 15, 2009.

97. Gene Healy and John Glaser, "Repeal, Don't Replace, the AUMF," Cato Institute Policy Report, July/August 2018; and Richard Fontaine and Vance Serchuk, "Congress Should Oversee America's Wars, Not Just Authorize Them," Lawfareblog.com, June 7, 2018.

98. Julie Hirschfeld Davis and Eric Schmitt, "Senate Votes to End Aid for Yemen Fight over Khashoggi Killing and Saudis' War Aims," *New York Times*, December 13, 2018.

99. Nick Cumming-Bruce, "War Crimes Report on Yemen Accuses Saudi Arabia and U.A.E.," *New York Times*, August 28, 2018.

100. Susan Ferrechio, "Paul Ryan Blocks House from Taking Up Yemen Bill," *Washington Examiner*, December 2, 2018.

101. Karoun Demirjian, "With Vote to End U.S. Involvement in Yemen's War, House Sets Up Trump's Second Veto," *Washington Post*, April 4, 2019.

102. James Goldgeier and Elizabeth N. Saunders, "The Unconstrained Presidency," *Foreign Affairs*, September/October 2018.

103. Alex Lo, "Donald Trump: Learning on the Job," *South China Morning Post*, March 2, 2017; and Jeff Shesol, "Can President Trump Learn on the Job?" *New Yorker*, April 22, 2017.

104. Pam Key, "McConnell: Trump Is 'Learning on the Job,'" Breitbart, April 13, 2017.

105. Gerard Baker, Carol E. Lee, and Michael C. Bender, "Trumps Says He Offered China Better Trade Terms in Exchange for Help on North Korea," *Wall Street Journal*, April 12, 2017.

106. Robert Schlesinger, "What Donald Trump Doesn't Know," *U.S. News & World Report*, April 28, 2017, https://www.usnews.com/opinion/thomas -jefferson-street/articles/2017-04-28/being-president-is-hard-and-other -obvious-things-donald-trump-didnt-know.

107. Aaron Blake, "President Trump's Full Washington Post Interview Transcript, Annotated," *Washington Post*, November 27, 2018.

108. Jenna Johnson, "Donald Trump Begs Iowans Not to Believe Ben Carson: 'Don't Be Fools, Okay?" *Washington Post*, November 13, 2015.

109. Woodward, *Fear*, p. 226.

110. Mark Landler and Julie Hirschfeld Davis, "After Another Week of Chaos, Trump Repairs to Palm Beach. No One Knows What Comes Next," *New York Times*, March 23, 2018.

111. Anne Gearan and Sarah Ellison, "How Trump Relies on His Cable News Cabinet As Much As the Real One," *Washington Post*, August 28, 2018.

112. Mike Allen, "Operation Normal: Trump Goes [Globe]-al," Axios, April 13, 2017, https://www.axios.com/operation-normal-trump-goes-al -1513301578-ec35cf4b-01a5-4f7e-9281-781220f64cc0.html.

113. George E. Condon Jr., "Trump's Historic National Security Staff Turnover," *National Journal*, October 12, 2018; and Helene Cooper, "Jim Mattis, Secretary of Defense, Resigns in Rebuke of Trump's Worldview," *New York Times*, December 20, 2018.

114. See, for example, Phil Levy, "Is President Trump's Protectionism a Savvy Negotiating Ploy?," Forbes.com, June 11, 2018; and Emily Landau, "The World Should Back Trump's Strategy on Iran," *National Interest*, November 13, 2018.

115. Tara Golshan and Ella Nilsen, "Trump Says a Shutdown Would Be a 'Great Political Issue' 2 Months from the Midterms," *Vox*, September 7, 2018; and Robert Schroeder, "Trump Today: President Threatens to Deploy Military to Close Border with Mexico," MarketWatch, October 18, 2018.

116. Patrick Porter, "Why America's Grand Strategy Has Not Changed: Power, Habit, and the US Foreign Policy Establishment," *International Security* 42, no. 4 (Spring 2018): 10, emphasis added.

117. David Samuels, "The Aspiring Novelist Who Became Obama's Foreign-Policy Guru," *New York Times Magazine*, May 5, 2016.

118. Stephen M. Walt, *The Hell of Good Intentions: America's Foreign Policy Elite and the Decline of U.S. Primacy* (New York: Farrar, Straus and Giroux, 2018); and Benjamin H. Friedman and Justin Logan, "Why Washington Doesn't Debate Grand Strategy," *Strategic Studies Quarterly* 10, no. 4 (Winter 2016): 14–45.

119. The exceptions included Rand Paul among Republicans and Bernie Sanders in the Democratic Party primary.

120. James Mann, "The Adults in the Room," *New York Review of Books*, October 26, 2017.

121. Anonymous, "I Am Part of the Resistance Inside the Trump Administration," *New York Times*, September 5, 2018.

122. Margaret Hartmann, "U.S. Officials Worked behind Trump's Back to Keep Him from Blowing Up NATO," Intelligencer, August 10, 2018; Karen DeYoung and Karoun Demirjian, "Contradicting Trump, Bolton Says No Withdrawal from Syria until ISIS Destroyed, Kurds' Safety Guaranteed," *Washington Post*, January 6, 2019; Thomas Gibbons-Neff and Helene Cooper, "Newest U.S. Strategy in Afghanistan Mirrors Past Plans for Retreat," *New York Times*, July 28, 2018; and Tal Axelrod, "Trump Wanted to Assassinate Assad after Chemical Attack: Woodward Book," The Hill, September 4, 2018.

123. Dan Mangan and Jacob Pramuk, "Gary Cohn Resigns as Trump's Top Economic Advisor," CNBC.com, March 6, 2018.

124. Porter, "Why America's Grand Strategy Has Not Changed," p. 45.

125. John Glaser, "Withdrawing from Overseas Bases: Why a Forward-Deployed Military Posture Is Unnecessary, Outdated, and Dangerous," Cato Institute Policy Analysis no. 816, July 18, 2017.

CHAPTER 5

1. Ian Bremmer, *Every Nation for Itself: Winners and Losers in a G-Zero World* (London: Penguin UK, 2012), p. 13.

2. Pew Research Center, "Public Sees U.S. Power Declining as Support for Global Engagement Slips," December 3, 2013; Pew Research Center, "Public Uncertain, Divided over America's Place in the World," May 5, 2016; and Dina Smeltz, Ivo Daalder, and Craig Kafura, *Foreign Policy in the Age of Retrenchment* (Chicago: Chicago Council on Global Affairs, 2014).

3. Hal Brands, *American Grand Strategy in the Age of Trump* (Washington: Brookings Institution Press, 2018), p. 91; Rebecca Friedman Lissner and Mira Rapp-Hooper, "The Day after Trump: American Strategy for a New International Order," *Washington Quarterly* 41, no. 1 (2018): 7–25; Robert Kagan, *The Jungle Grows Back: America and Our Imperiled World* (New York: Knopf, 2018); and A. Trevor Thrall and Erik Goepner, "Millennials and U.S. Foreign Policy: The Next Generation's Attitudes toward Foreign Policy and War (and Why They Matter)," Cato Institute White Paper, June 16, 2015.

4. Robert Kagan, "'America First' Has Won," *New York Times*, September 24, 2018.

5. Dina Smeltz et al., *What Americans Think about America First* (Chicago: Chicago Council on Global Affairs, 2017); and A. Trevor Thrall and John Glaser, "America First? Not So Fast! What We've Learned from 100 Days of Trump Foreign Policy," War on the Rocks, April 27, 2017.

6. Smeltz, Daalder, and Kafura, *Age of Retrenchment*, p. 7.

7. Dina Smeltz, *Foreign Policy in the New Millennium* (Chicago: Chicago Council on Global Affairs, 2012), p. 8.

8. Afghanistan poll data compiled by Pollingreport.com: http://www.pollingreport.com/afghan.htm; Iraq poll data compiled by Pollingreport.com: http://www.pollingreport.com/iraq.htm. For the Gallup Poll "mistake" question, see Andrew Dugan, "Fewer in U.S. View Iraq, Afghanistan Wars as Mistakes," Gallup.com, June 12, 2015. See also Gary Jacobson, "A Tale of Two Wars: Public Opinion on the U.S. Military Interventions in Afghanistan and Iraq," *Presidential Studies Quarterly* 40, no. 4 (December 2010): 585–610.

9. Smeltz, Daalder, and Kafura, *Age of Retrenchment*, p. 8.

10. Eugene R. Wittkopf, *Faces of Internationalism: Public Opinion and American Foreign Policy* (Durham, NC: Duke University Press, 1990).

11. Smeltz et al., *What Americans Think about America First*; and A. Trevor Thrall et al., "The Clash of Generations? Intergenerational Change and American Foreign Policy Views," Chicago Council on Global Affairs, June 25, 2018.

12. Pew Research Center, "Iran Nuclear Agreement Meets with Public Skepticism," July 21, 2015.

13. Thrall et al., "Clash of Generations?," p. 19.

14. Thrall and Goepner, "Millennials and U.S. Foreign Policy."

15. Thrall and Goepner, "Millennials and U.S. Foreign Policy."

16. Eugene R. Wittkopf, "The Structure of Foreign Policy Attitudes: An Alternate View," *Social Science Quarterly* 62, no. 1 (1981): 108; and Joshua D. Kertzer, and Kathleen M. McGraw, "Folk Realism: Testing the Microfoundations of Realism in Ordinary Citizens," *International Studies Quarterly* 56, no. 2 (2012): 245–58.

17. Karl Mannheim, "The Problem of Generations," *Psychoanalytic Review* 57, no. 3 (1970): 378–404; Michael X. Delli Carpini, "Age and History: Generations and Sociopolitical Change," in *Political Learning in Adulthood: A Sourcebook of Theory and Research*, ed. R. S. Sigel, (Chicago: University of Chicago Press, 1989), pp. 11–55; Paul R. Abramson and Ronald F. Inglehart, *Value Change in Global Perspective* (Ann Arbor, MI: University of Michigan Press, 2009); and M. Kent Jennings and Richard G. Niemi, *Generations and Politics: A Panel Study of Young Adults and Their Parents* (Princeton, NJ: Princeton University Press, 2014).

18. Lynn Vavreck, "Younger Americans Are Less Patriotic. At Least, in Some Ways," *New York Times*, July 4, 2014, https://www.nytimes.com/2014/07/05/upshot/younger-americans-are-less-patriotic-at-least-in-some-ways.html.

19. Nathaniel P. Flannery, "Is Donald Trump Right about NAFTA?" Forbes.com, August 28, 2017.

20. Dina Smeltz et al., *America Engaged* (Chicago: Chicago Council on Global Affairs, 2018), p. 5.

21. David Ljunggren, "Exclusive: Canada Increasingly Convinced Trump Will Pull Out of NAFTA," Reuters, January 10, 2018.

22. Smeltz et al., *America Engaged*, p. 5.

23. Tal Kopan, "What Donald Trump Has Said about Mexico and Vice Versa," CNN.com, August 31, 2016.

24. Smeltz et al., *America Engaged*.

25. Gallup.com, Historical Trends, "Immigration."

26. Quinnipiac University Poll, "Dreamers Should Stay," September 28, 2017. See also Kathy Frankovic, "Compromise on Immigration Reform Faces an Uncompromising Partisan Public," YouGov.com, January 11, 2018.

27. Quinnipiac University Poll, January 11, 2018, https://poll.qu.edu/national/release-detail?ReleaseID=2512. See question 30.

28. Gallup.com, Historical Trends, "Presidential Ratings—Issues Approval."

29. See PollingReport.com for Quinnipiac University Poll trend data on immigration: http://www.pollingreport.com/immigration.htm.

30. Mark Hensch, "Poll: Few Support Syrian Refugees Entering US," *The Hill*, August 15, 2016, https://thehill.com/blogs/blog-briefing-room/news/291471-poll-most-reject-syrian-refugees-entering-us.

31. Steven Shepard, "Poll: Majority of Voters Back Trump Travel Ban," *Politico*, July 5, 2017.

Conclusion

1. See, for example, Hal Brands, *American Grand Strategy in the Age of Trump* (Washington: Brookings Institution Press, 2018).

2. Christopher Fettweis, "Unipolarity, Hegemony and the New Peace," *Security Studies* 26, no. 3 (Fall 2017): 423–51.

3. Robert Jervis, *The Meaning of the Nuclear Revolution: Statecraft and the Prospect of Armageddon* (Ithaca, NY: Cornell University Press, 1990), p. 8.

4. Stephen M. Walt, "Rethinking the 'Nuclear Revolution,'" *Foreign Policy*, August 3, 2010.

5. Francis Fukuyama, "The End of History?," *National Interest* no. 16 (Summer 1989): 3–18.

6. Duncan Snidal, "The Limits of Hegemonic Stability Theory," *International Organization* 39, no. 4 (Autumn 1985): 579–614.

7. Sameer Lalwani and Joshua Shifrinson, "Whither Command of the Commons? Choosing Security over Control," New America Foundation, September 2011.

8. Lydia Saad, "Demand Wanes for Higher Defense Spending," Gallup.com, March 12, 2019, https://news.gallup.com/poll/247622/demand-wanes-higher-defense-spending.aspx. See also Sarah Kreps, *Taxing Wars: The American Way of War Finance and the Decline of Democracy* (Ithaca, NY: Cornell University Press, 2018).

9. Stephen M. Walt, *The Hell of Good Intentions: America's Foreign Policy Elite and the Decline of U.S. Primacy* (New York: Farrar, Straus and Giroux, 2018).

10. John Kasich, "Reclaiming Global Leadership," *Foreign Affairs*, July/August 2018: 102–112; Brands, *American Grand Strategy*; Eliot Cohen, *The Big Stick: The Limits of Soft Power and the Necessity of Military Force* (New York: Basic Books, 2017); Colin Dueck, *Hard Line: The Republican Party and U.S. Foreign Policy since World War II* (Princeton University Press: 2010); and Colin Dueck et al., "Policy Roundtable: The Future of Conservative Foreign Policy," *Texas National Security Review*, November 30, 2018.

11. Elizabeth Warren, "A Foreign Policy for All," *Foreign Affairs*, January/February 2019: 50–61.

12. Bernie Sanders, "American Foreign Policy Speech at Westminster College," New Wilmington, PA, *Vox*, September 21, 2017.

13. Peter Beinart, "America Needs an Entirely New Foreign Policy for the Trump Age," *The Atlantic*, September 16, 2018. See also Van Jackson et al., "Policy Roundtable: The Future of Progressive Foreign Policy," *Texas National Security Review*, December 4, 2018; and Daniel Nexon, "Toward a Neo-Progressive Foreign Policy: The Case for an Internationalist Left," *Foreign Affairs*, September 4, 2018.

14. Emma Ashford and A. Trevor Thrall, "The Battle Inside the Political Parties for the Future of U.S. Foreign Policy," War on the Rocks, December 12, 2018; Mike Gallagher and Colin Dueck, "The Conservative Case for NATO," *National Review* (Online), January 30, 2019.

15. Making this argument is Joshua Shifrinson, "Should the United States Fear China's Rise?" *Washington Quarterly* 41, no. 4 (2018): 65–83. See also Charles L. Glaser, "A US-China Grand Bargain? The Hard Choice between Military Competition and Accommodation," *International Security* 39, no. 4 (2015): 49–90.

16. See, for example, Ian Bremmer, "Americans Want a Less Aggressive Foreign Policy. It's Time Lawmakers Listened to Them," Time.com, February 19, 2019.

17. Patrick Porter, "A World Imagined: Nostalgia and Liberal Order," Cato Institute Policy Analysis no. 843, June 5, 2018.

18. James Goldgeier, "When President Trump Heads to Europe, Discussion Turns to Burden-Sharing," *Washington Post*, November 14, 2018.

19. See, for example, John Mueller and Mark G. Stewart, *Chasing Ghosts: The Policing of Terrorism* (New York: Oxford University Press, 2015).

20. Kenneth N. Waltz, "The Emerging Structure of International Politics," *International Security* 18 (1993): 44–79.

21. Congressional Research Service, *Instances of Use of United States Armed Forces Abroad, 1798–2018*, CRS Report R42738, updated December 28, 2018.

22. Reid J. Epstein, "Kerry: Russia Behaving Like It's the 19th Century," *Politico*, March 2, 2014.

23. Martha Finnemore, "Legitimacy, Hypocrisy, and the Social Structure of Unipolarity," *World Politics* 61, no. 1 (January 2009): 73–74.

24. Robert Jervis, *System Effects: Complexity in Political and Social Life* (Princeton, NJ: Princeton University Press, 1997), p. 144.

INDEX

Note: Illustrations are indicated by f (figure) or t (table) after the page number(s).

ABOUT THE AUTHORS

John Glaser is the director of foreign policy studies at the Cato Institute. His research interests include grand strategy, U.S. foreign policy in the Middle East, the rise of China, and the role of status and prestige motivations in international politics. He has been a guest on a variety of television and radio programs, including Fox News, MSNBC, and National Public Radio, and has had his work published in the *New York Times*, the *Washington Post*, *USA Today*, the *Los Angeles Times*, and *Foreign Affairs*, among other outlets. Glaser earned a master of arts in international security at the Schar School of Policy and Government at George Mason University and a bachelor of arts in political science from the University of Massachusetts Amherst.

Christopher A. Preble is the vice president for defense and foreign policy studies at the Cato Institute. He is the author of four books, including *Peace, War, and Liberty: Understanding U.S. Foreign Policy* (Libertarianism.org, 2019) and *The Power Problem: How American Military Dominance Makes Us Less Safe, Less Prosperous, and Less Free* (Cornell University Press, 2009). Preble has also published articles in major publications, including the *New York Times*, the *Los Angeles Times*, *National Review*, *the National Interest*, and *Foreign Policy*. In addition to his work at Cato, Preble teaches the U.S. foreign policy elective at the University of California, Washington Center, and he is the cohost of the *Net Assessment* podcast at War on the Rocks. Preble was a commissioned officer in the U.S. Navy and holds a PhD in history from Temple University.

A. Trevor Thrall is a senior fellow for the Cato Institute's defense and foreign policy department and an associate professor at George Mason University's Schar School of Policy and Government, where he teaches courses in international security. Thrall's recent research includes work on shifting American attitudes toward foreign policy, an analysis of the role of arms sales in U.S. foreign policy, and *U.S. Grand Strategy in the 21st Century: The Case for Restraint* (Routledge, 2018), an edited volume (with Ben Friedman) that presents a cutting-edge critique of primacy and a comprehensive outline of the case for restraint in U.S. foreign policy. Thrall has published articles in a range of academic journals, and his shorter commentary on foreign affairs has appeared in a number of publications, including the *Atlantic*, the *Washington Post*, *Foreign Policy*, the *Detroit News*, the *Huffington Post*, and *War on the Rocks*, and he is the cohost of the *Power Problems* podcast. Thrall holds a PhD in political science from MIT.

ABOUT THE CATO INSTITUTE

Founded in 1977, the Cato Institute is a public policy research foundation dedicated to broadening the parameters of policy debate to allow consideration of more options that are consistent with the principles of limited government, individual liberty, and peace. To that end, the Institute strives to achieve greater involvement of the intelligent, concerned lay public in questions of policy and the proper role of government.

The Institute is named for *Cato's Letters*, libertarian pamphlets that were widely read in the American Colonies in the early 18th century and played a major role in laying the philosophical foundation for the American Revolution.

Despite the achievement of the nation's Founders, today virtually no aspect of life is free from government encroachment. A pervasive intolerance for individual rights is shown by government's arbitrary intrusions into private economic transactions and its disregard for civil liberties. And while freedom around the globe has notably increased in the past several decades, many countries have moved in the opposite direction, and most governments still do not respect or safeguard the wide range of civil and economic liberties.

To address those issues, the Cato Institute undertakes an extensive publications program on the complete spectrum of policy issues. Books, monographs, and shorter studies are commissioned to examine the federal budget, Social Security, regulation, military spending, international trade, and myriad other issues. Major policy conferences are held throughout the year, from which papers are published thrice yearly in the *Cato Journal*. The Institute also publishes the quarterly magazine *Regulation*.

In order to maintain its independence, the Cato Institute accepts no government funding. Contributions are received from foundations, corporations, and individuals, and other revenue is generated from the sale of publications. The Institute is a nonprofit, tax-exempt, educational foundation under Section 501(c)3 of the Internal Revenue Code.

CATO INSTITUTE
1000 Massachusetts Ave., NW
Washington, DC 20001
www.cato.org